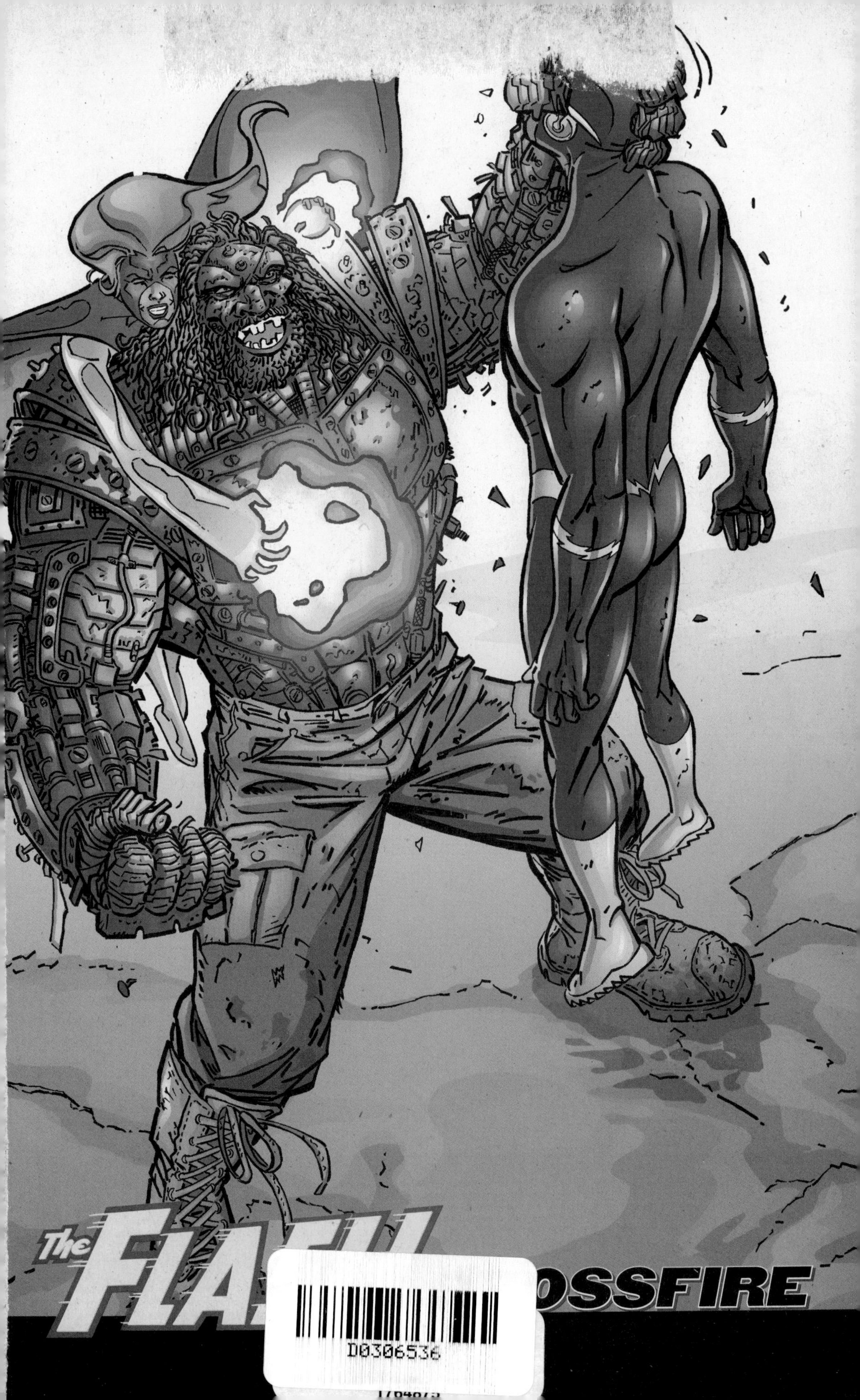
The FLA
OSSFIRE

Dan DiDio VP-Editorial Joey Cavalieri Editor-original series Bob Greenberger Senior Editor-Collected Edition
Robbin Brosterman Senior Art Director Paul Levitz President & Publisher Georg Brewer VP-Design & Retail Product Development
Richard Bruning Senior VP-Creative Director Patrick Caldon Senior VP-Finance & Operations Chris Caramalis VP-Finance
Terri Cunningham VP-Managing Editor Alison Gill VP-Manufacturing Lillian Laserson Senior VP & General Counsel
Jim Lee Editorial Director-Wildstorm David McKillips VP- Advertising & Custom Publishing John Nee VP-Business Development
Cheryl Rubin VP-Brand Management Bob Wayne VP-Sales & Marketing

THE FLASH: CROSSFIRE

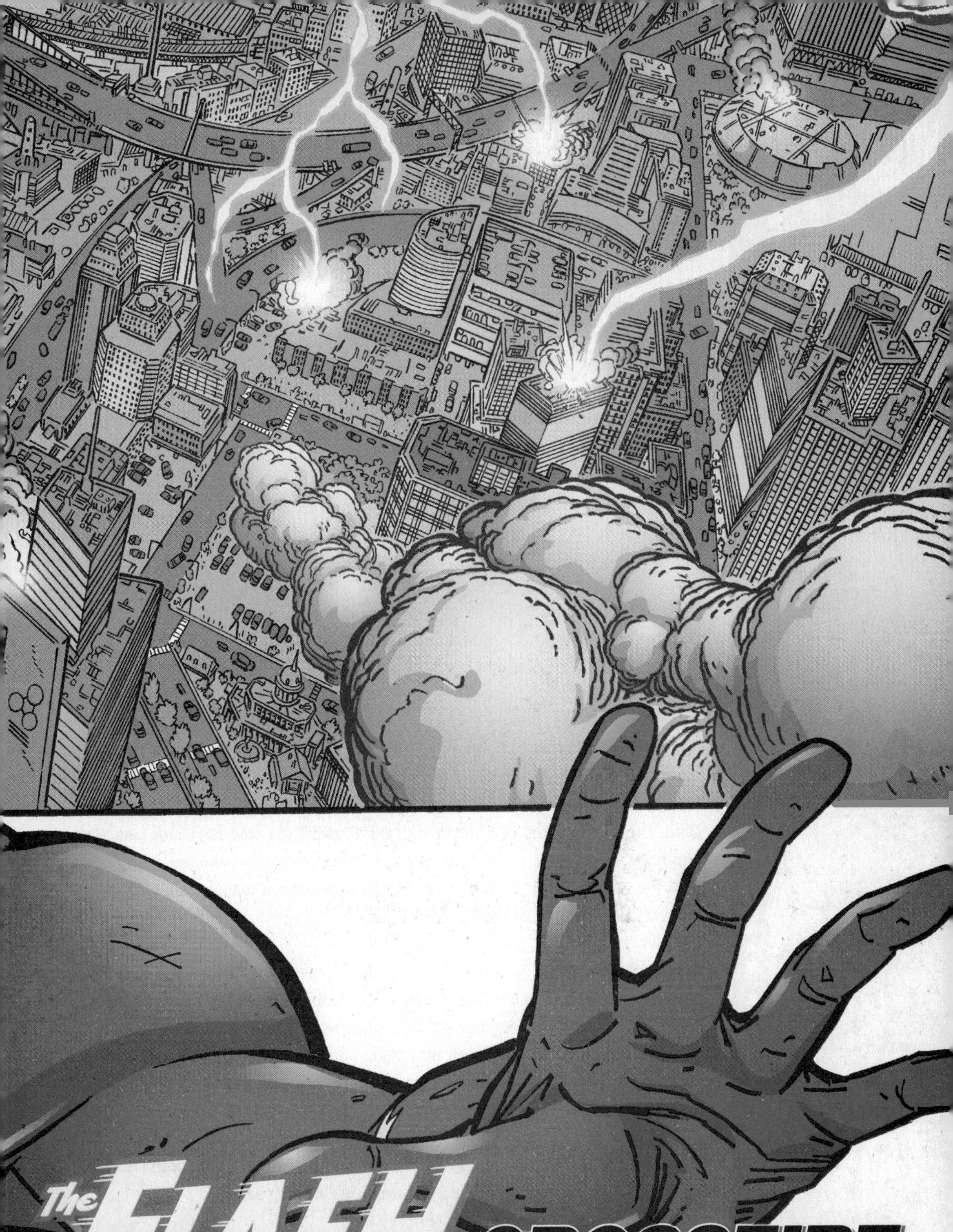

The FLASH CROSSFIRE

GEOFF JOHNS Writer

SCOTT KOLINS RICH BURCHETT JUSTINIANO Pencillers

DOUG HAZLEWOOD DAN PANOSIAN WALDEN WONG Inkers

JAMES SINCLAIR Colorist **GASPAR SALADINO BILL OAKLEY** Letterers

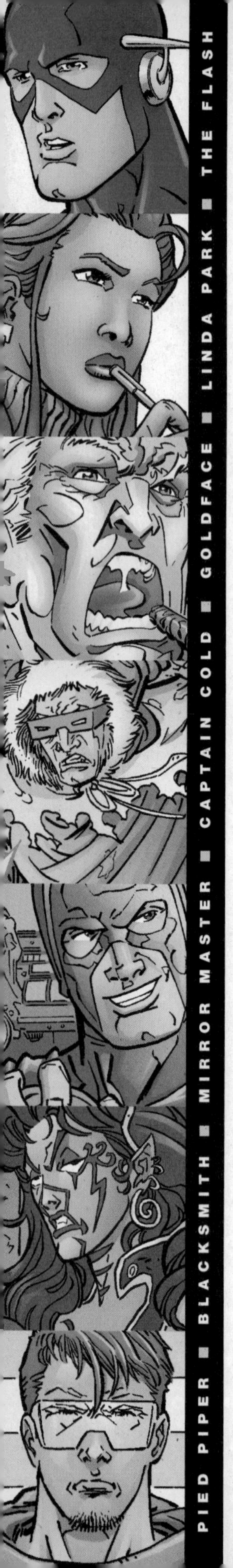
PIED PIPER ■ BLACKSMITH ■ MIRROR MASTER ■ CAPTAIN COLD ■ GOLDFACE ■ LINDA PARK ■ THE FLASH

C H A R A C T E R B I O S

THE FLASH: Caught in a bizarre accident, teenager Wally West was struck by an erratic bolt of lightning and bestowed with the gift of incredible super-speed. After years of training as Kid Flash to Barry Allen's Flash, Wally inherited the mantle of the Scarlet Speedster following the death of his mentor. Now, protecting Keystone City, he carries on the legacy of the fastest man alive — Wally West is the Flash!

LINDA PARK: Linda Park originally thought Wally to be brash and arrogant — which he was. But Linda also saw something else in him, the spark of a better man. As their relationship developed, that spark turned into a flame of love that led them to marry. So strong is their bond that it has enabled Flash to find his way home, regardless of time, dimension, or location. Recently, Linda has enrolled at Central City Medical College.

GOLDFACE: Keith Kenyon was a simple chemist who discovered a powerful elixir derived from ancient gold. It altered Kenyon, giving him enhanced strength and a golden skin tone. He turned to crime to pay for his experiments and crossed paths first with Green Lantern, and then the Flash. While in Iron Heights, Kenyon's skin turned from flesh into organic metal. Upon his release, Kenyon followed his father's path and became a union leader, now the head of Union 242, Keystone City's largest work force.

CAPTAIN COLD: Leonard Snart was never more than a common thief until the day he was taken down by the Flash. In prison, Len promised himself he would face the Flash when he got out. The opportunity came after he stole an experimental cryogenic engine. Snart created a cold-gun and renamed himself Captain Cold. During his years of battling with the Flash, Cold saw his sister Lisa slide into his shadow as the villainous Golden Glider. Today, he remains guilt-ridden over her death and has grown even colder towards his fellow man. Cold is the most underestimated of the Flash's Rogues.

MIRROR MASTER: Just as Wally is the third generation Flash, there have been several incarnations of the Mirror Master. Currently wearing the costume is Evan McCulloch. Hired and equipped by the government as an enforcer, he quickly outgrew the need for direction and banished his superiors to a mirror world. He has used the reflecting ability of mirrors in ways that Sam Scudder, the original Mirror Master, never dreamt of. McCulloch will do anything for a price.

BLACKSMITH: Almost nothing is known about the female leader of the Rogues, save that she has been operating in Keystone City for years.

PIED PIPER: Hartley Rathaway was born deaf, but after modern medical science restored his hearing he fell in love with music. That love of music fueled an interest in sonics that ultimately led the wealthy youth to assume the costumed guise of the Pied Piper. Rathaway seemed more interested in challenging the second Flash than in committing crimes, and he ultimately turned away from that path. Today, as a friend to Wally West, he is a champion of civil and social rights across Keystone and Central City.

WEATHER WIZARD: Mark Mardon was a small-time crook who either got lucky or was a murderer. A prison escapee, Mardon headed to his older brother's observatory for shelter, where he either found his brother dead (from a heart attack) or killed him. What is indisputable is that he took possession of his brother's invention, a "weather wand" capable of controlling weather. Using the wand, Mardon became the thief known as Weather Wizard. He has battled various incarnations of the Flash, improving his control over the wand's properties with experience.

MURMUR: Dr. Michael Christian Amar was a surgeon, well-respected throughout the twin cities of Keystone and Central. But Amar was also a costumed serial killer, nicknamed "Murmur" by the local papers for his constant muttering, a nervous tic he could not control. He was caught by Keystone Police, identified by his speech impediment. In order to insure he never incriminate himself again, Murmur cut out his own tongue. Murmur recently was the catalyst for a massive breakout in Iron Heights.

MAGENTA: Frances Kane's metahuman magnetic abilities manifested themselves at the worst time conceivable. While in the car with her father and brother, Kane's powers kicked in, causing a terrible accident that left both men dead. From then on, whenever Kane would use her magnetic abilities, a twisted side of her psyche, later dubbed Magenta, would emerge. Over the years, Magenta has switched sides between good and evil, most recently reemerging more in control of her powers and more focused on toying with her ex-lover, The Flash.

GIRDER: After steelworker Tony Woodward assaulted a young female at work, a riot ensued and he was thrown into a vat of molten steel by angry co-workers. No ordinary metal, it was, in fact, scrap from S.T.A.R. Labs that had undergone several mysterious experiments. Woodward rose up from the pit in the metallic form of Girder. Endowed with incredible strength, Girder's greatest enemy is rust, which painfully eats away more of his body each day.

PLUNDER: While trapped in a "mirror world" within his wife's diamond ring, the Flash was tracked by a bounty hunter calling himself Plunder. Realizing he was trapped in a reflection, which was destined to fade away, Plunder escaped "Wonderland" on the heels of the Flash. Plunder's true identity is unknown, but he is a "reflection" of somebody in the real world.

...and introducing a brand new **TRICKSTER.**

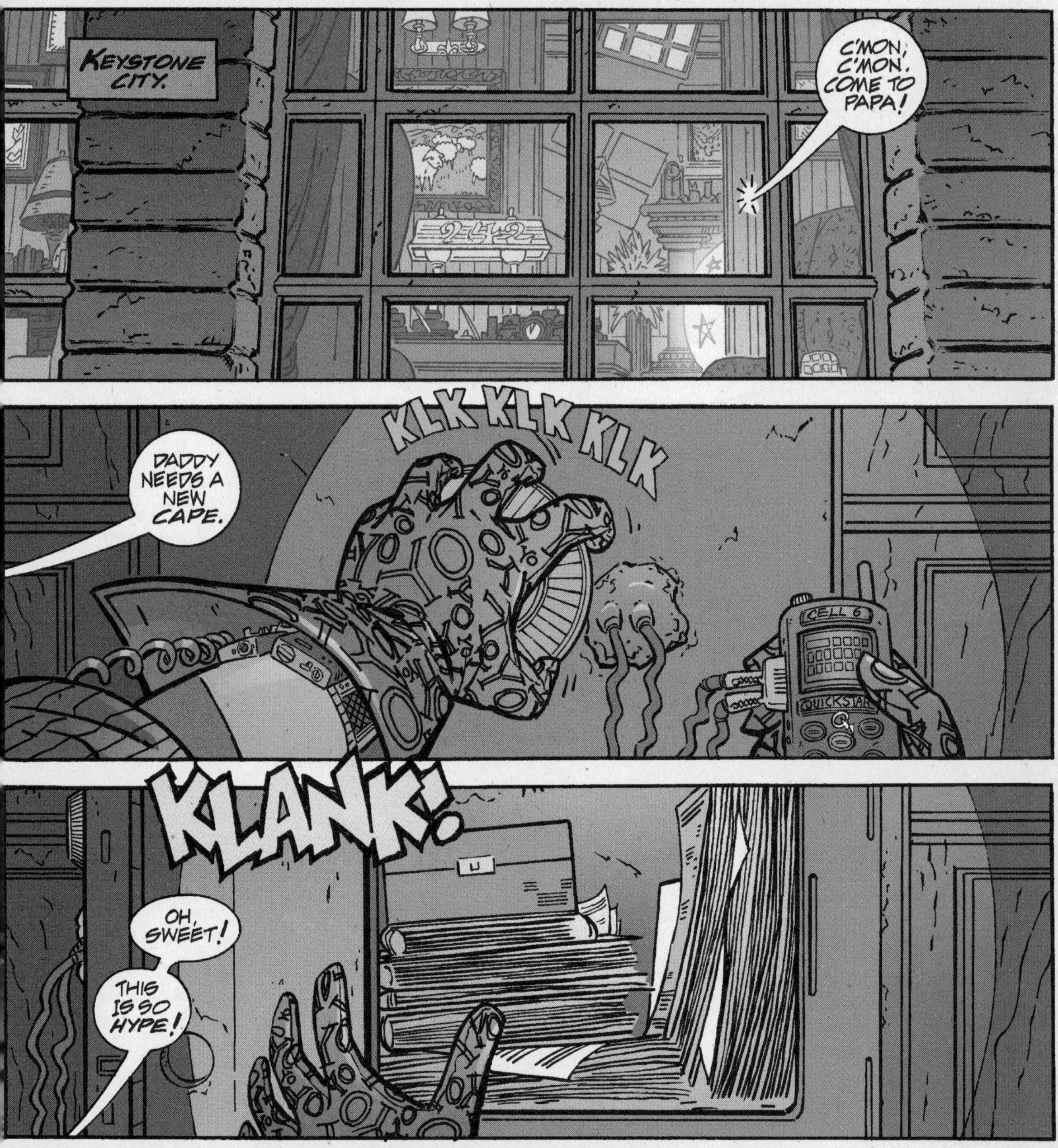
KEYSTONE CITY.
C'MON, C'MON. COME TO PAPA!
KLK KLK KLK
DADDY NEEDS A NEW CAPE.
CELL 6
QUICKSTART
KLANK!
OH, SWEET!
THIS IS SO HYPE!
WHA--? I'M BUSTED?!
YOU'RE KIDDIN'?
DON'T MOVE, PAL! YOU'RE BUSTED!
The NETWORK

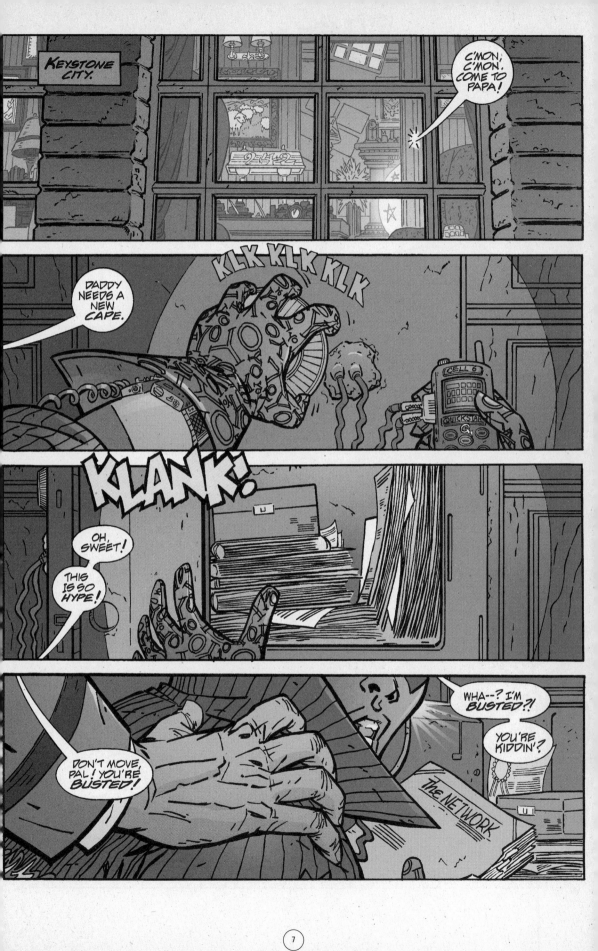

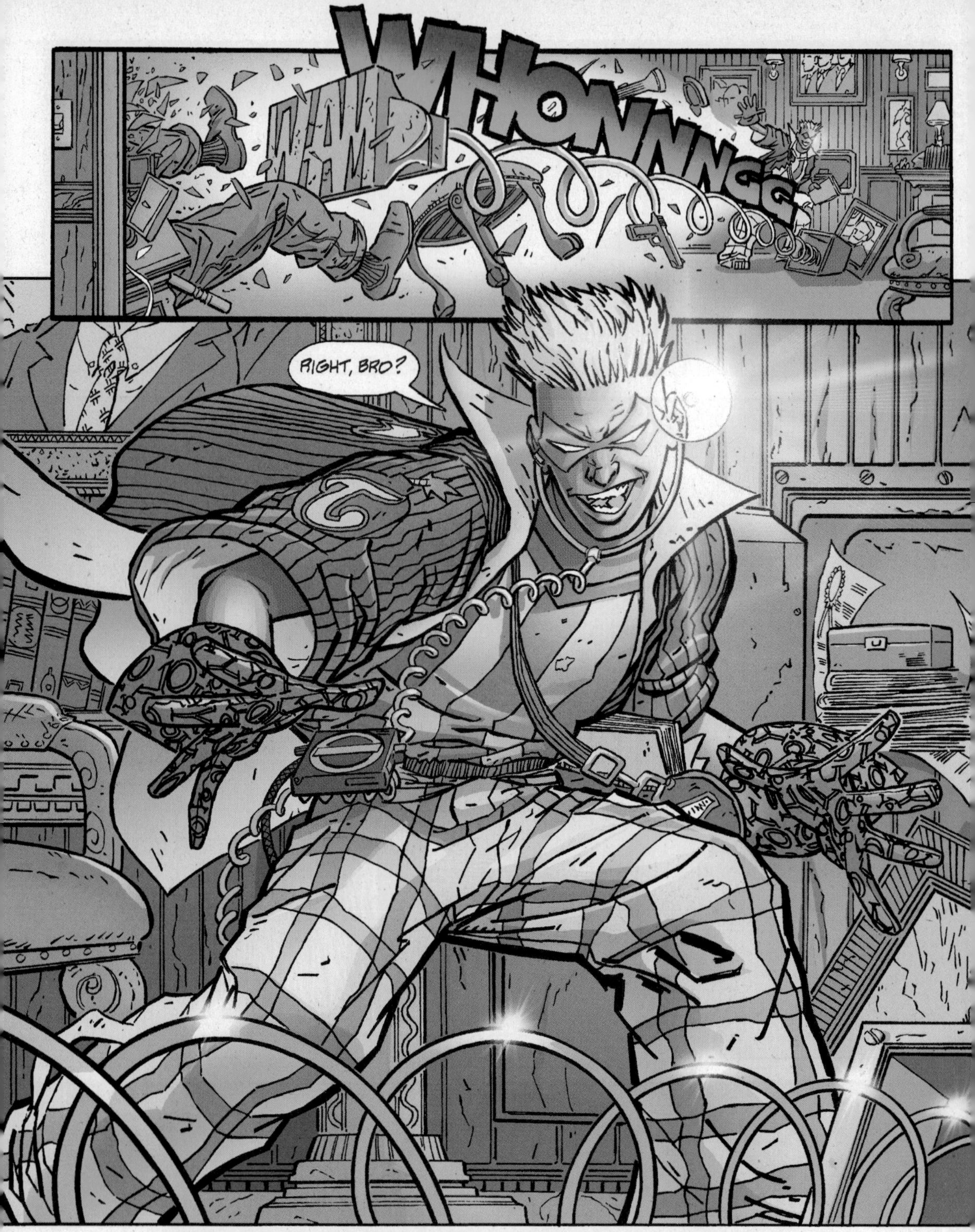
WHONNNGG
WAM
RIGHT, BRO?

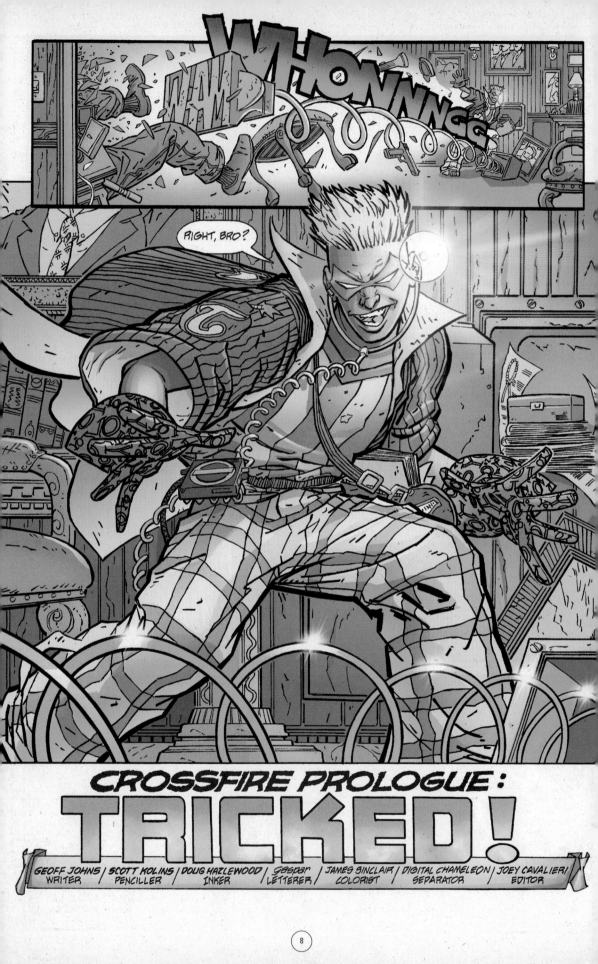

CROSSFIRE PROLOGUE: TRICKED!

GEOFF JOHNS / WRITER | SCOTT KOLINS / PENCILLER | DOUG HAZLEWOOD / INKER | Gaspar / LETTERER | JAMES SINCLAIR / COLORIST | DIGITAL CHAMELEON / SEPARATOR | JOEY CAVALIERI / EDITOR

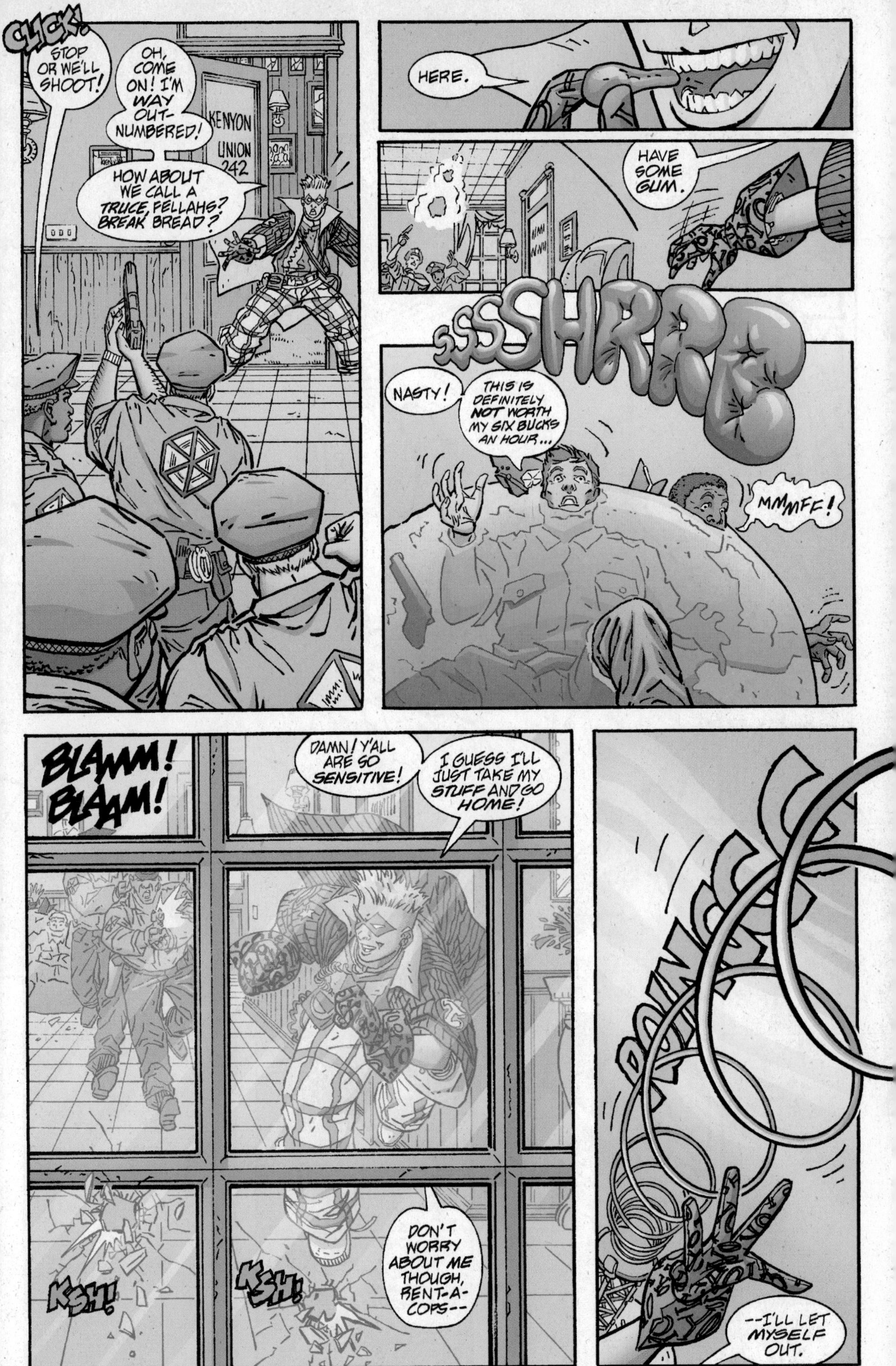
CLICK!
STOP OR WE'LL SHOOT!
OH, COME ON! I'M WAY OUT-NUMBERED!
HOW ABOUT WE CALL A TRUCE, FELLAHS? BREAK BREAD?
KENYON UNION 242
HERE.
HAVE SOME GUM.
SSSSHRRRB
NASTY!
THIS IS DEFINITELY NOT WORTH MY SIX BUCKS AN HOUR...
MMMFF!
BLAMM! BLAAM!
DAMN! Y'ALL ARE SO SENSITIVE!
I GUESS I'LL JUST TAKE MY STUFF AND GO HOME!
DON'T WORRY ABOUT ME THOUGH, RENT-A-COPS--
KSH!
KSH!
--I'LL LET MYSELF OUT.

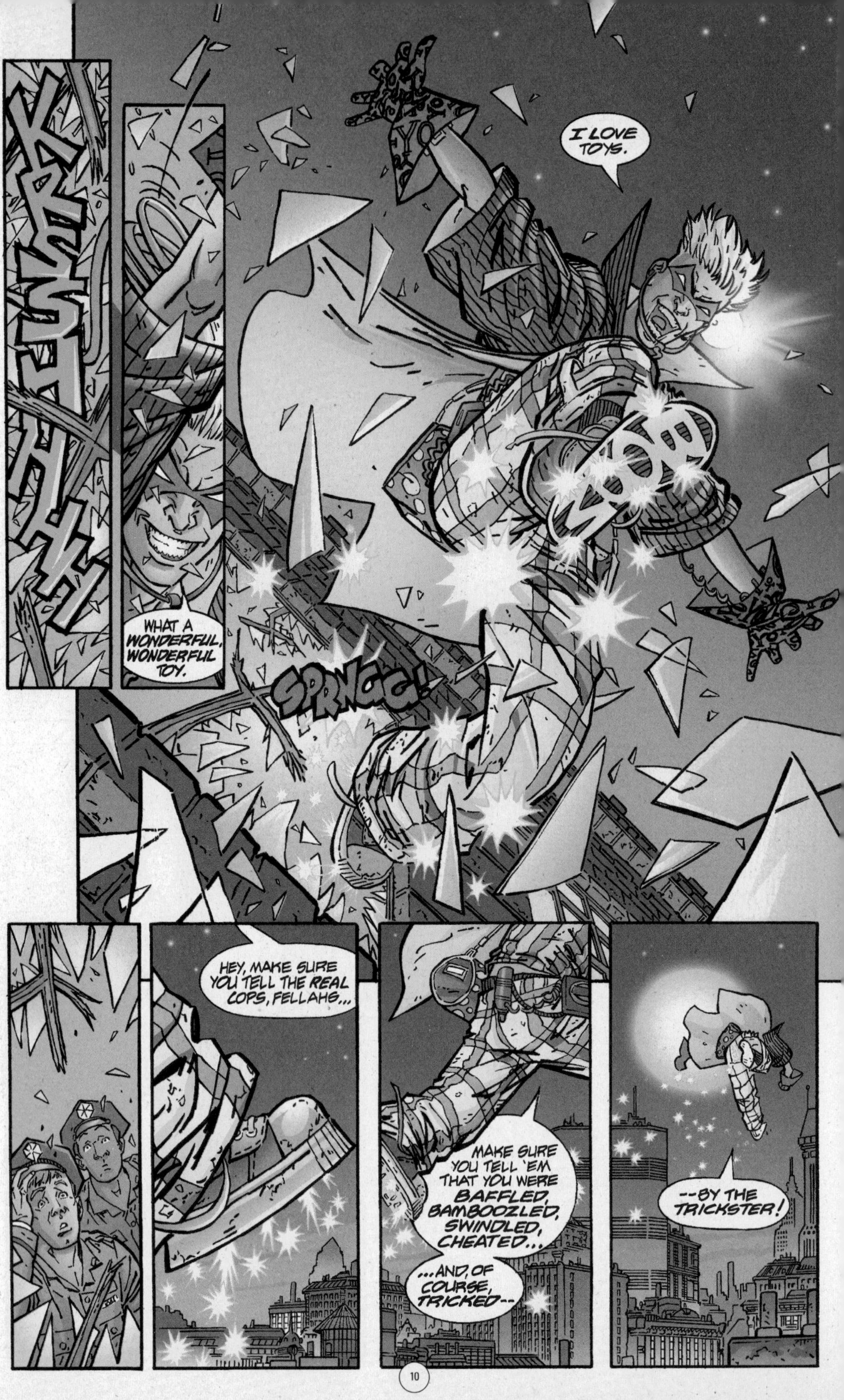
KRSSHHH!
WHAT A WONDERFUL, WONDERFUL TOY.
I LOVE TOYS.
SPRNGG!
HEY, MAKE SURE YOU TELL THE REAL COPS, FELLAHS...
MAKE SURE YOU TELL 'EM THAT YOU WERE BAFFLED, BAMBOOZLED, SWINDLED, CHEATED...
...AND, OF COURSE, TRICKED--
--BY THE TRICKSTER!

THE *TRICKSTER*? I THOUGHT HE *RETIRED*. DIDN'T HE *RETIRE*, MORILLO?

DAMMIT, I WANT THAT *ROGUE* FOUND, OFFICER CHYRE. THE TRICKSTER STOLE *TOP SECRET* DOCUMENTS. UNION PLANS. THIS COULD HAVE DISASTROUS EFFECTS--

ON *YOU*, GOLDFACE?

ON *EVERYONE* IN KEYSTONE. I'M TRYING TO *PROTECT* MY UNION. PROTECT THIS *CITY*.

AND THE *NAME* ISN'T GOLDFACE. IT'S COMMISSIONER KENYON.

uh-huh. MORILLO, YOU WANT TO...

YO, MORILLO! YOU COME HERE FOR THE FREE COFFEE OR THE VIEW?

WHAT?

OH...

WE'VE TAKEN OUR REPORT AND FORENSICS HAS WHAT THEY NEED. IT'LL ALL BE GIVEN TO OUR ROGUE PROFILER,...AND THE FLASH HAS BEEN NOTIFIED.

WE'LL SEE WHAT WE CAN DO.

WHAT?

THAT'S *NOT* GOOD ENOUGH.

IT'S GOING TO HAVE TO BE, KENYON. WE'VE GOT A *STACK* OF METAHUMAN CAGES TO GET THROUGH TODAY, AND QUITE *HONESTLY* YOU'RE DAMN *LOW* ON MY PRIORITY LIST.

NEED MORE SUGAR IN YOUR COFFEE, MORILLO?

I'M FINE, FRED.

FRED?

SCHOOL'S GOOD. A LITTLE *TOUGH* GETTING BACK INTO IT.

BUT IT'S *FUN.*

HOW'S IT GOING FOR YOU, IRIS? WITH JOSH?

IT'S A CHALLENGE. BEEN SO LONG SINCE I RAISED CHILDREN OF MY OWN.

AND I DID THAT IN THE *FUTURE.* WITH HELP FROM ROBOTIC DEVICES YOU WOULDN'T BELIEVE.

RING RING

NEVER CHANGED A SINGLE DIAPER. NOW...NOW I'VE CHANGED PLENTY.

WELCOME BACK TO THE *STONE AGE.*

ACTUALLY, I NEVER *DID* TAKE TO THE *FUTURE.*

ARE YOU *SURE*? HOW DID--

WALLY? WILL YOU *STOP* THAT? THE *WHOLE* APARTMENT'S SHAKING!

BARRY AND I SPENT A LOT OF TIME IN OUR *V.R.* ROOM.

SET TO THE LATE 20TH CENTURY.

AND AFTER BARRY DIED, AND THEN MY KIDS, THE *TWINS*... THERE WAS NOTHING LEFT FOR ME THERE.

THAT WAS JESSE QUICK.

WHAT'S *WRONG?*

HER COMPANY. QUICK-START'S ACCOUNTS JUST WENT *DRY.* FIVE HUNDRED *MILLION* DOLLARS VANISHED WITHOUT A TRACE.

I'M HEADING DOWN TO THE STATION. WORK TO DO.

SOMETIMES THAT MAN--

WAAA! WAA!

--IS STILL JUST A *BOY.*

SHE MIGHT NOT MAKE IT TO JAY'S TONIGHT. I ASKED IF SHE WANTED MY HELP, BUT YOU KNOW HOW JESSE IS.

FIRST MAX MERCURY GOES MISSING, NOW THIS.

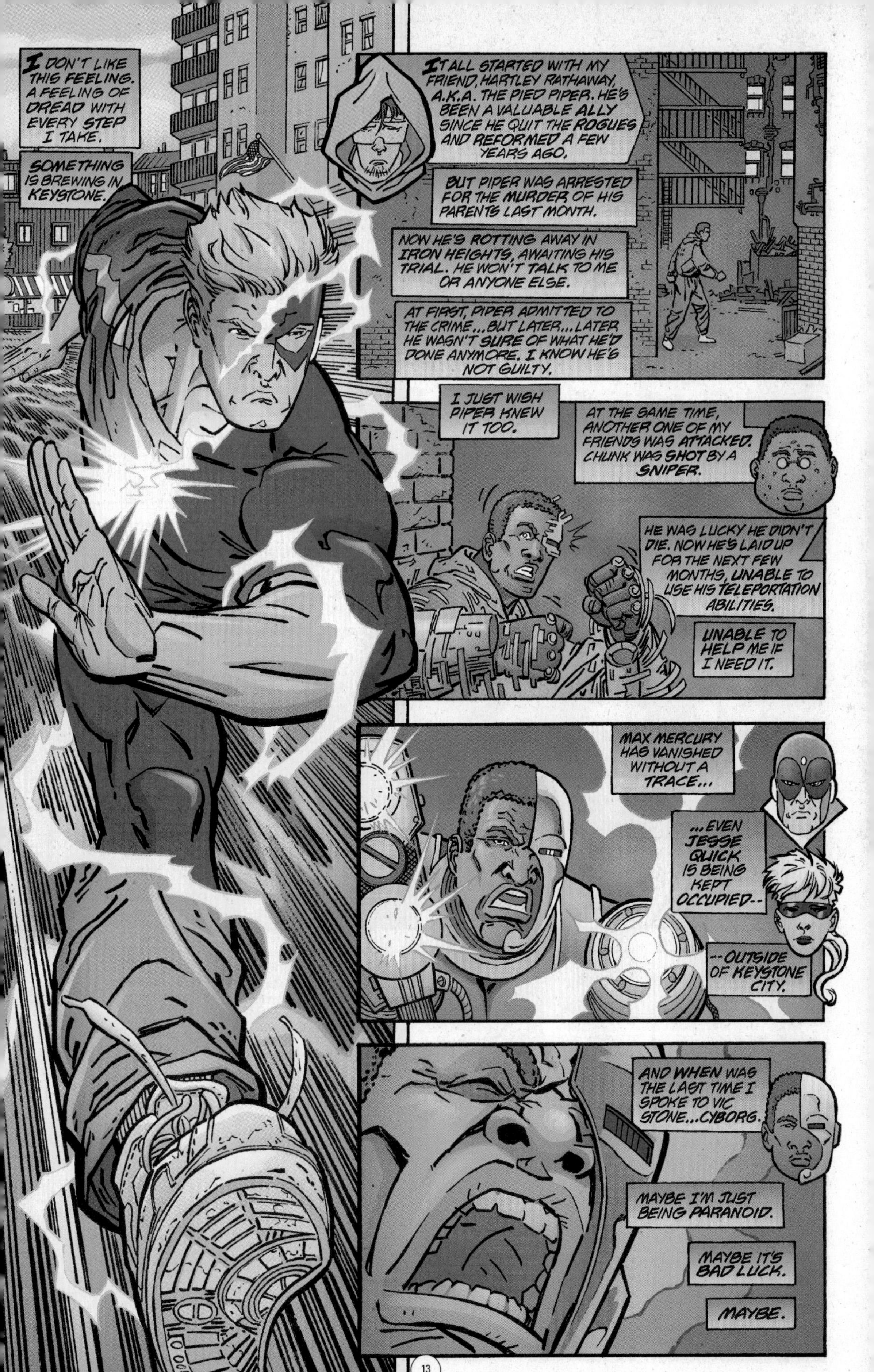
I DON'T LIKE THIS FEELING. A FEELING OF DREAD WITH EVERY STEP I TAKE.
SOMETHING IS BREWING IN KEYSTONE.
IT ALL STARTED WITH MY FRIEND, HARTLEY RATHAWAY, A.K.A. THE PIED PIPER. HE'S BEEN A VALUABLE ALLY SINCE HE QUIT THE ROGUES AND REFORMED A FEW YEARS AGO.
BUT PIPER WAS ARRESTED FOR THE MURDER OF HIS PARENTS LAST MONTH.
NOW HE'S ROTTING AWAY IN IRON HEIGHTS, AWAITING HIS TRIAL. HE WON'T TALK TO ME OR ANYONE ELSE.
AT FIRST, PIPER ADMITTED TO THE CRIME... BUT LATER... LATER HE WASN'T SURE OF WHAT HE'D DONE ANYMORE. I KNOW HE'S NOT GUILTY.
I JUST WISH PIPER KNEW IT TOO.
AT THE SAME TIME, ANOTHER ONE OF MY FRIENDS WAS ATTACKED. CHUNK WAS SHOT BY A SNIPER.
HE WAS LUCKY HE DIDN'T DIE. NOW HE'S LAID UP FOR THE NEXT FEW MONTHS, UNABLE TO USE HIS TELEPORTATION ABILITIES.
UNABLE TO HELP ME IF I NEED IT.
MAX MERCURY HAS VANISHED WITHOUT A TRACE...
...EVEN JESSE QUICK IS BEING KEPT OCCUPIED--
--OUTSIDE OF KEYSTONE CITY.
AND WHEN WAS THE LAST TIME I SPOKE TO VIC STONE...CYBORG.
MAYBE I'M JUST BEING PARANOID.
MAYBE IT'S BAD LUCK.
MAYBE.

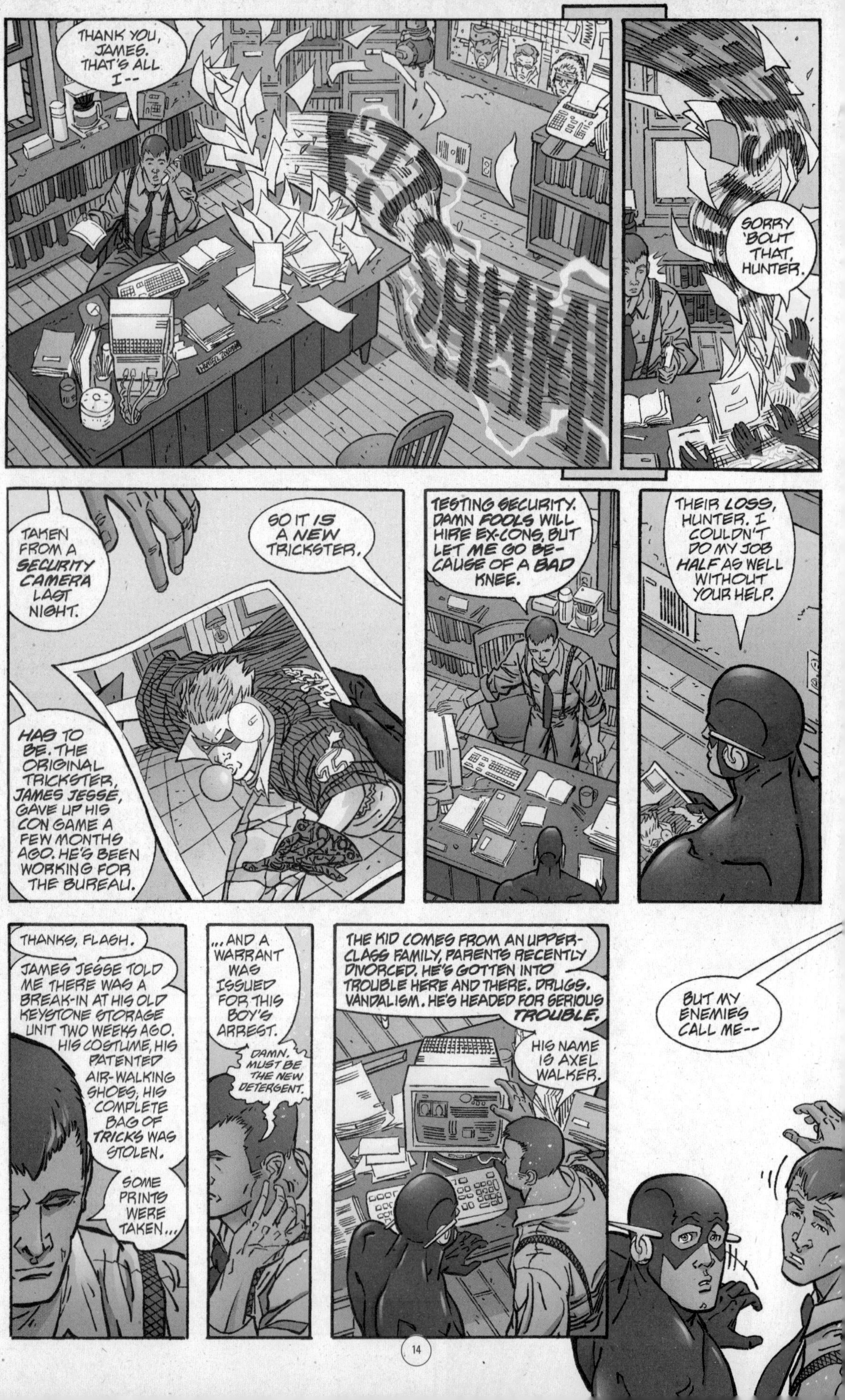
THANK YOU, JAMES. THAT'S ALL I--
SORRY 'BOUT THAT, HUNTER.
TAKEN FROM A SECURITY CAMERA LAST NIGHT.
SO IT IS A NEW TRICKSTER.
HAS TO BE. THE ORIGINAL TRICKSTER, JAMES JESSE, GAVE UP HIS CON GAME A FEW MONTHS AGO. HE'S BEEN WORKING FOR THE BUREAU.
TESTING SECURITY. DAMN FOOLS WILL HIRE EX-CONS, BUT LET ME GO BECAUSE OF A BAD KNEE.
THEIR LOSS, HUNTER. I COULDN'T DO MY JOB HALF AS WELL WITHOUT YOUR HELP.
THANKS, FLASH.
JAMES JESSE TOLD ME THERE WAS A BREAK-IN AT HIS OLD KEYSTONE STORAGE UNIT TWO WEEKS AGO. HIS COSTUME, HIS PATENTED AIR-WALKING SHOES, HIS COMPLETE BAG OF TRICKS WAS STOLEN.
SOME PRINTS WERE TAKEN...
...AND A WARRANT WAS ISSUED FOR THIS BOY'S ARREST.
DAMN. MUST BE THE NEW DETERGENT.
THE KID COMES FROM AN UPPER-CLASS FAMILY, PARENTS RECENTLY DIVORCED. HE'S GOTTEN INTO TROUBLE HERE AND THERE. DRUGS. VANDALISM. HE'S HEADED FOR SERIOUS TROUBLE.
HIS NAME IS AXEL WALKER.
BUT MY ENEMIES CALL ME--

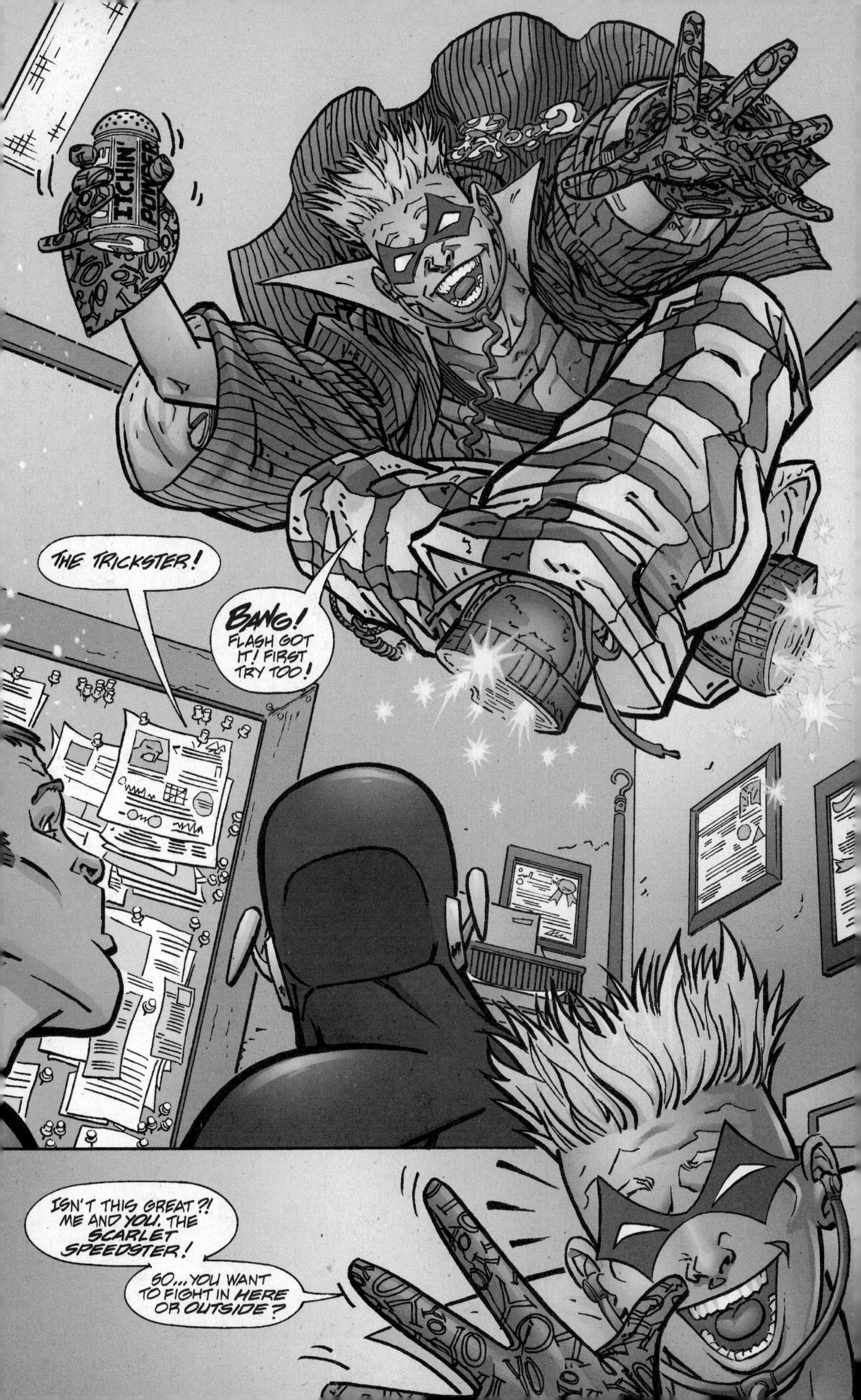
ITCHIN' POWDER
THE TRICKSTER!
BANG! FLASH GOT IT! FIRST TRY TOO!
ISN'T THIS GREAT?! ME AND YOU. THE SCARLET SPEEDSTER!
SO... YOU WANT TO FIGHT IN HERE OR OUTSIDE?

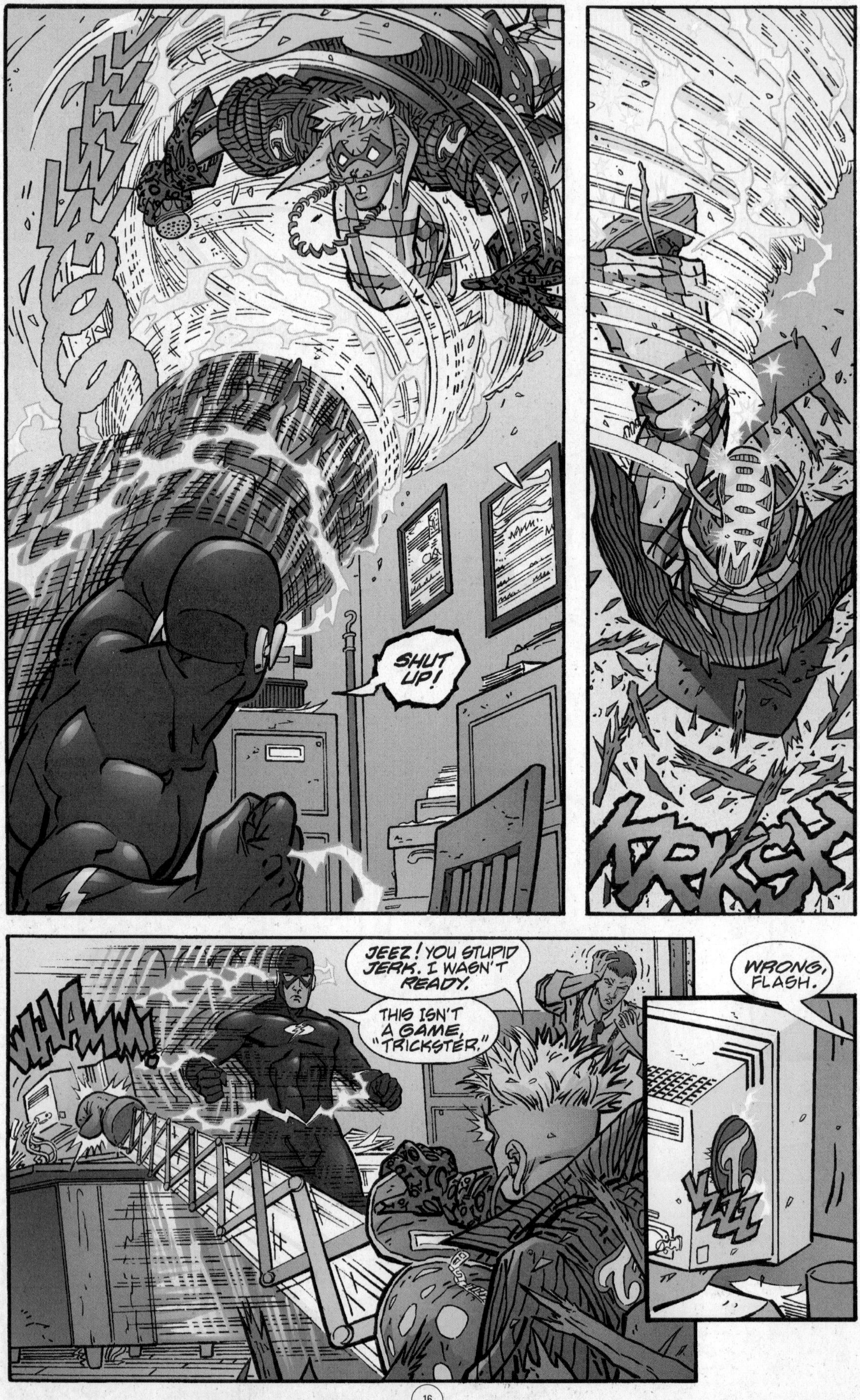
SHUT UP!
WHAMM!
JEEZ! YOU STUPID JERK. I WASN'T READY.
THIS ISN'T A GAME, "TRICKSTER."
WRONG, FLASH.

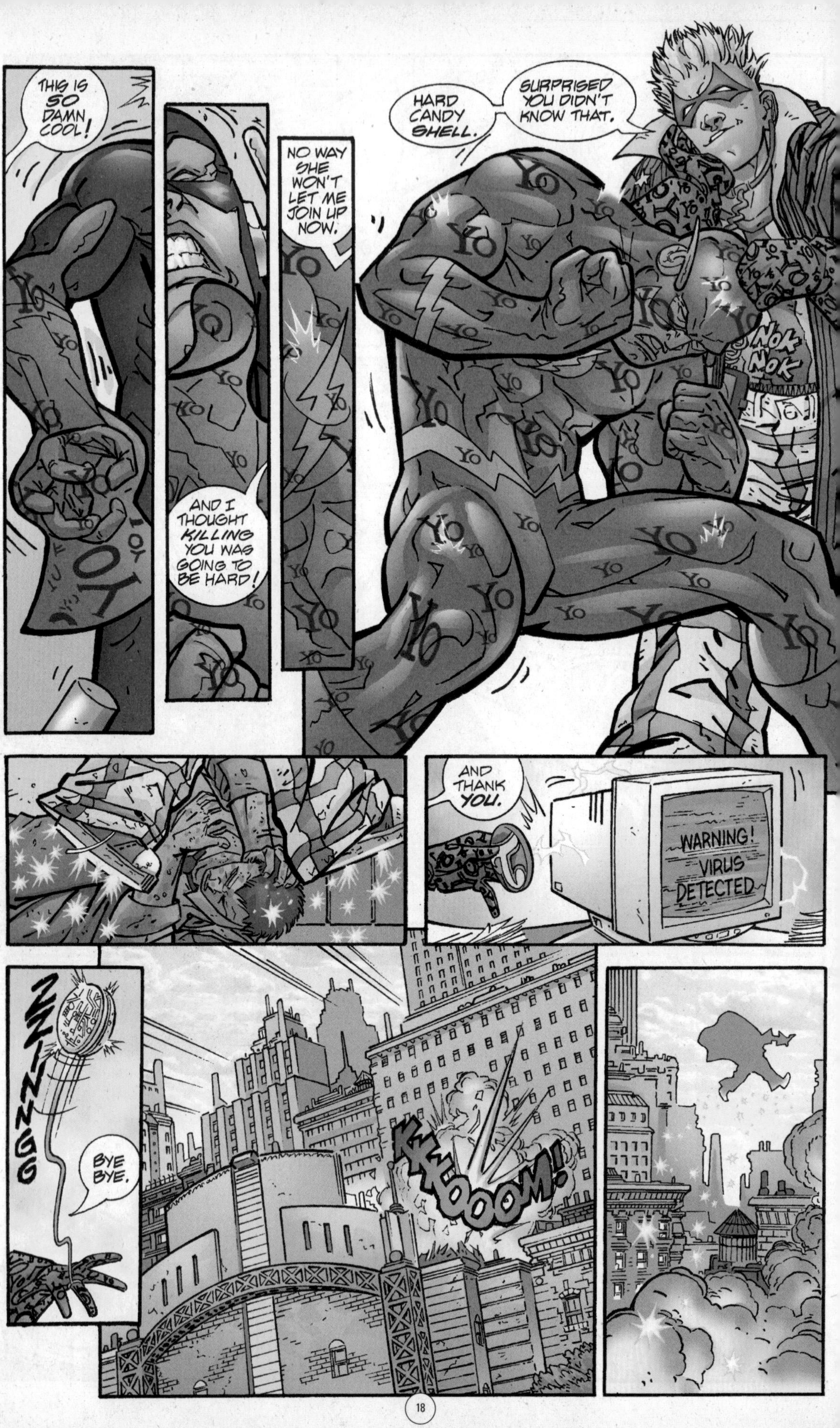
THIS IS SO DAMN COOL!
NO WAY SHE WON'T LET ME JOIN UP NOW.
HARD CANDY SHELL.
SURPRISED YOU DIDN'T KNOW THAT.
AND I THOUGHT KILLING YOU WAS GOING TO BE HARD!
NOK NOK
AND THANK YOU.
WARNING! VIRUS DETECTED
ZZINNGG
BYE BYE.
KKTHOOOM!

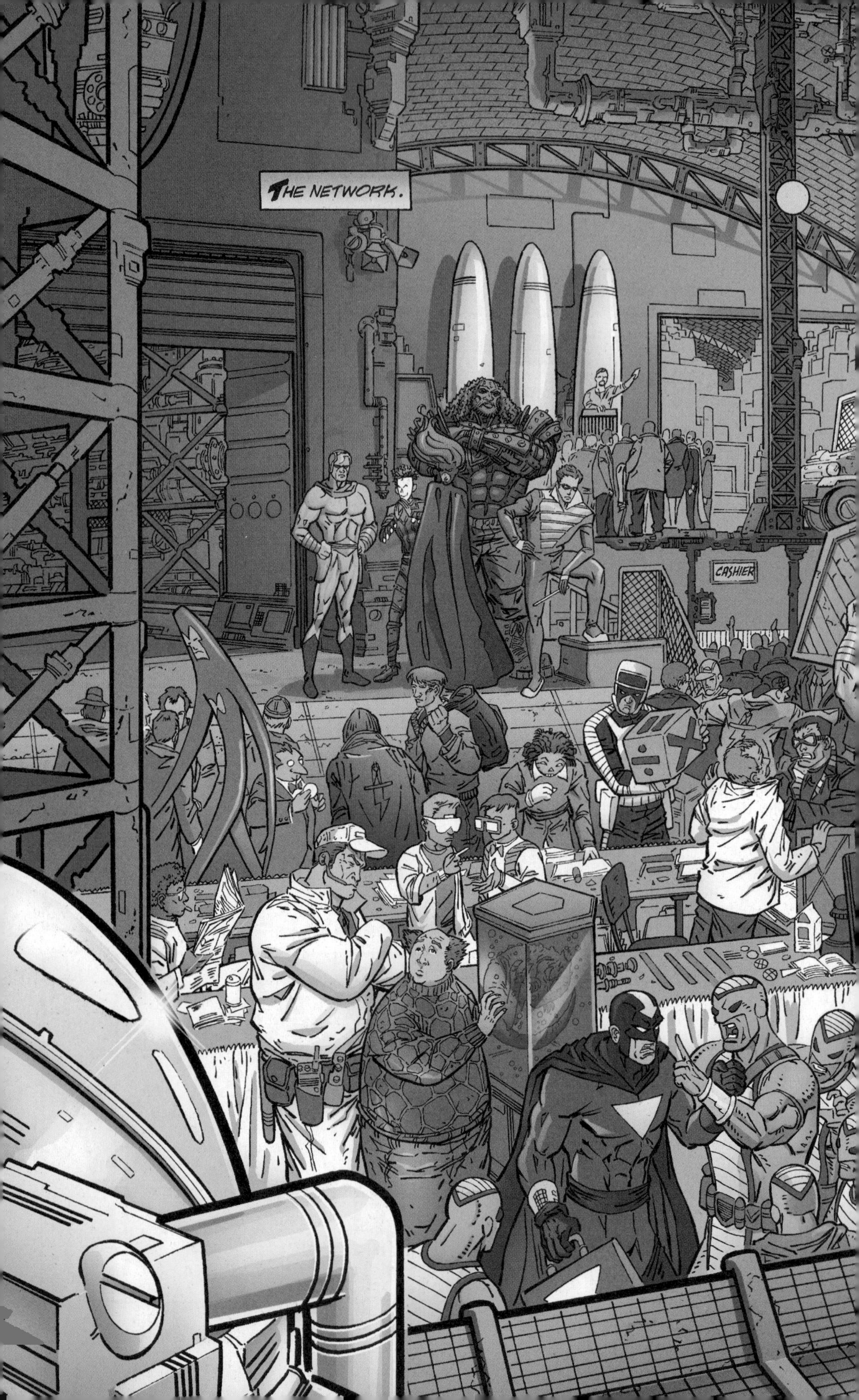
THE NETWORK.
CASHIER

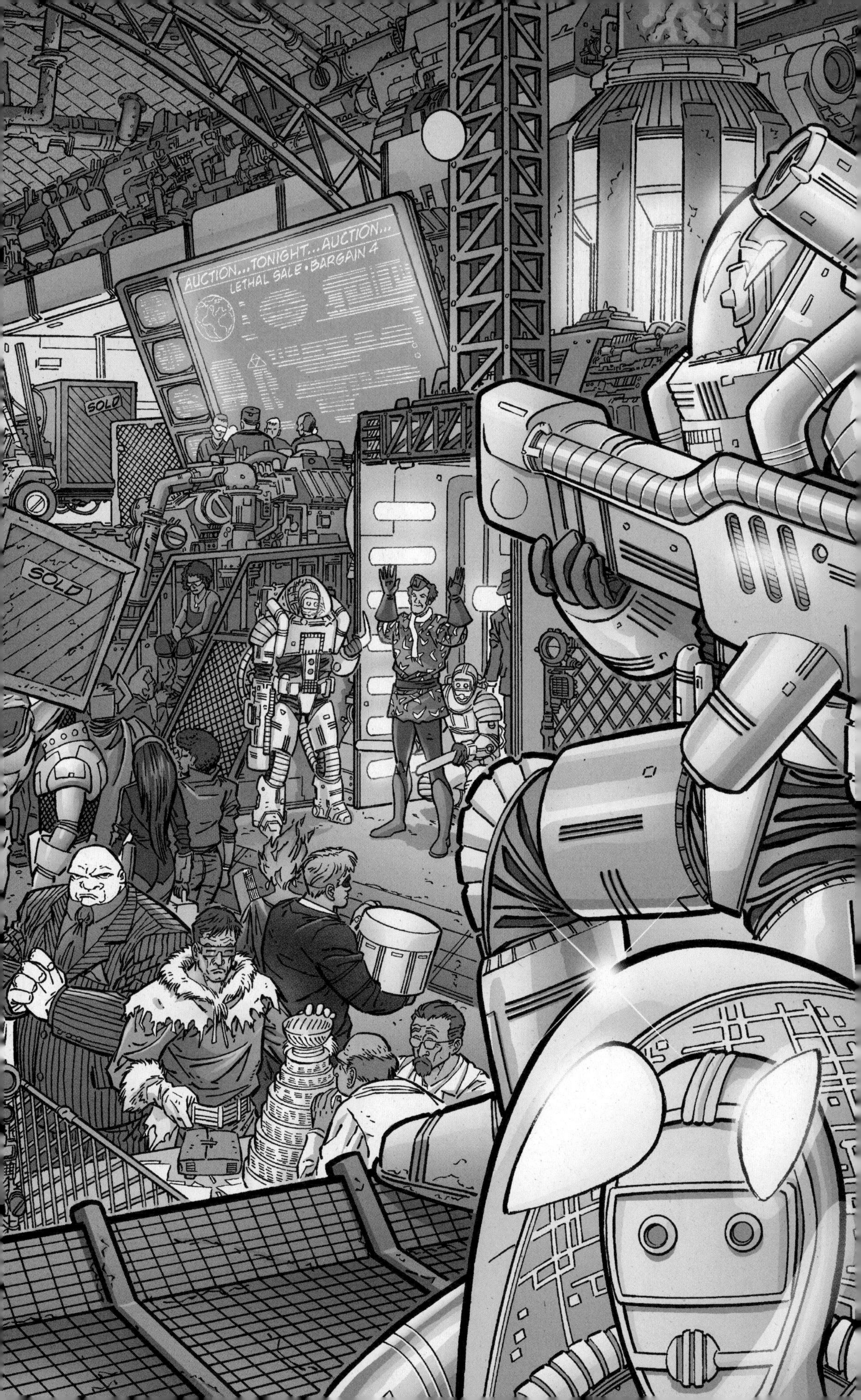
AUCTION...TONIGHT...AUCTION...
LETHAL SALE • BARGAIN 4
SOLD
SOLD

THIS IS *COOL* AS HELL! I HEARD RUMORS OF A *BLACK MARKET* IN KEYSTONE, BUT I HAD NO IDEA.

SO AM I *IN*? WITH MIRROR MASTER AND THE *OTHERS*?

YOU'VE SEEN THE NETWORK. IF YOU *WEREN'T* IN, YOU'D BE *DEAD*.

YOU DID *WELL*, TRICKSTER.

COME ON, BLACKSMITH. WHAT'S HE SUPPOSED TO BE? OUR *MASCOT*? YOU WANT A TRICKSTER, WE'LL DRAG OL' JAMES BACK TO KEYSTONE.

HAW!

THIS "MASCOT" MAY HAVE *SAVED* MY ENTIRE OPERATION, WEATHER WIZARD. HE'S KEEPING YOU *ROGUES* IN BUSINESS.

GOLDFACE WAS READY TO *STRIKE*, HUNTER ZOLOMON WAS ABOUT TO PIECE EVERYTHING TOGETHER AND *EXPOSE* THE NETWORK.

I'M NOT ABOUT TO THROW *FIFTEEN* YEARS AWAY.

HANDS *OFF*, GIRDER.

VMMM

BLACKSMITH! WE HAVE *TROUBLE*!

WHAT'S GOING ON?

COMPUTRON UNIT EIGHT REPORTING. IT'S THE *RAIDER* AGAIN. STIRRING UP *TROUBLE*.

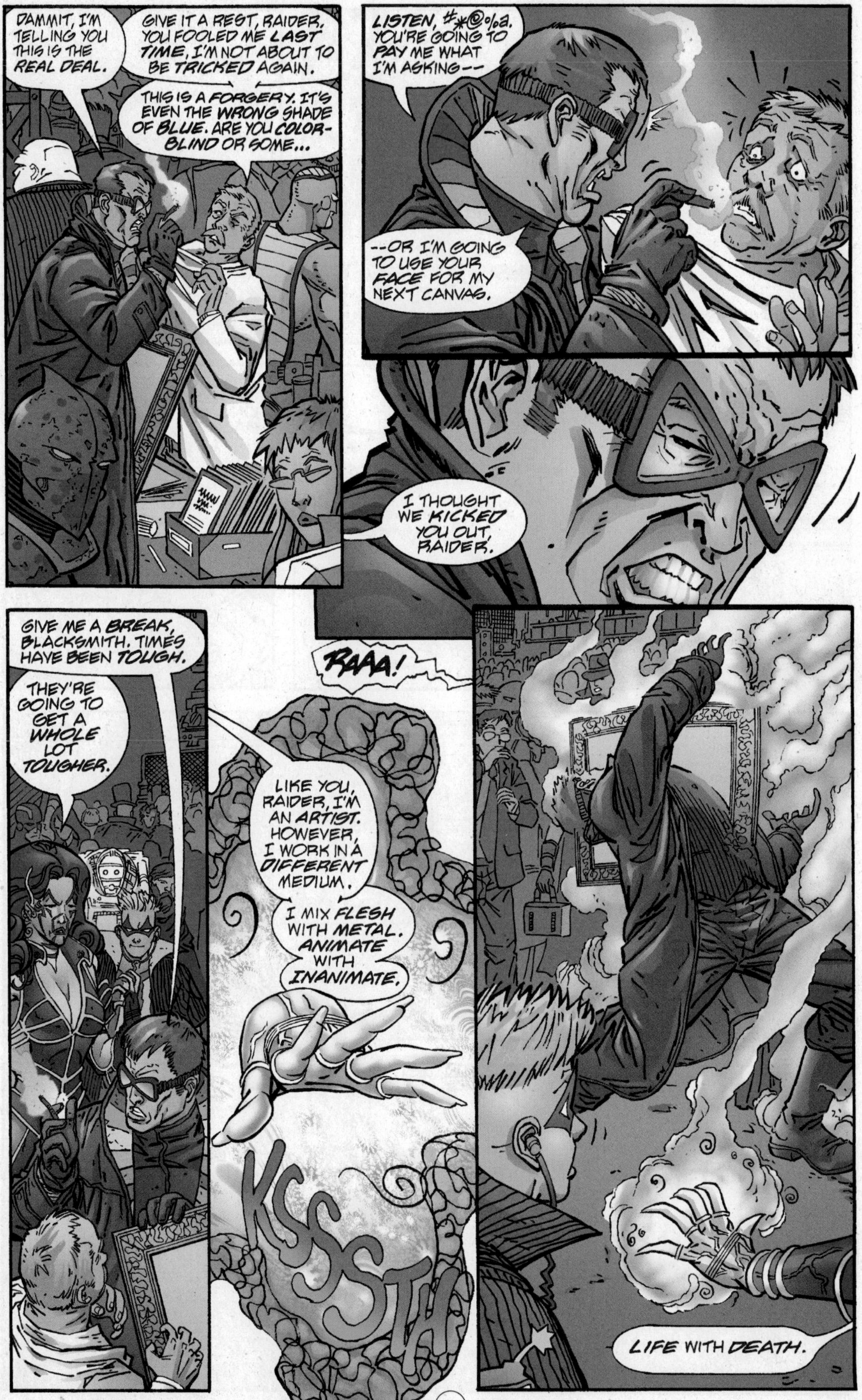
DAMMIT, I'M TELLING YOU THIS IS THE REAL DEAL.
GIVE IT A REST, RAIDER. YOU FOOLED ME LAST TIME, I'M NOT ABOUT TO BE TRICKED AGAIN.
THIS IS A FORGERY. IT'S EVEN THE WRONG SHADE OF BLUE. ARE YOU COLOR-BLIND OR SOME...
LISTEN, #*@%a. YOU'RE GOING TO PAY ME WHAT I'M ASKING--
--OR I'M GOING TO USE YOUR FACE FOR MY NEXT CANVAS.
I THOUGHT WE KICKED YOU OUT, RAIDER.
GIVE ME A BREAK, BLACKSMITH. TIMES HAVE BEEN TOUGH.
THEY'RE GOING TO GET A WHOLE LOT TOUGHER.
RAAA!
LIKE YOU, RAIDER, I'M AN ARTIST. HOWEVER, I WORK IN A DIFFERENT MEDIUM.
I MIX FLESH WITH METAL. ANIMATE WITH INANIMATE.
KSSSTH
LIFE WITH DEATH.

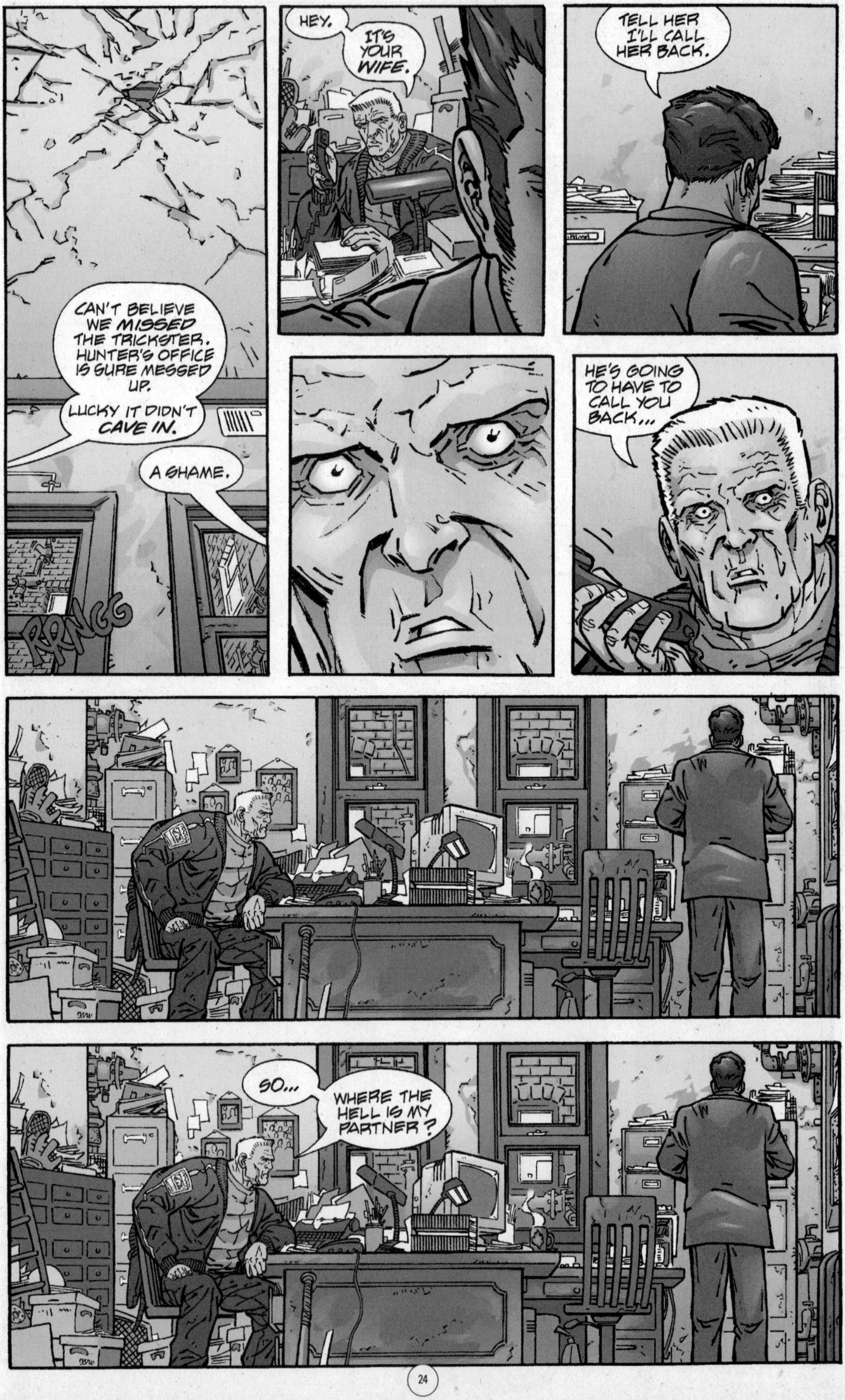
CAN'T BELIEVE WE MISSED THE TRICKSTER. HUNTER'S OFFICE IS SURE MESSED UP.
LUCKY IT DIDN'T CAVE IN.
A SHAME.
RRNGG
HEY.
IT'S YOUR WIFE.
TELL HER I'LL CALL HER BACK.
HE'S GOING TO HAVE TO CALL YOU BACK...
SO...
WHERE THE HELL IS MY PARTNER?

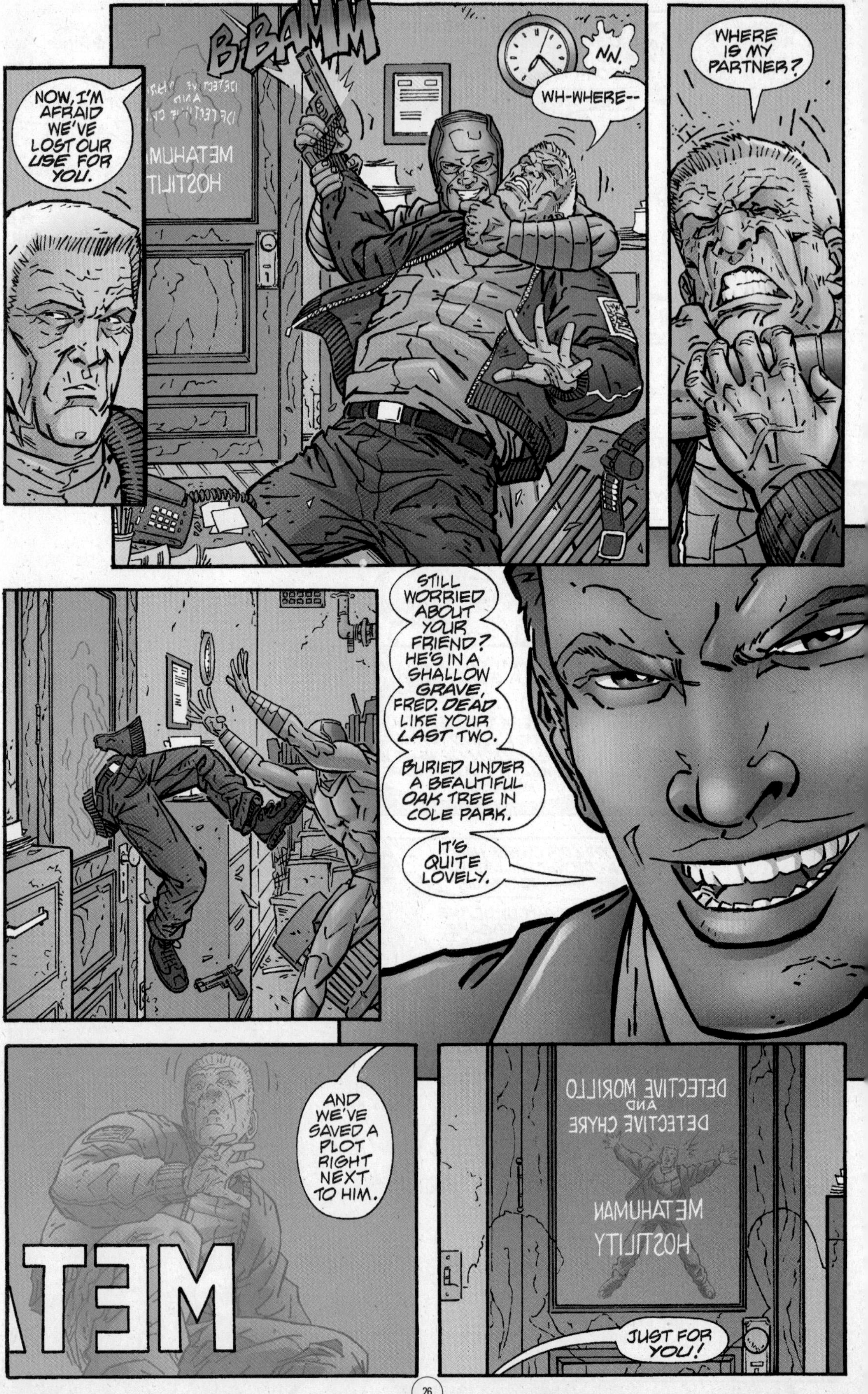
NOW, I'M AFRAID WE'VE LOST OUR USE FOR YOU.
B-BAMM
NN.
WH-WHERE--
WHERE IS MY PARTNER?
STILL WORRIED ABOUT YOUR FRIEND? HE'S IN A SHALLOW GRAVE, FRED. DEAD LIKE YOUR LAST TWO.
BURIED UNDER A BEAUTIFUL OAK TREE IN COLE PARK.
IT'S QUITE LOVELY.
AND WE'VE SAVED A PLOT RIGHT NEXT TO HIM.
JUST FOR YOU!

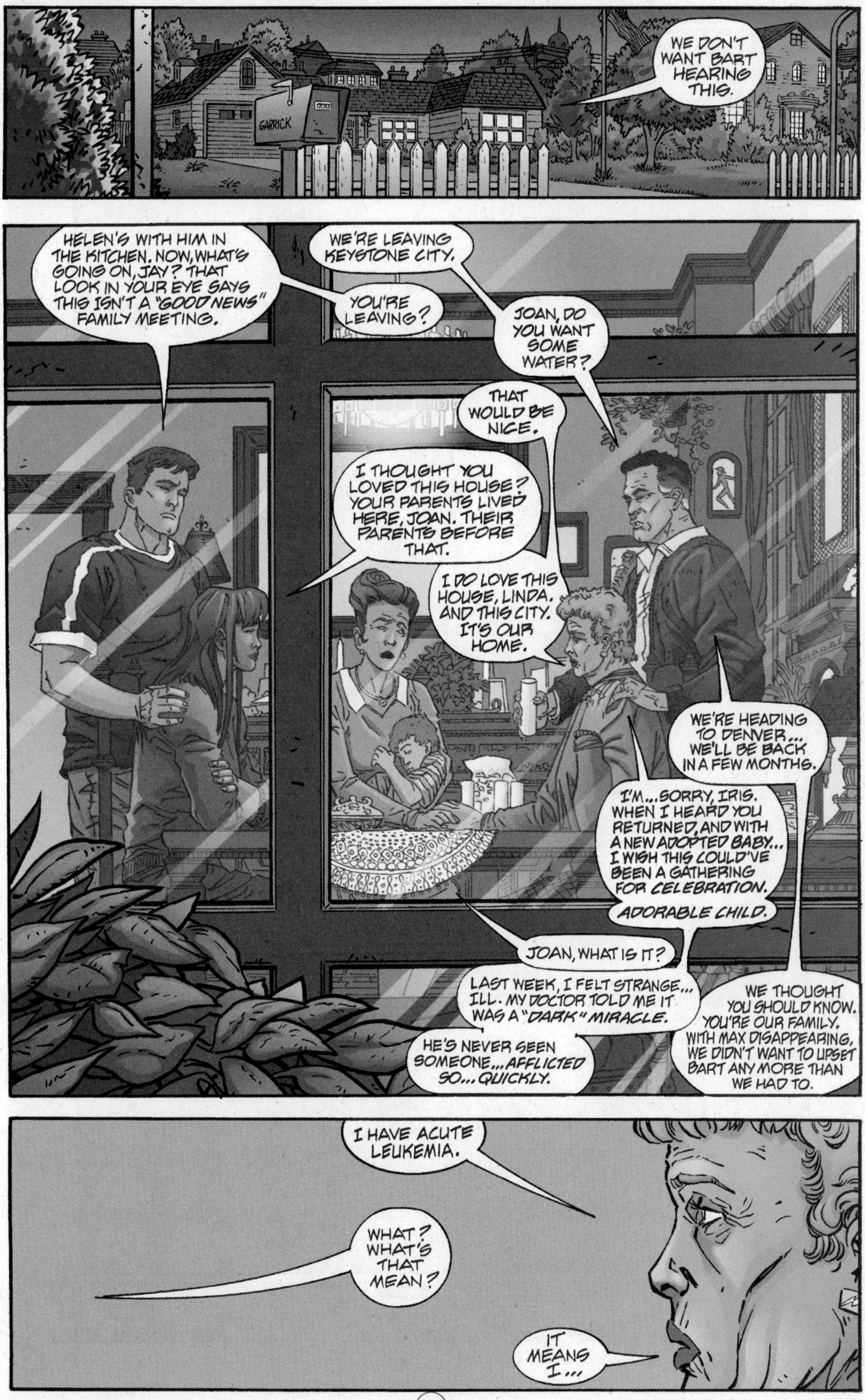
GARRICK
WE DON'T WANT BART HEARING THIS.
HELEN'S WITH HIM IN THE KITCHEN. NOW, WHAT'S GOING ON, JAY? THAT LOOK IN YOUR EYE SAYS THIS ISN'T A "GOOD NEWS" FAMILY MEETING.
WE'RE LEAVING KEYSTONE CITY.
YOU'RE LEAVING?
JOAN, DO YOU WANT SOME WATER?
THAT WOULD BE NICE.
I THOUGHT YOU LOVED THIS HOUSE? YOUR PARENTS LIVED HERE, JOAN. THEIR PARENTS BEFORE THAT.
I DO LOVE THIS HOUSE, LINDA. AND THIS CITY. IT'S OUR HOME.
WE'RE HEADING TO DENVER... WE'LL BE BACK IN A FEW MONTHS.
I'M... SORRY, IRIS. WHEN I HEARD YOU RETURNED, AND WITH A NEW ADOPTED BABY... I WISH THIS COULD'VE BEEN A GATHERING FOR CELEBRATION.
ADORABLE CHILD.
JOAN, WHAT IS IT?
LAST WEEK, I FELT STRANGE... ILL. MY DOCTOR TOLD ME IT WAS A "DARK" MIRACLE.
HE'S NEVER SEEN SOMEONE... AFFLICTED SO... QUICKLY.
WE THOUGHT YOU SHOULD KNOW. YOU'RE OUR FAMILY. WITH MAX DISAPPEARING, WE DIDN'T WANT TO UPSET BART ANY MORE THAN WE HAD TO.
I HAVE ACUTE LEUKEMIA.
WHAT? WHAT'S THAT MEAN?
IT MEANS I...

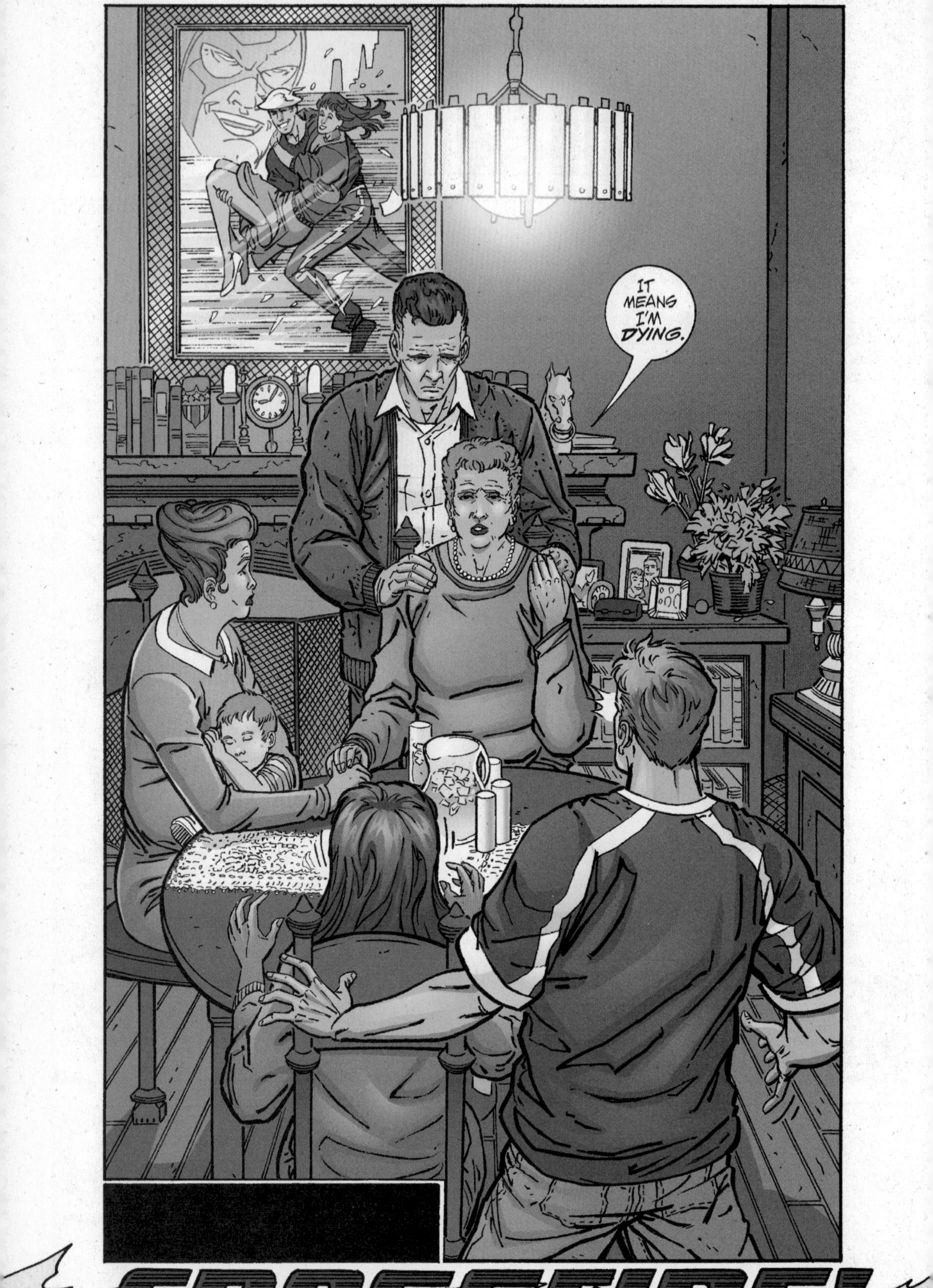
IT MEANS I'M DYING.
CROSSFIRE!

KEYSTONE CITY.

THE CITY OF INDUSTRY.

BUILT IN KEYSTONE

TIKA TIKA TAC TAC

AND HOME TO THE FLASH.

YOU'RE AWFULLY QUIET, WALLY.

SO IS KEYSTONE.

I KNOW YOU'RE WORRIED ABOUT THE GARRICKS, BUT IRIS TALKED TO THEM THIS MORNING. JAY'S IMPRESSED WITH THE CANCER SPECIALIST JOAN'S SEEING.

IT'S MORE THAN THAT, LINDA.

THE GARRICKS AREN'T THE ONLY ONES TO BE HIT BY A STROKE OF BAD LUCK.

PIPER, CHUNK AND JESSE QUICK ARE OUT OF COMMISSION. MAX MERCURY IS STILL MISSING.

AND CYBORG... VIC HASN'T CALLED ME BACK, HAS HE?

NO. HE HASN'T.

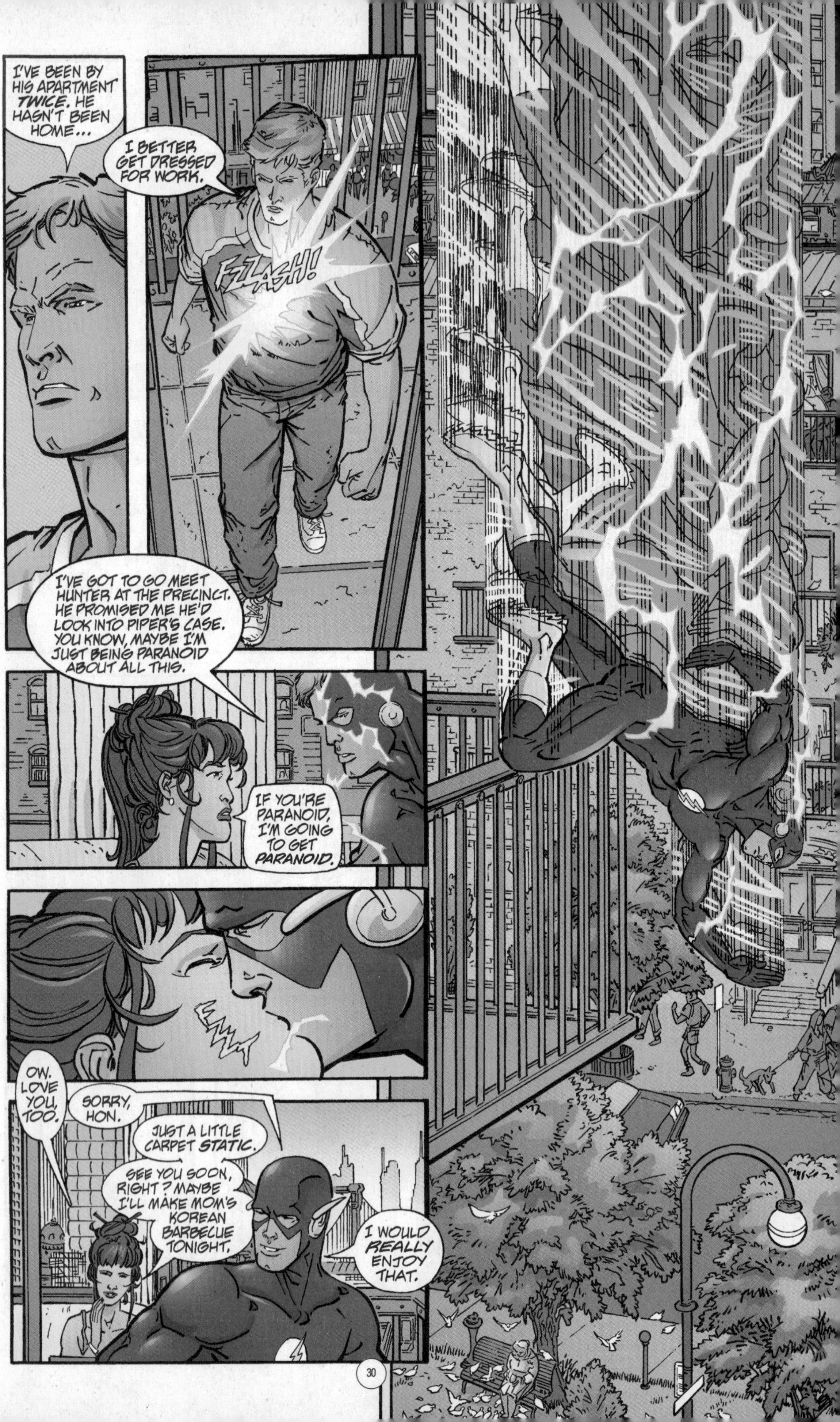
I'VE BEEN BY HIS APARTMENT TWICE. HE HASN'T BEEN HOME...
I BETTER GET DRESSED FOR WORK.
FLASH!
I'VE GOT TO GO MEET HUNTER AT THE PRECINCT. HE PROMISED ME HE'D LOOK INTO PIPER'S CASE. YOU KNOW, MAYBE I'M JUST BEING PARANOID ABOUT ALL THIS.
IF YOU'RE PARANOID, I'M GOING TO GET PARANOID.
OW. LOVE YOU, TOO.
SORRY, HON.
JUST A LITTLE CARPET STATIC.
SEE YOU SOON, RIGHT? MAYBE I'LL MAKE MOM'S KOREAN BARBECUE TONIGHT.
I WOULD REALLY ENJOY THAT.

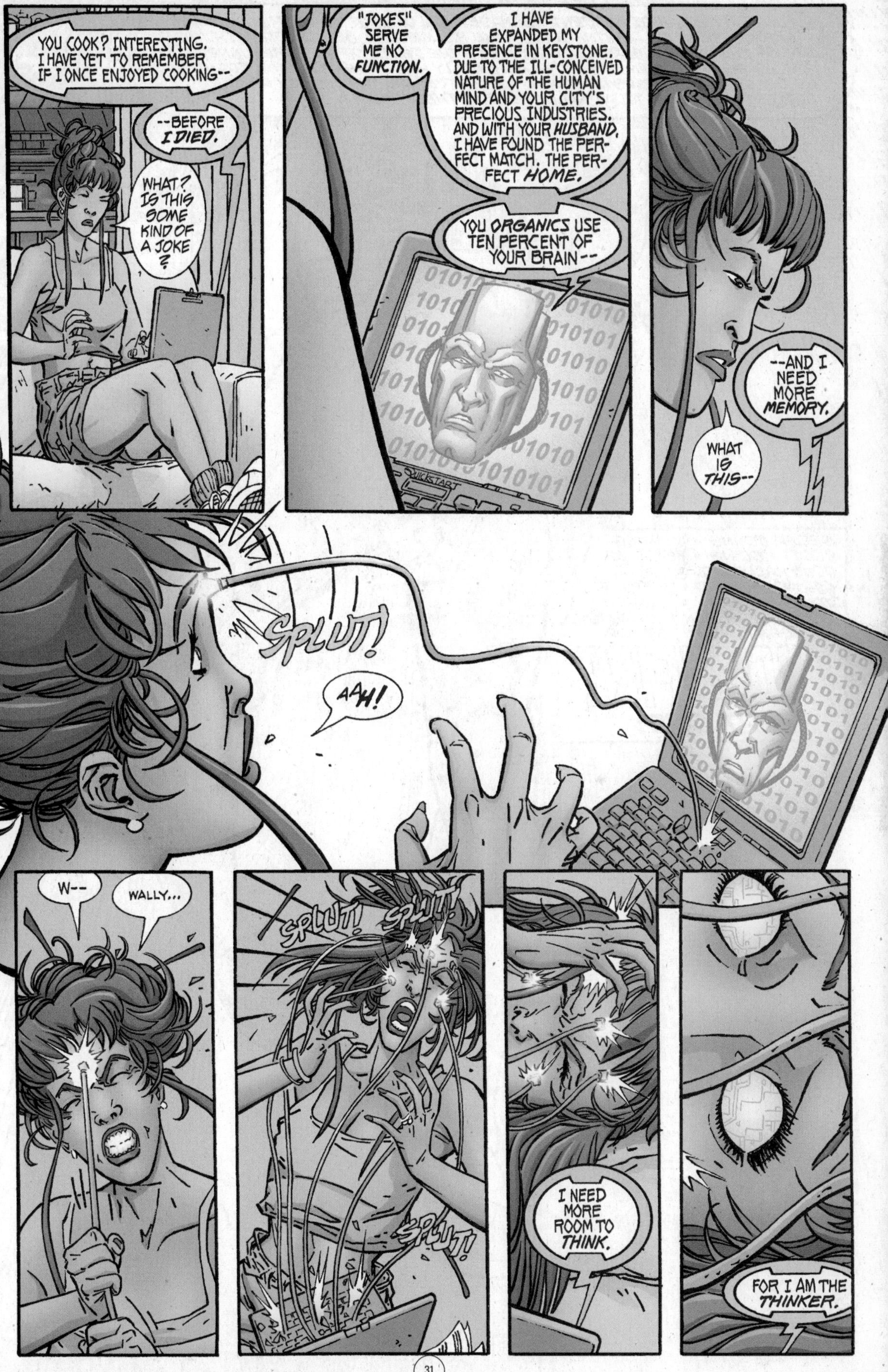
YOU COOK? INTERESTING. I HAVE YET TO REMEMBER IF I ONCE ENJOYED COOKING--
--BEFORE I DIED.
WHAT? IS THIS SOME KIND OF A JOKE?
"JOKES" SERVE ME NO FUNCTION.
I HAVE EXPANDED MY PRESENCE IN KEYSTONE. DUE TO THE ILL-CONCEIVED NATURE OF THE HUMAN MIND AND YOUR CITY'S PRECIOUS INDUSTRIES. AND WITH YOUR HUSBAND, I HAVE FOUND THE PERFECT MATCH. THE PERFECT HOME.
YOU ORGANICS USE TEN PERCENT OF YOUR BRAIN--
--AND I NEED MORE MEMORY.
WHAT IS THIS--
SPLUT!
AAH!
W--
WALLY...
SPLUT! SPLUT!
SPLUT!
I NEED MORE ROOM TO THINK.
FOR I AM THE THINKER.

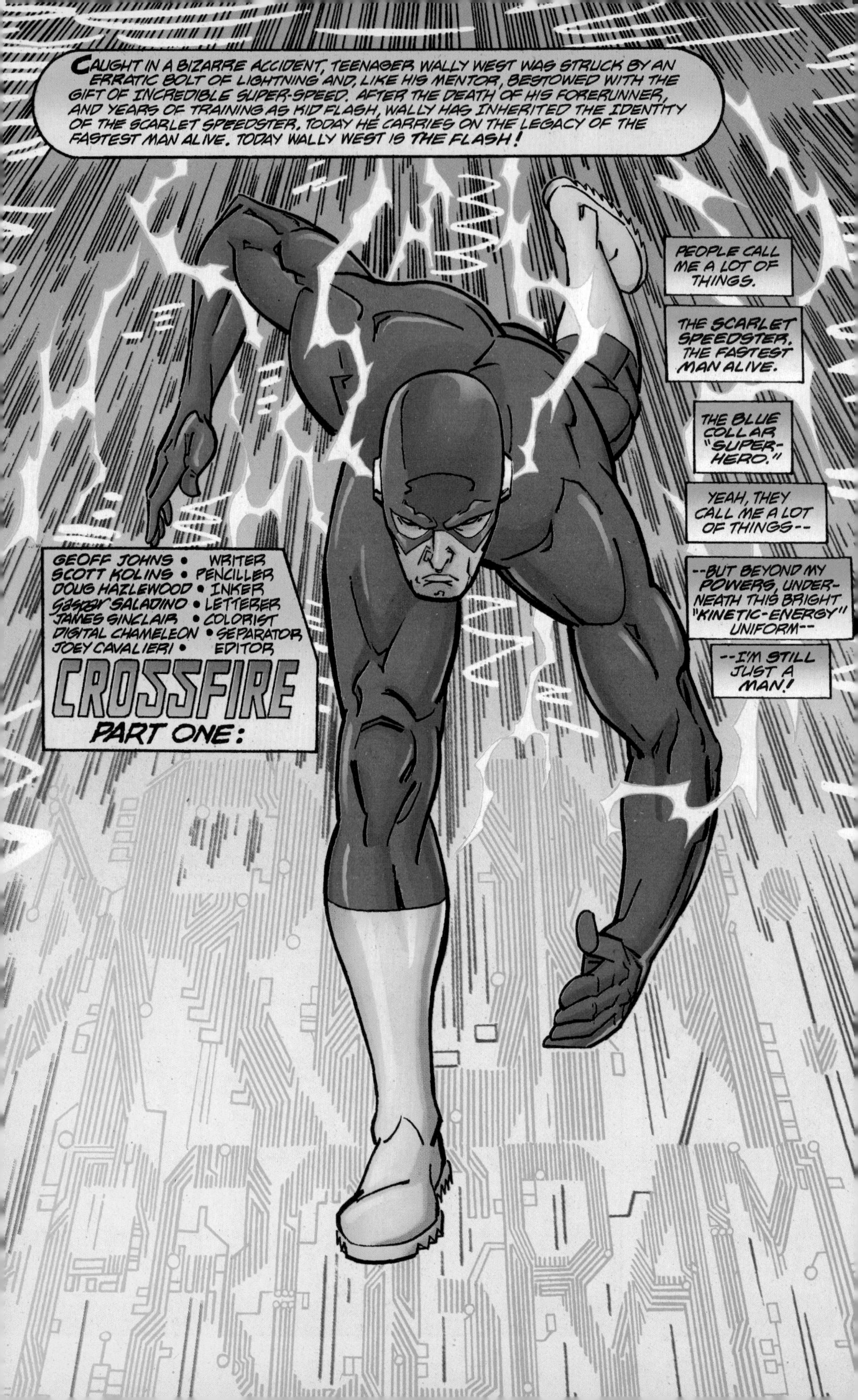
CAUGHT IN A BIZARRE ACCIDENT, TEENAGER WALLY WEST WAS STRUCK BY AN ERRATIC BOLT OF LIGHTNING AND, LIKE HIS MENTOR, BESTOWED WITH THE GIFT OF INCREDIBLE SUPER-SPEED. AFTER THE DEATH OF HIS FORERUNNER, AND YEARS OF TRAINING AS KID FLASH, WALLY HAS INHERITED THE IDENTITY OF THE SCARLET SPEEDSTER. TODAY HE CARRIES ON THE LEGACY OF THE FASTEST MAN ALIVE. TODAY WALLY WEST IS THE FLASH!
PEOPLE CALL ME A LOT OF THINGS.
THE SCARLET SPEEDSTER. THE FASTEST MAN ALIVE.
THE BLUE COLLAR "SUPER-HERO."
YEAH, THEY CALL ME A LOT OF THINGS--
--BUT BEYOND MY POWERS, UNDERNEATH THIS BRIGHT "KINETIC-ENERGY" UNIFORM--
--I'M STILL JUST A MAN!
GEOFF JOHNS • WRITER
SCOTT KOLINS • PENCILLER
DOUG HAZLEWOOD • INKER
GASPAR SALADINO • LETTERER
JAMES SINCLAIR • COLORIST
DIGITAL CHAMELEON • SEPARATOR
JOEY CAVALIERI • EDITOR
CROSSFIRE
PART ONE:

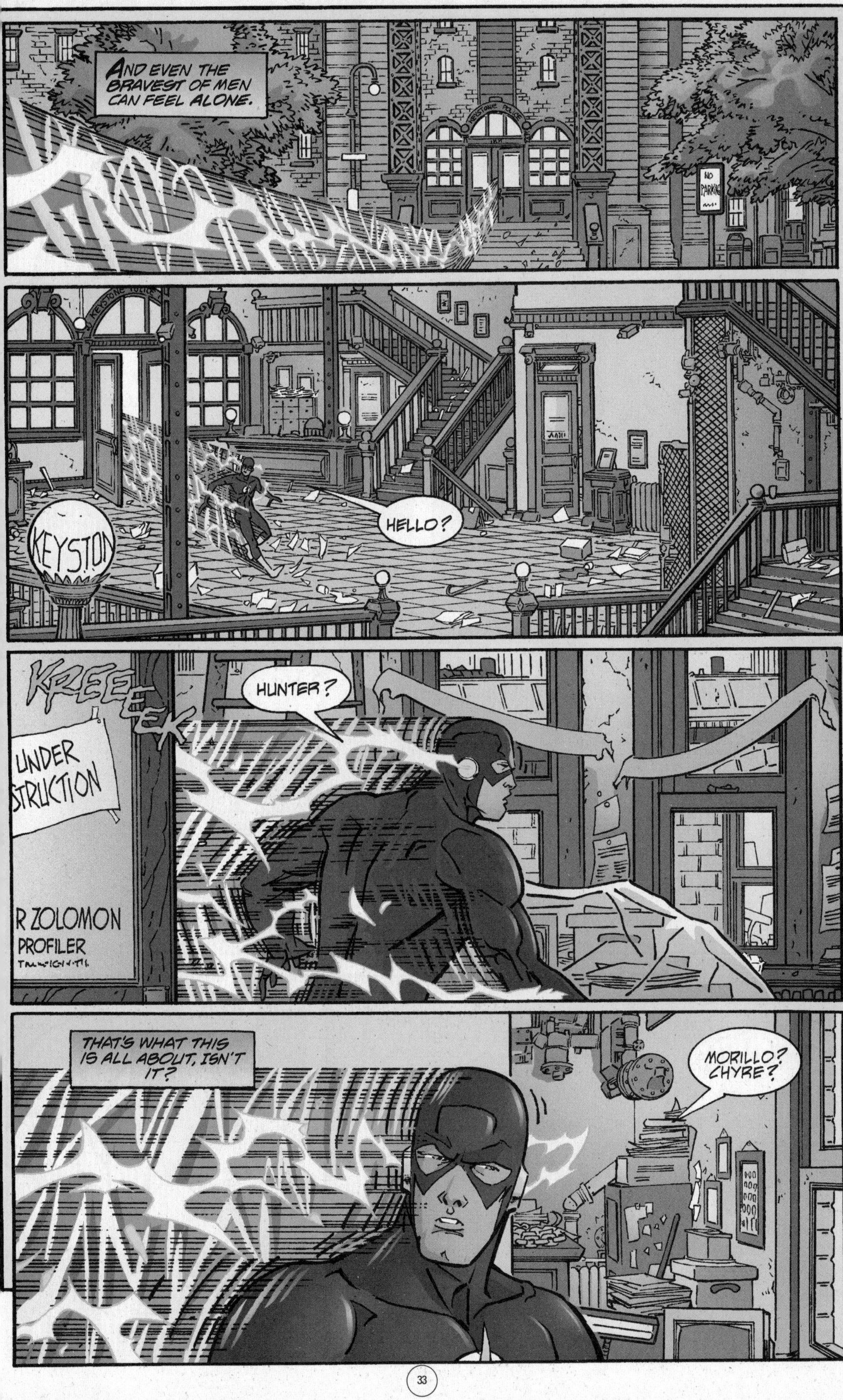
AND EVEN THE BRAVEST OF MEN CAN FEEL ALONE.
NO PARKING
KEYSTON
HELLO?
KREEEEEK
HUNTER?
UNDER
STRUCTION
R ZOLOMON
PROFILER
THAT'S WHAT THIS IS ALL ABOUT, ISN'T IT?
MORILLO? CHYRE?

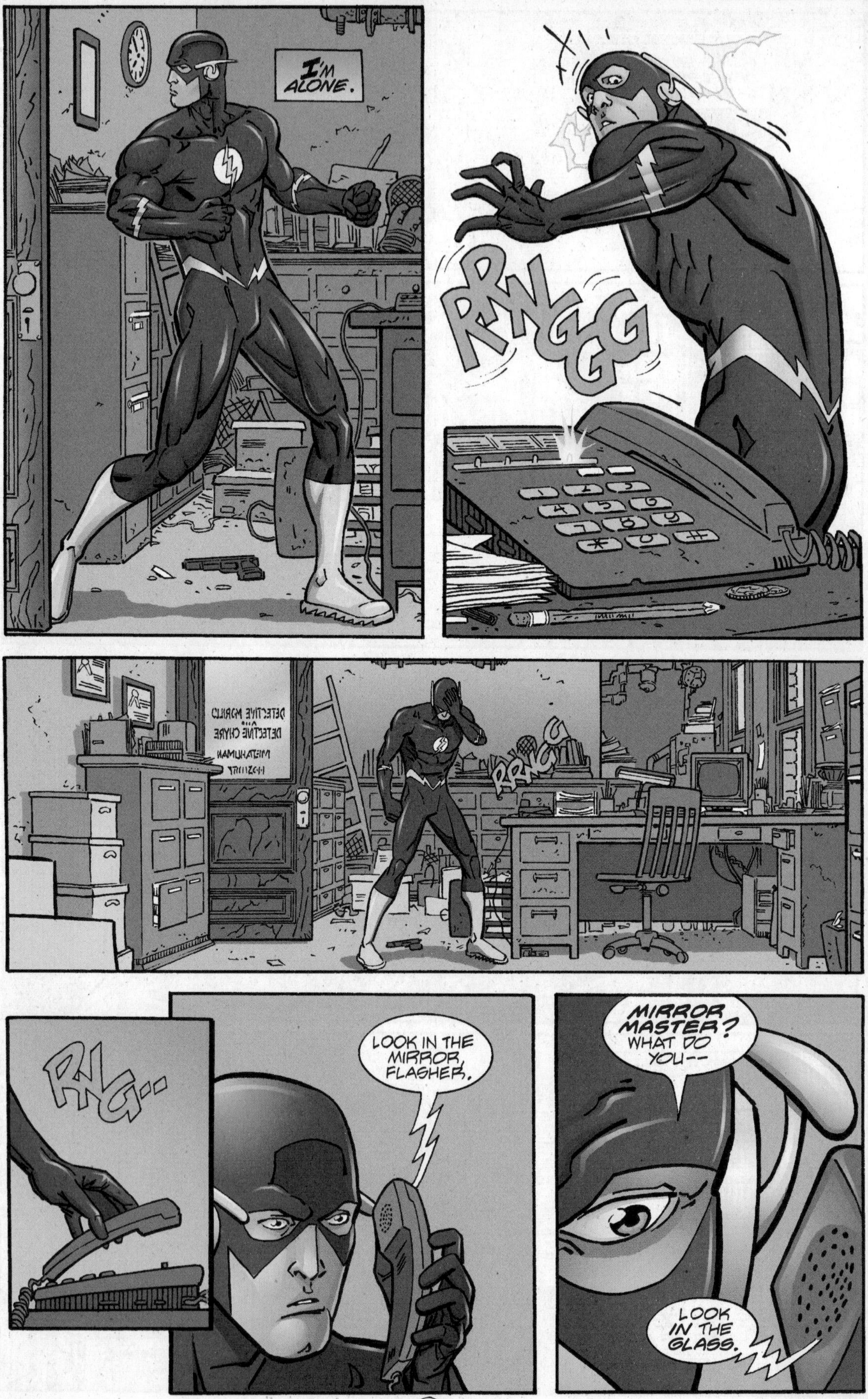
I'M ALONE.
RRNGGG
RRNG
RNG..
LOOK IN THE MIRROR, FLASHER.
MIRROR MASTER? WHAT DO YOU--
LOOK IN THE GLASS.

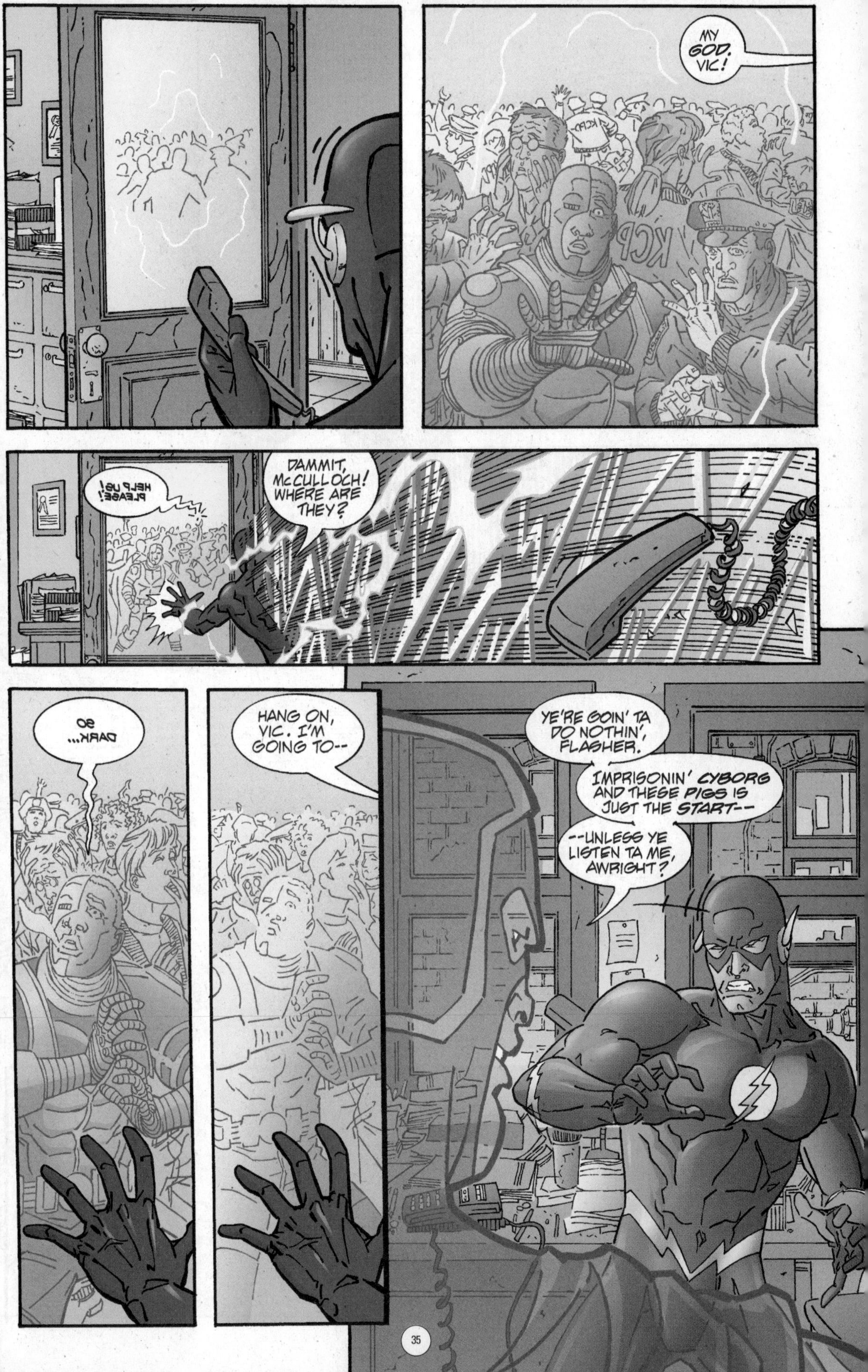

MY GOD. VIC!
HELP US! PLEASE!
DAMMIT, McCULLOCH! WHERE ARE THEY?
SO DARK...
HANG ON, VIC. I'M GOING TO--
YE'RE GOIN' TA DO NOTHIN', FLASHER.
IMPRISONIN' CYBORG AND THESE PIGS IS JUST THE START--
--UNLESS YE LISTEN TA ME, AWRIGHT?

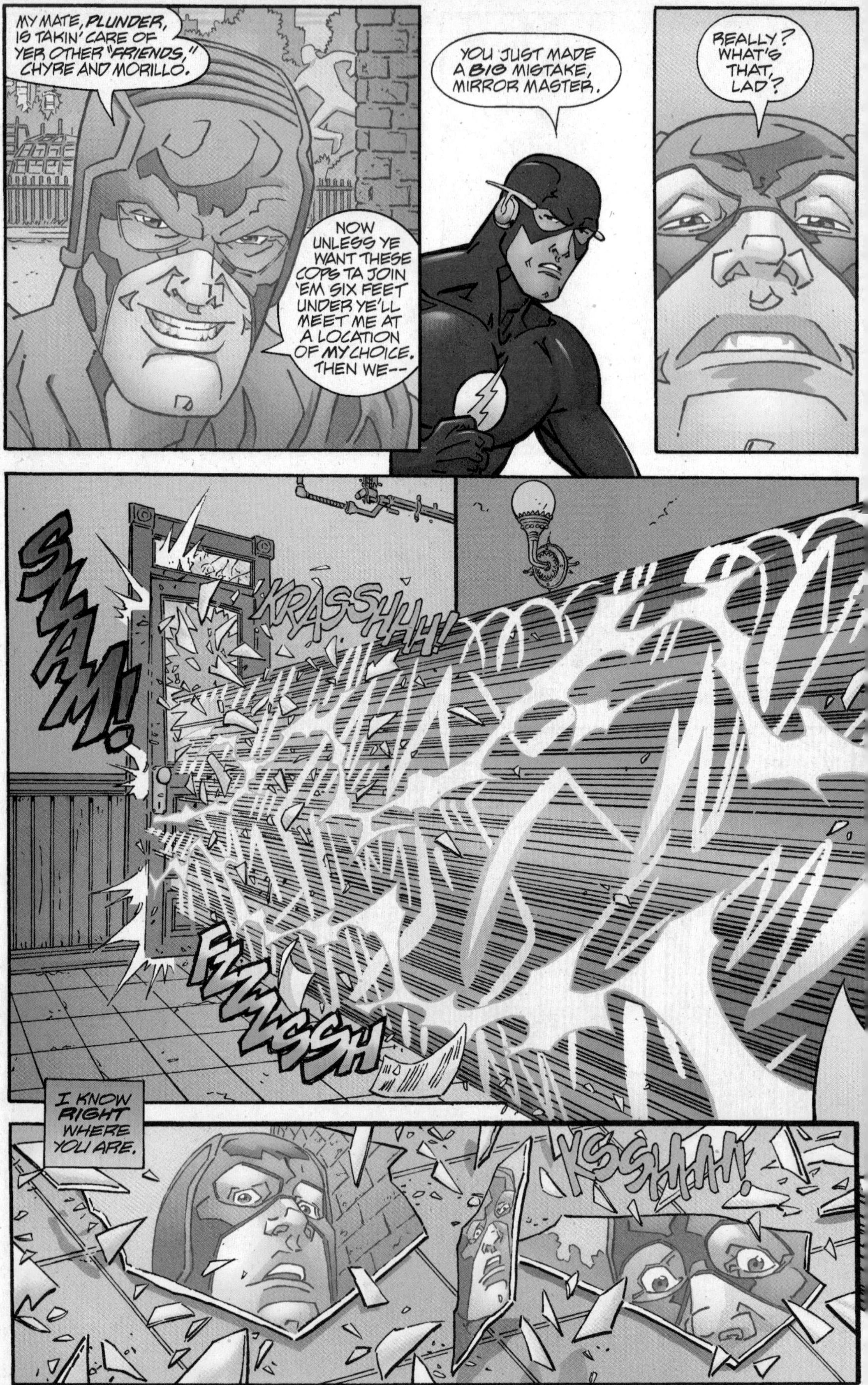
MY MATE, PLUNDER, IS TAKIN' CARE OF YER OTHER "FRIENDS," CHYRE AND MORILLO.
NOW UNLESS YE WANT THESE COPS TA JOIN 'EM SIX FEET UNDER YE'LL MEET ME AT A LOCATION OF MY CHOICE. THEN WE--
YOU JUST MADE A BIG MISTAKE, MIRROR MASTER.
REALLY? WHAT'S THAT, LAD?
SHAM!
KRASSHHH!
FZZWSSH
I KNOW RIGHT WHERE YOU ARE.
KSSHHH!

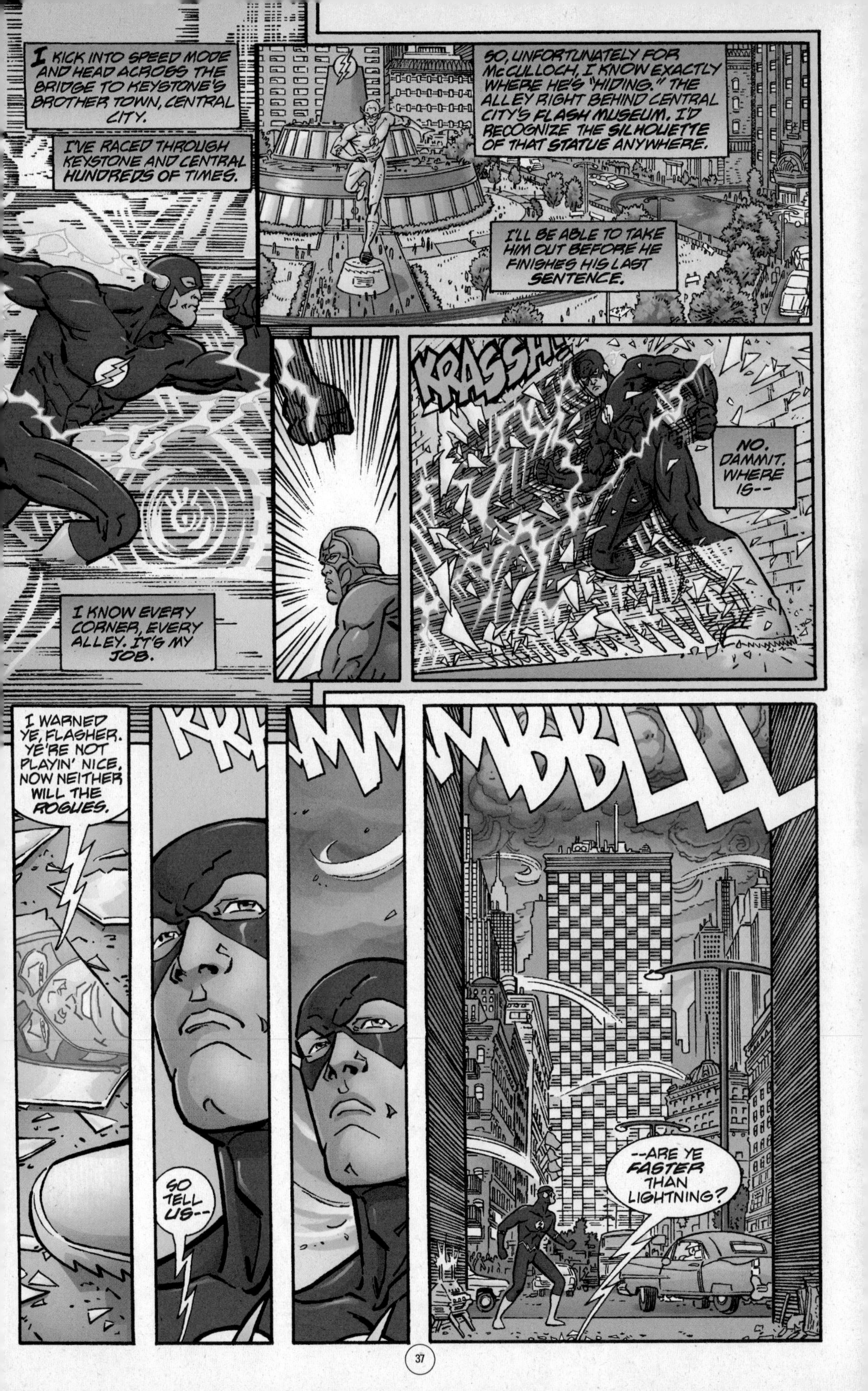
I KICK INTO SPEED MODE AND HEAD ACROSS THE BRIDGE TO KEYSTONE'S BROTHER TOWN, CENTRAL CITY.
I'VE RACED THROUGH KEYSTONE AND CENTRAL HUNDREDS OF TIMES.
I KNOW EVERY CORNER, EVERY ALLEY. IT'S MY JOB.
SO, UNFORTUNATELY FOR McCULLOCH, I KNOW EXACTLY WHERE HE'S "HIDING." THE ALLEY RIGHT BEHIND CENTRAL CITY'S FLASH MUSEUM. I'D RECOGNIZE THE SILHOUETTE OF THAT STATUE ANYWHERE.
I'LL BE ABLE TO TAKE HIM OUT BEFORE HE FINISHES HIS LAST SENTENCE.
KRASSH!
NO. DAMMIT. WHERE IS--
I WARNED YE, FLASHER. YE'RE NOT PLAYIN' NICE, NOW NEITHER WILL THE ROGUES.
KRAAMMMBBLLL
SO TELL US--
--ARE YE FASTER THAN LIGHTNING?

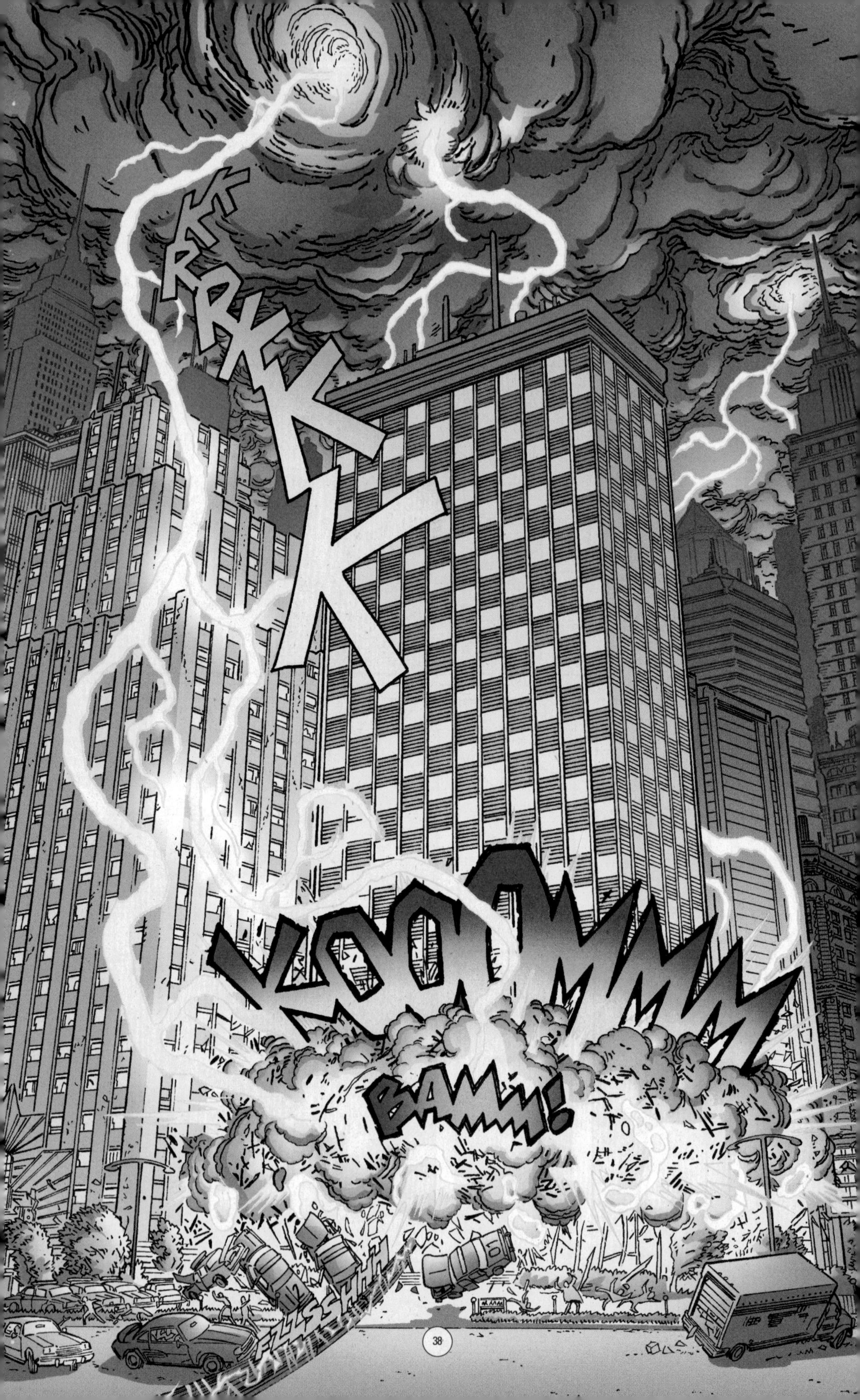
KOOMMMM
BAMM!
FZZZSSHHH

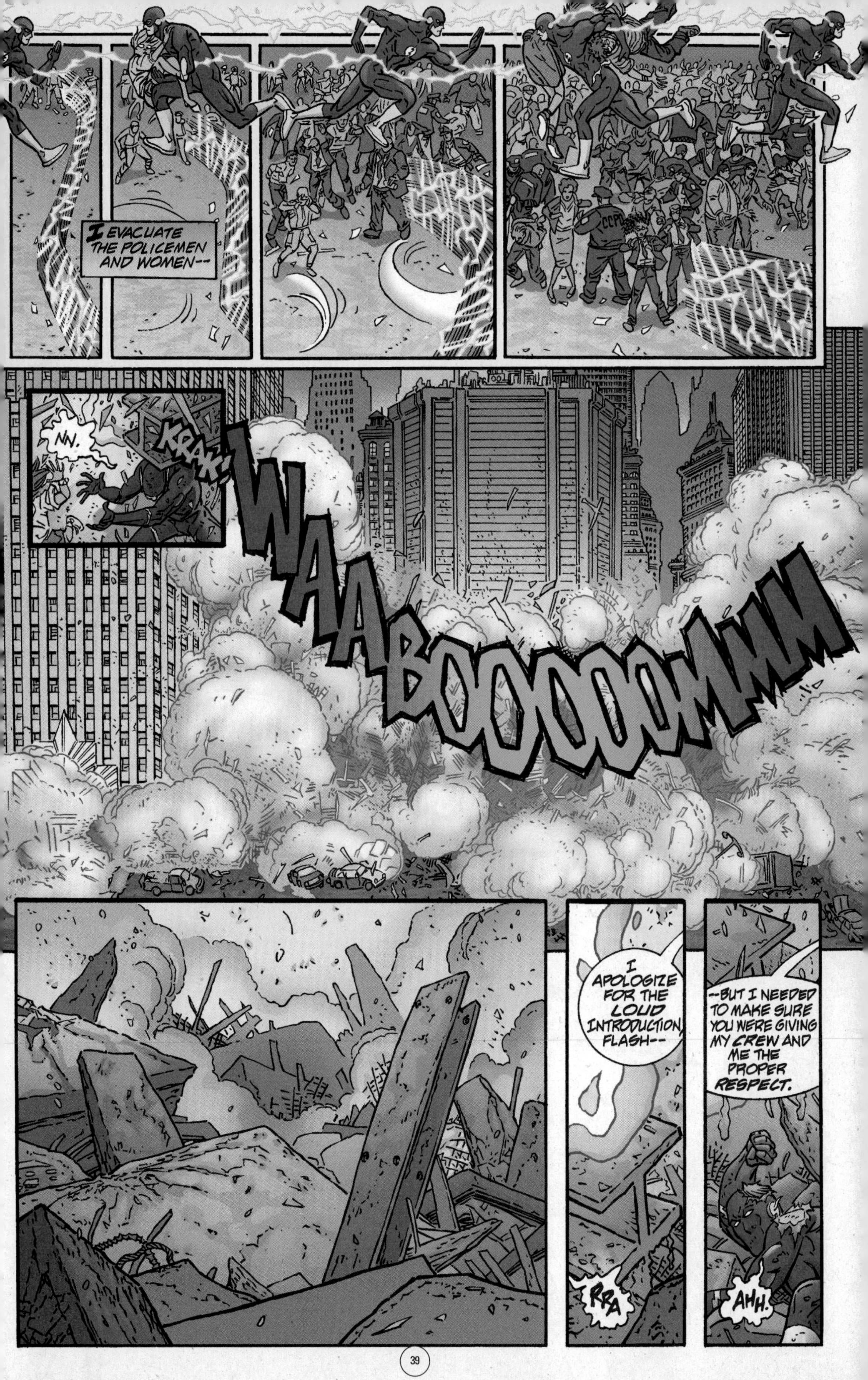
I EVACUATE THE POLICEMEN AND WOMEN--
CCPD
NN.
KRAK!
WAABOOOOOMMM
I APOLOGIZE FOR THE LOUD INTRODUCTION, FLASH--
RRA
--BUT I NEEDED TO MAKE SURE YOU WERE GIVING MY CREW AND ME THE PROPER RESPECT.
AHH.

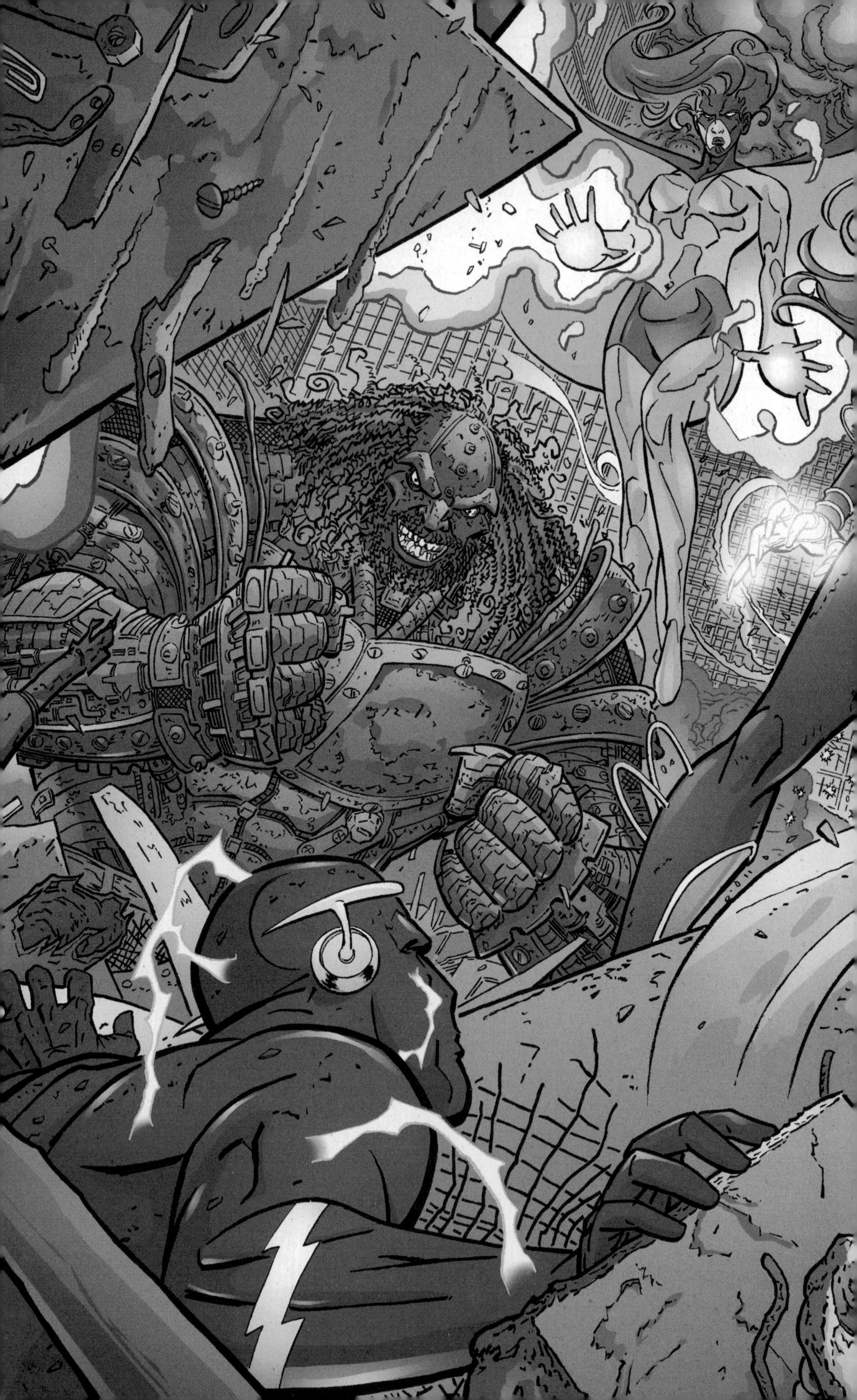

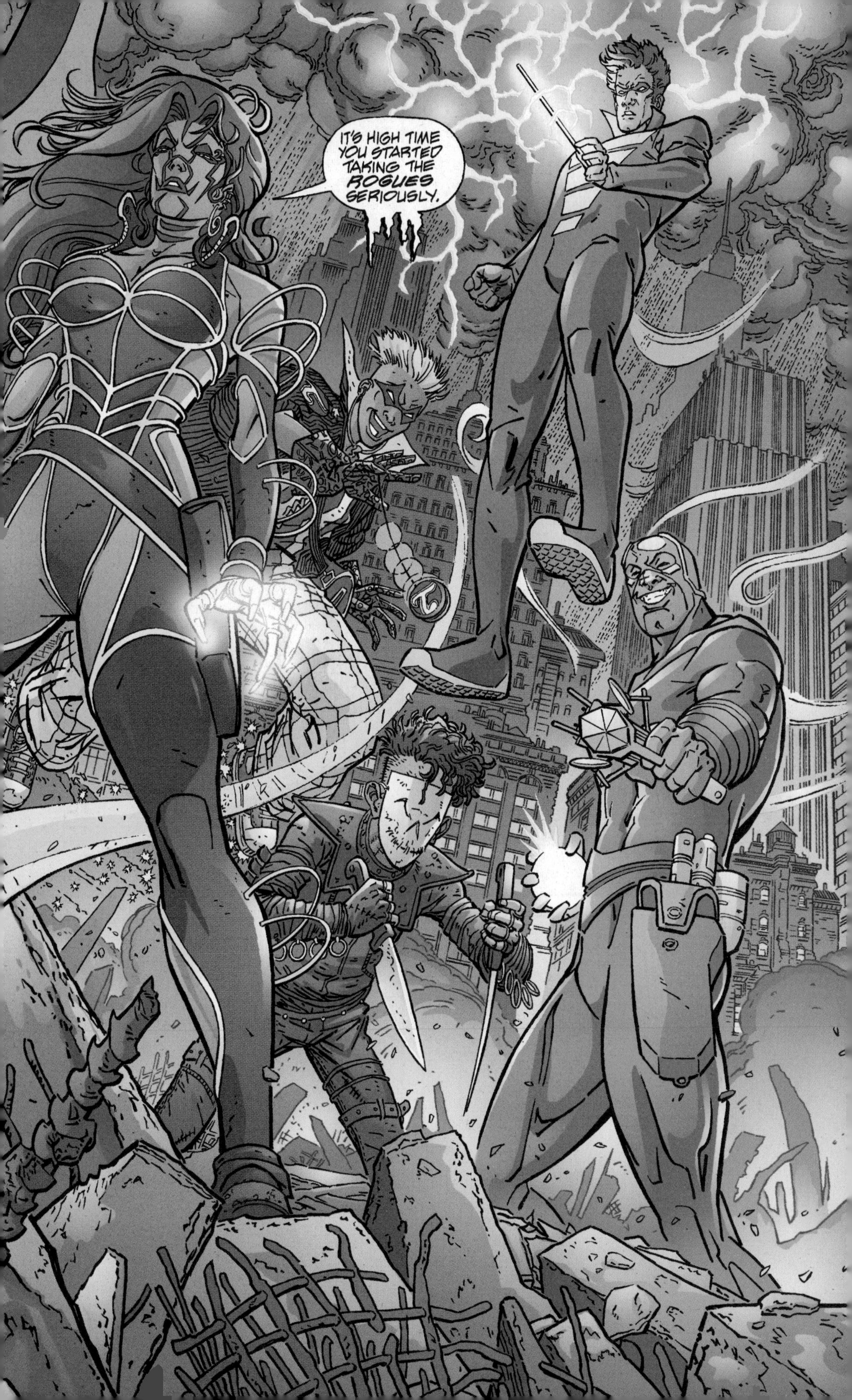
IT'S HIGH TIME YOU STARTED TAKING THE ROGUES SERIOUSLY.

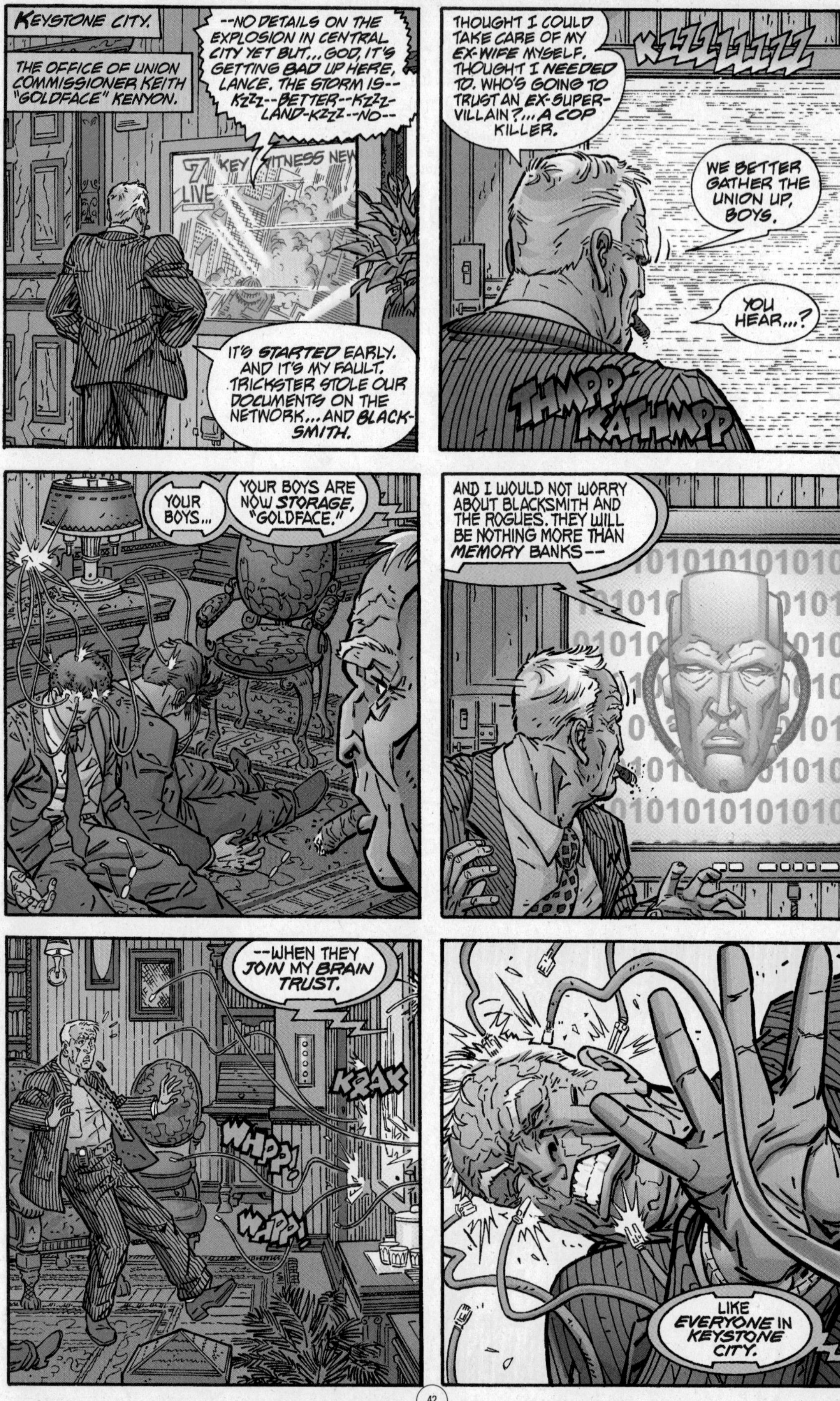

KEYSTONE CITY.
THE OFFICE OF UNION COMMISSIONER KEITH "GOLDFACE" KENYON.
--NO DETAILS ON THE EXPLOSION IN CENTRAL CITY YET BUT... GOD, IT'S GETTING BAD UP HERE, LANCE. THE STORM IS--KZZZ--BETTER--KZZZ-LAND-KZZZ--NO--
7 LIVE
KEY ...ITNESS NEW
IT'S STARTED EARLY. AND IT'S MY FAULT. TRICKSTER STOLE OUR DOCUMENTS ON THE NETWORK... AND BLACKSMITH.
THOUGHT I COULD TAKE CARE OF MY EX-WIFE MYSELF. THOUGHT I NEEDED TO. WHO'S GOING TO TRUST AN EX-SUPER-VILLAIN?... A COP KILLER.
KZZZZZZZ
WE BETTER GATHER THE UNION UP, BOYS.
YOU HEAR...?
THMPP KATHMPP
YOUR BOYS...
YOUR BOYS ARE NOW STORAGE, "GOLDFACE."
AND I WOULD NOT WORRY ABOUT BLACKSMITH AND THE ROGUES. THEY WILL BE NOTHING MORE THAN MEMORY BANKS--
--WHEN THEY JOIN MY BRAIN TRUST.
KRAK
WHPP!
WAPP!
LIKE EVERYONE IN KEYSTONE CITY.

EVERYONE.

DETECTIVE HUNTER ZOLOMON. ROGUE PROFILER.

IRIS WEST. JOSHUA JACKAM. THE FLASH'S AUNT AND HER ADOPTED CHILD. (SEE SUBFILE, WEATHER WIZARD.)

EXIT

LEONARD SNART. (SEE SUBFILE, CAPTAIN COLD.)

YSTONE MOTORS

EVERYONE.

COLE CEMETERY EST. 1810

FWMMP?

THERE YOU GO, OFFICER CHYRE. AS PROMISED.

RIGHT NEXT TO YOUR PARTNER.

MORILLO...

I REALLY HAVE BEEN LOOKING FORWARD TO THIS. ANY LAST WORDS YOU--

CHAK

BEEP! FIZZZZ!

WHAT THE HELL IS THAT?

43

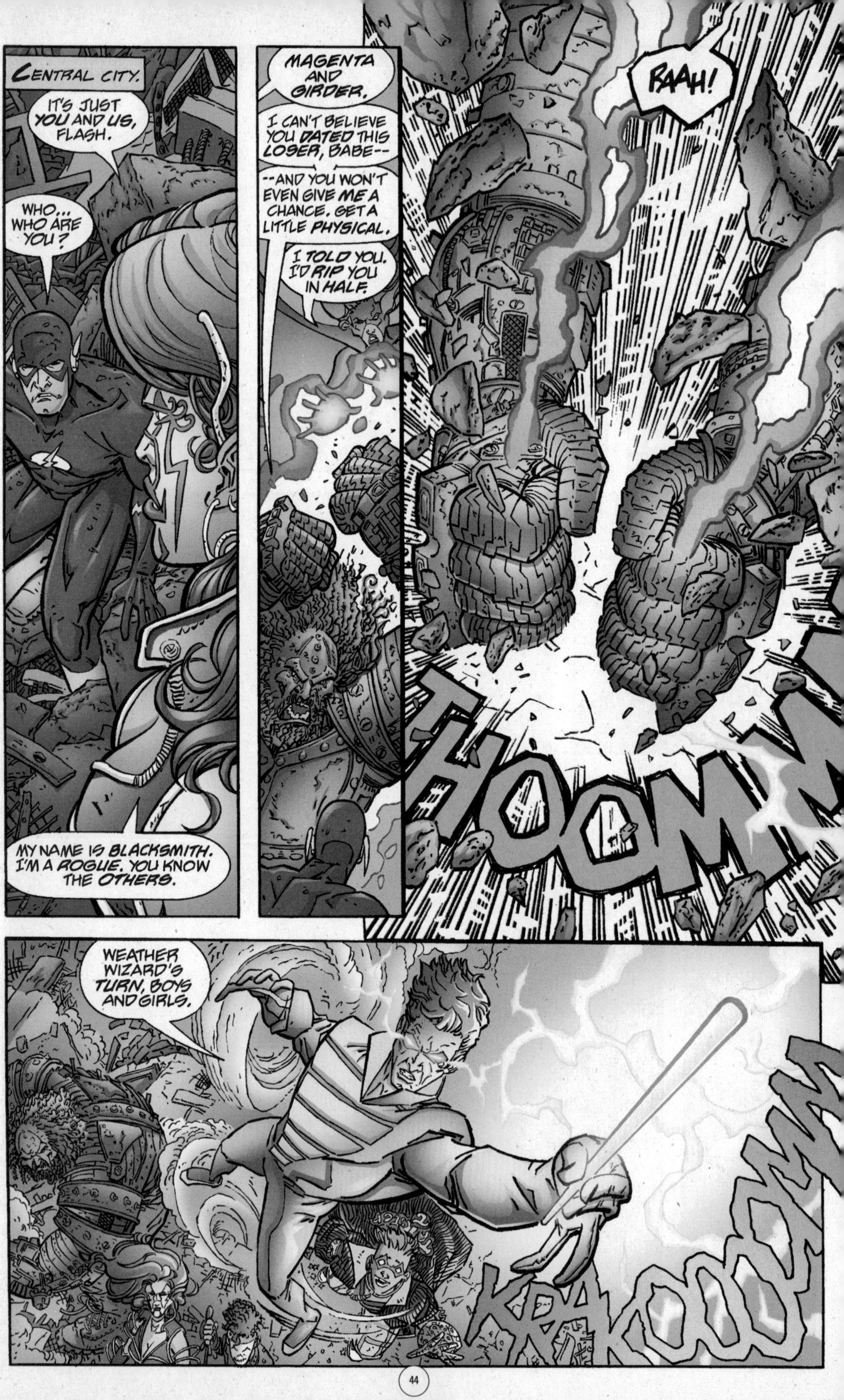

CENTRAL CITY.
IT'S JUST YOU AND US, FLASH.
WHO... WHO ARE YOU?
MY NAME IS BLACKSMITH. I'M A ROGUE. YOU KNOW THE OTHERS.
MAGENTA AND GIRDER.
I CAN'T BELIEVE YOU DATED THIS LOSER, BABE--
--AND YOU WON'T EVEN GIVE ME A CHANCE. GET A LITTLE PHYSICAL.
I TOLD YOU. I'D RIP YOU IN HALF.
RAAH!
THOOM
WEATHER WIZARD'S TURN, BOYS AND GIRLS.
KRAKOOOOM

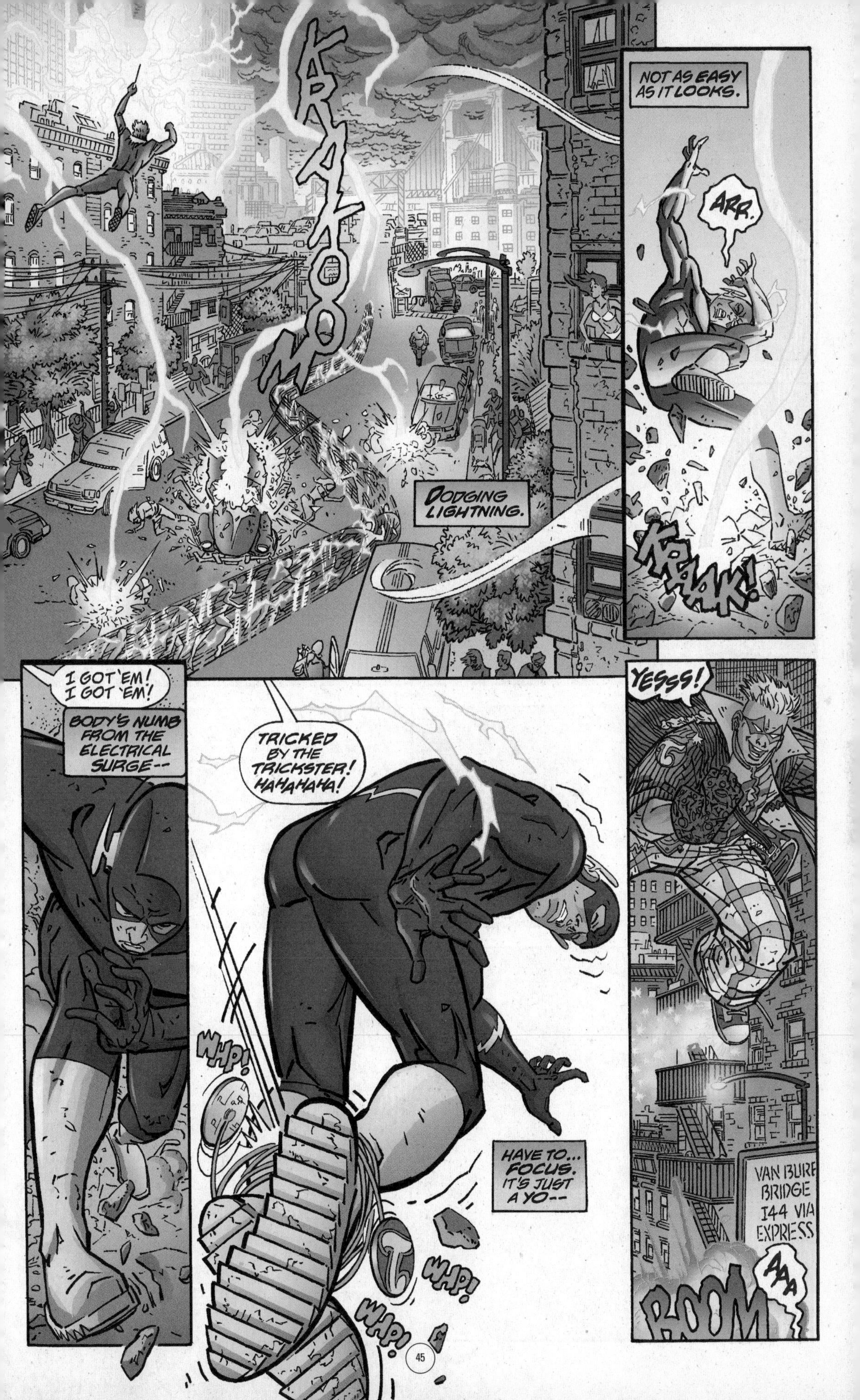
KRAKOOM
DODGING LIGHTNING.
NOT AS EASY AS IT LOOKS.
ARR.
KRAAK!
I GOT 'EM! I GOT 'EM!
BODY'S NUMB FROM THE ELECTRICAL SURGE--
TRICKED BY THE TRICKSTER! HAHAHAHA!
WHP!
HAVE TO... FOCUS. IT'S JUST A YO--
WHP!
WHP!
YESSS!
VAN BURE
BRIDGE
I44 VIA
EXPRESS
AAA
BOOM

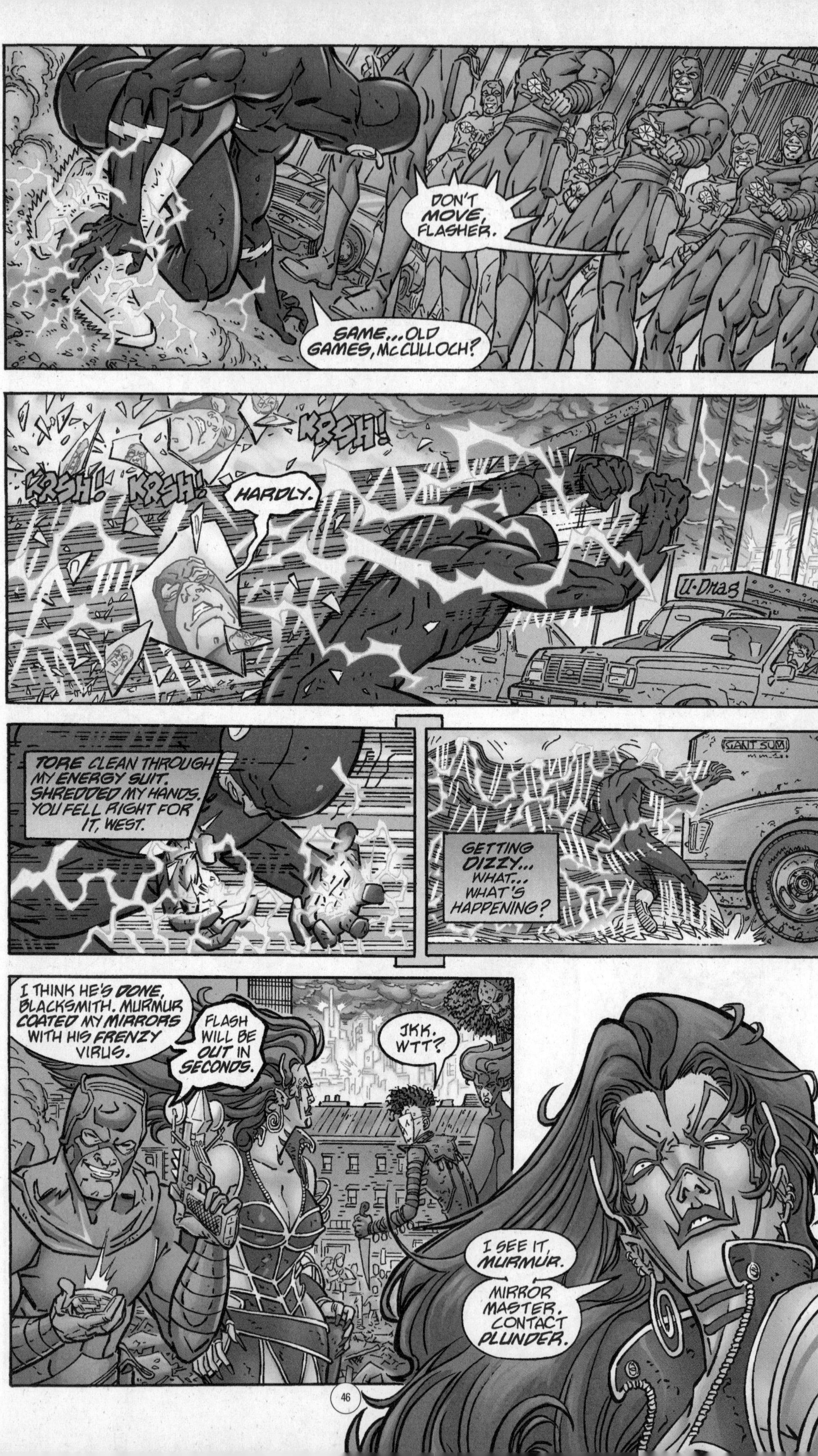
DON'T MOVE, FLASHER.
SAME... OLD GAMES, McCULLOCH?
KRSH!
KRSH!
KRSH!
HARDLY.
U-Drag
TORE CLEAN THROUGH MY ENERGY SUIT. SHREDDED MY HANDS. YOU FELL RIGHT FOR IT, WEST.
GIANT SUM
GETTING DIZZY... WHAT... WHAT'S HAPPENING?
I THINK HE'S DONE, BLACKSMITH. MURMUR COATED MY MIRRORS WITH HIS FRENZY VIRUS.
FLASH WILL BE OUT IN SECONDS.
JKK. WTT?
I SEE IT, MURMUR.
MIRROR MASTER. CONTACT PLUNDER.

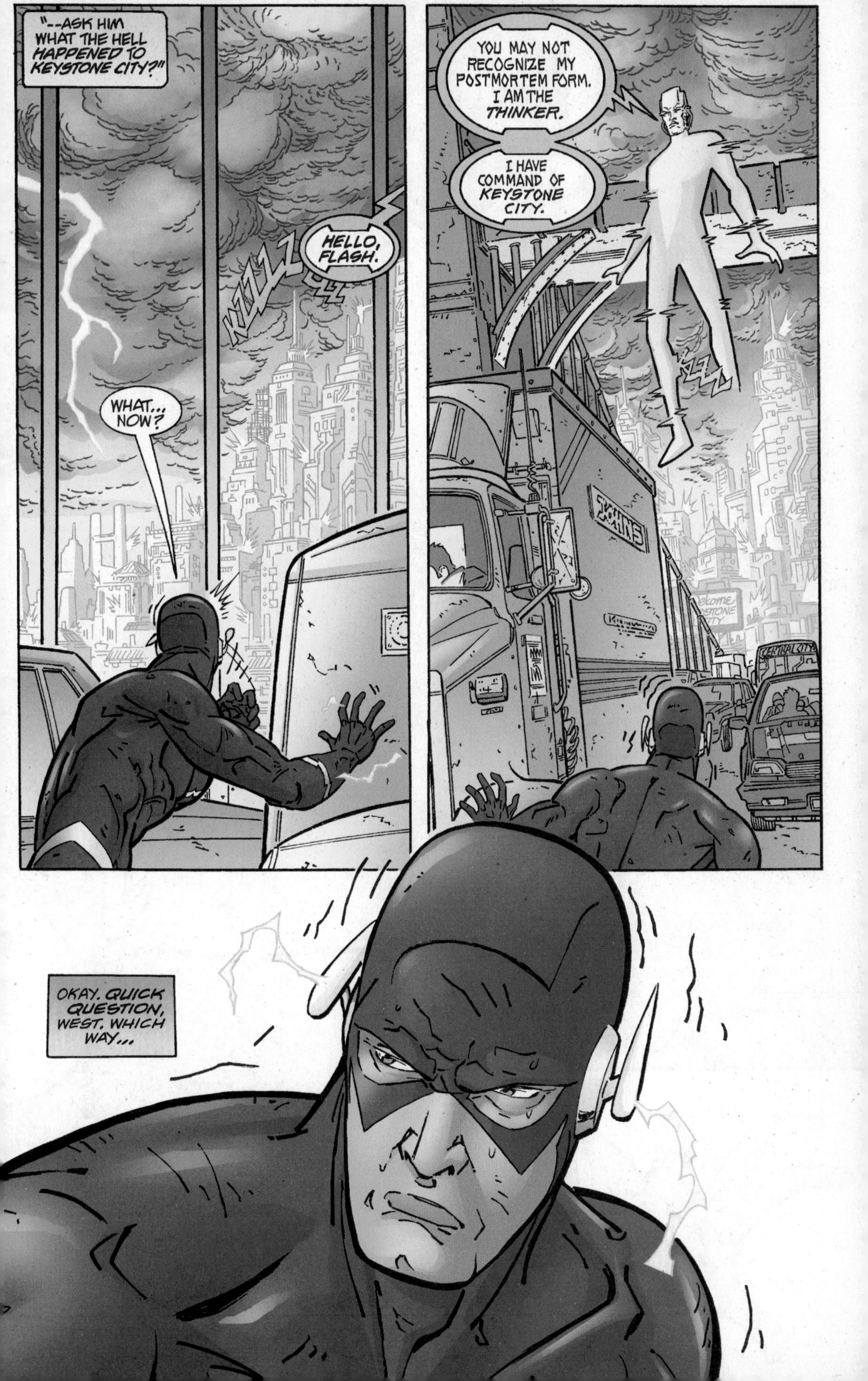
"--ASK HIM WHAT THE HELL HAPPENED TO KEYSTONE CITY?"
HELLO, FLASH.
KZZZZ
WHAT... NOW?
YOU MAY NOT RECOGNIZE MY POSTMORTEM FORM. I AM THE THINKER.
I HAVE COMMAND OF KEYSTONE CITY.
OKAY. QUICK QUESTION, WEST. WHICH WAY...

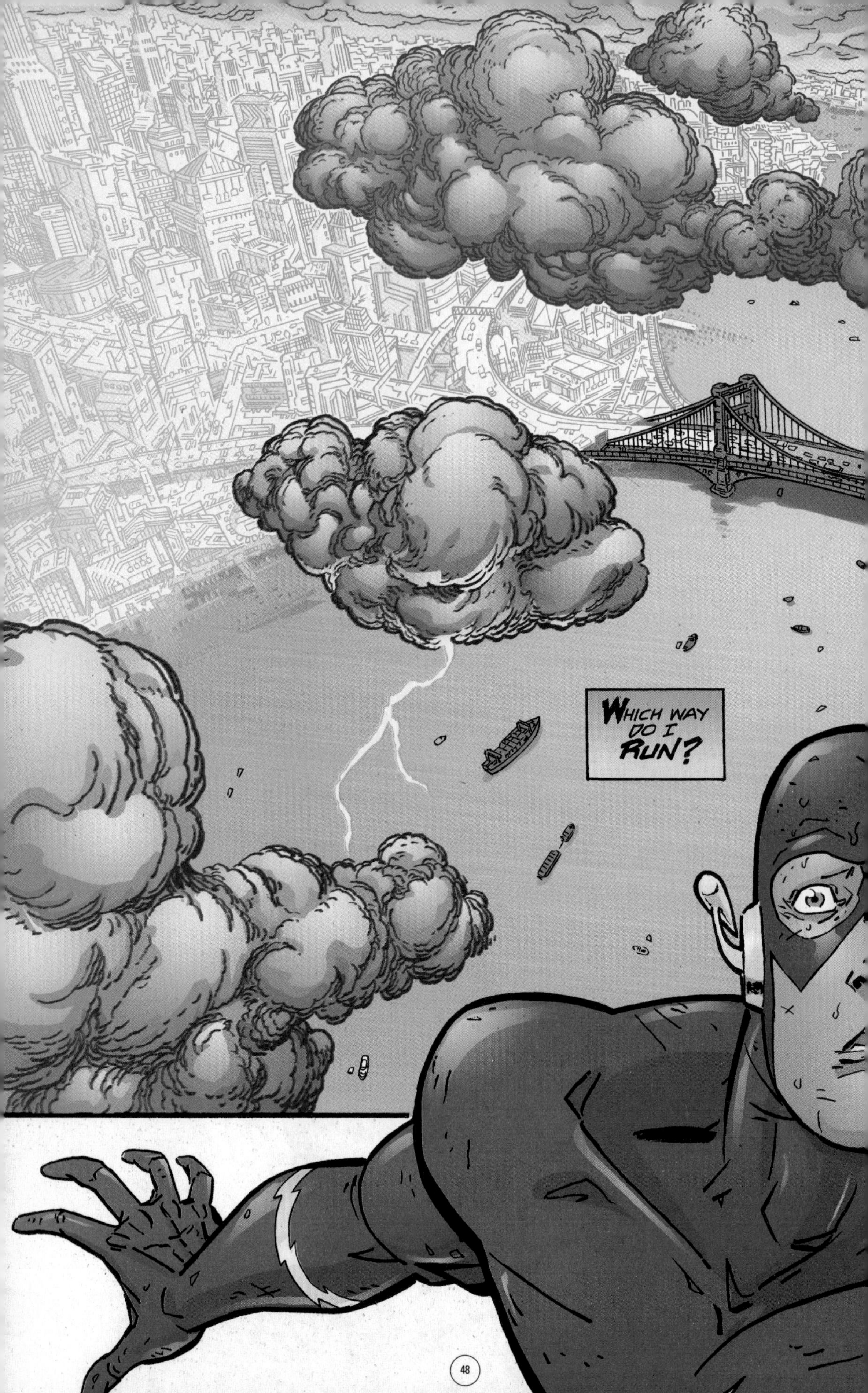
WHICH WAY DO I RUN?

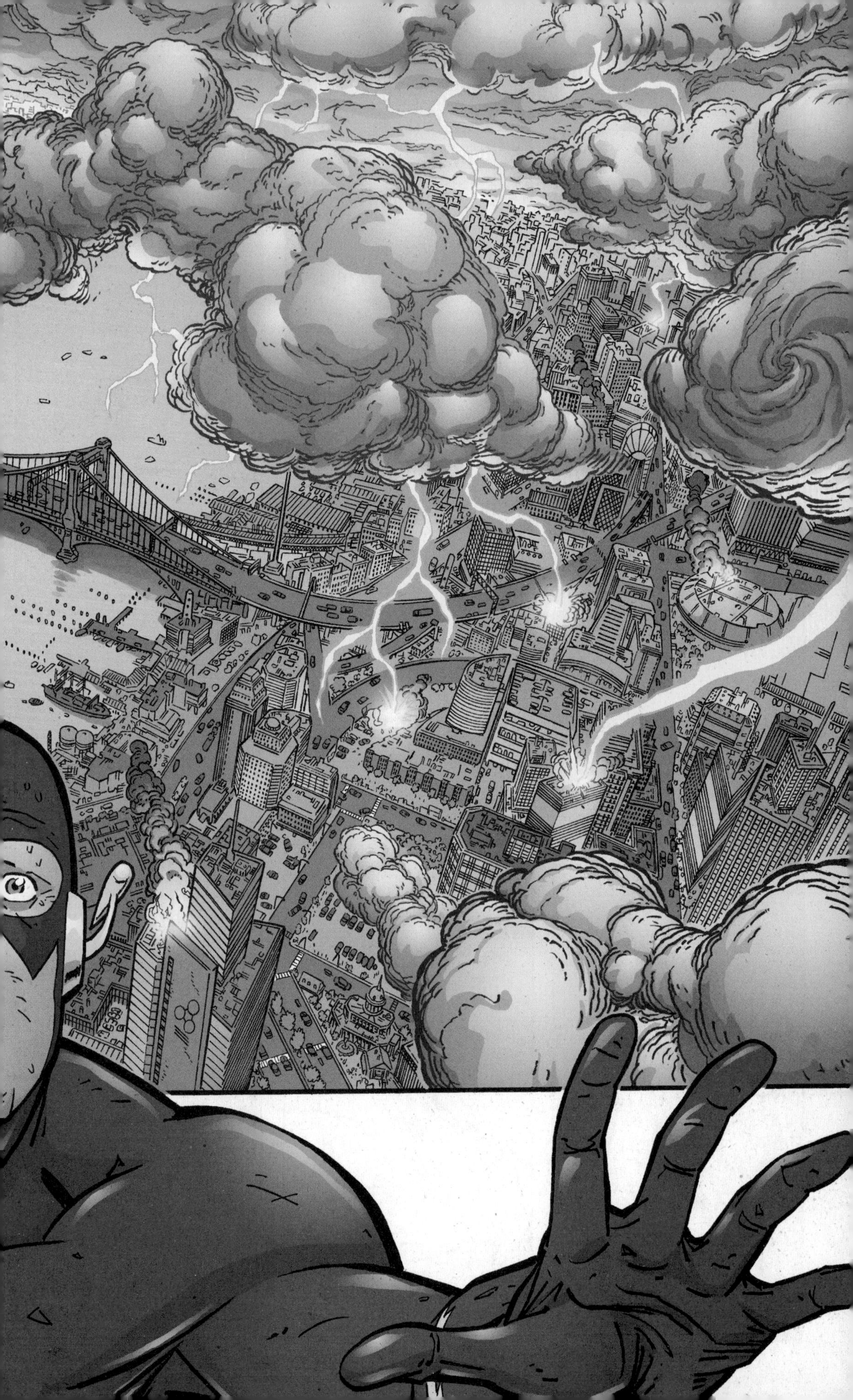

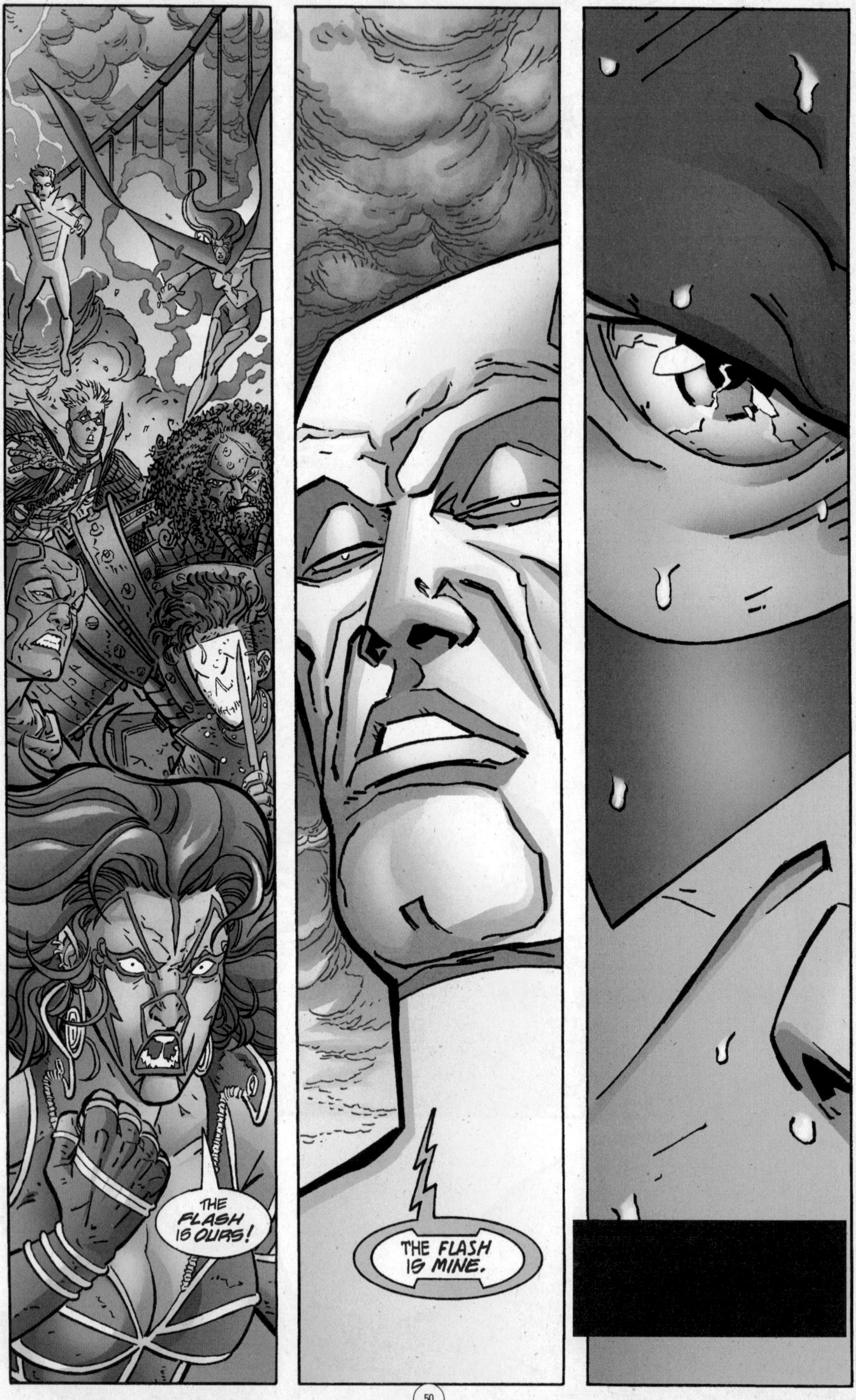
THE FLASH IS OURS!
THE FLASH IS MINE.
[redacted]

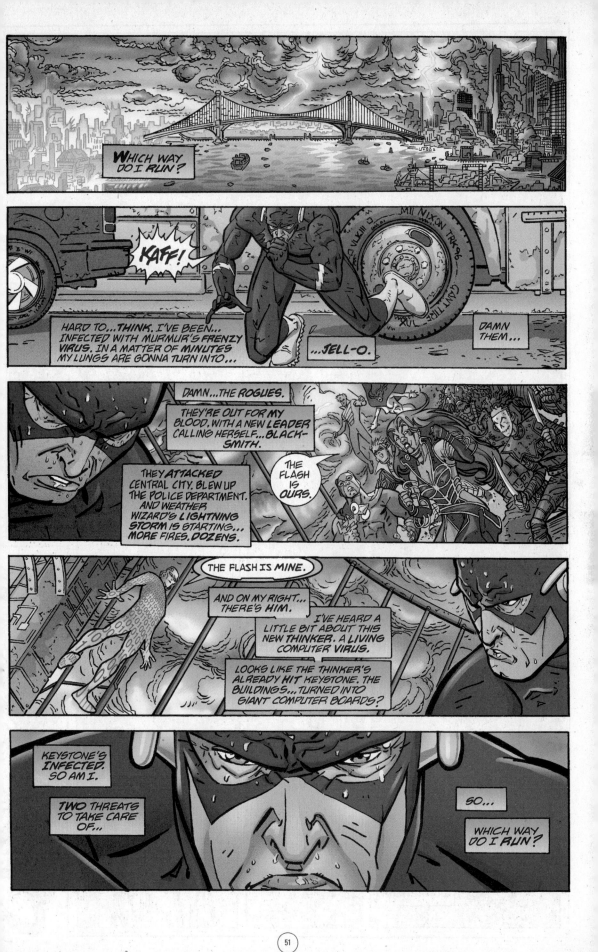

WHICH WAY DO I RUN?

KAFF!

HARD TO...THINK. I'VE BEEN... INFECTED WITH MURMUR'S FRENZY VIRUS. IN A MATTER OF MINUTES MY LUNGS ARE GONNA TURN INTO...

...JELL-O.

DAMN THEM...

DAMN...THE ROGUES. THEY'RE OUT FOR MY BLOOD, WITH A NEW LEADER CALLING HERSELF...BLACK-SMITH.

THE FLASH IS OURS.

THEY ATTACKED CENTRAL CITY. BLEW UP THE POLICE DEPARTMENT. AND WEATHER WIZARD'S LIGHTNING STORM IS STARTING... MORE FIRES. DOZENS.

THE FLASH IS MINE.

AND ON MY RIGHT... THERE'S HIM.

I'VE HEARD A LITTLE BIT ABOUT THIS NEW THINKER. A LIVING COMPUTER VIRUS.

LOOKS LIKE THE THINKER'S ALREADY HIT KEYSTONE. THE BUILDINGS...TURNED INTO GIANT COMPUTER BOARDS?

KEYSTONE'S INFECTED. SO AM I.

TWO THREATS TO TAKE CARE OF...

SO...

WHICH WAY DO I RUN?

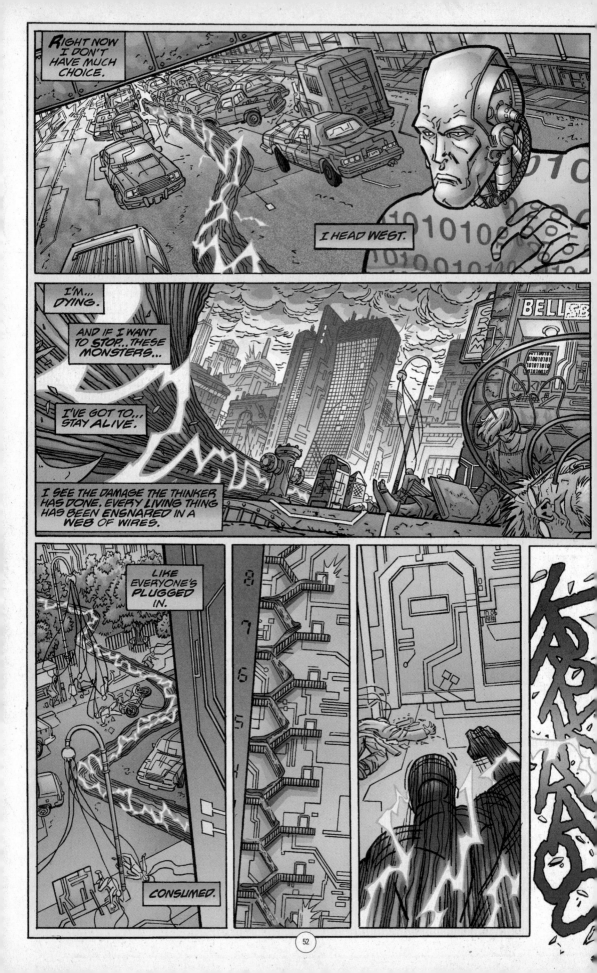

RIGHT NOW I DON'T HAVE MUCH CHOICE.

I HEAD WEST.

I'M... DYING.

AND IF I WANT TO STOP...THESE MONSTERS...

I'VE GOT TO... STAY ALIVE.

I SEE THE DAMAGE THE THINKER HAS DONE. EVERY LIVING THING HAS BEEN ENSNARED IN A WEB OF WIRES.

LIKE EVERYONE'S PLUGGED IN.

CONSUMED.

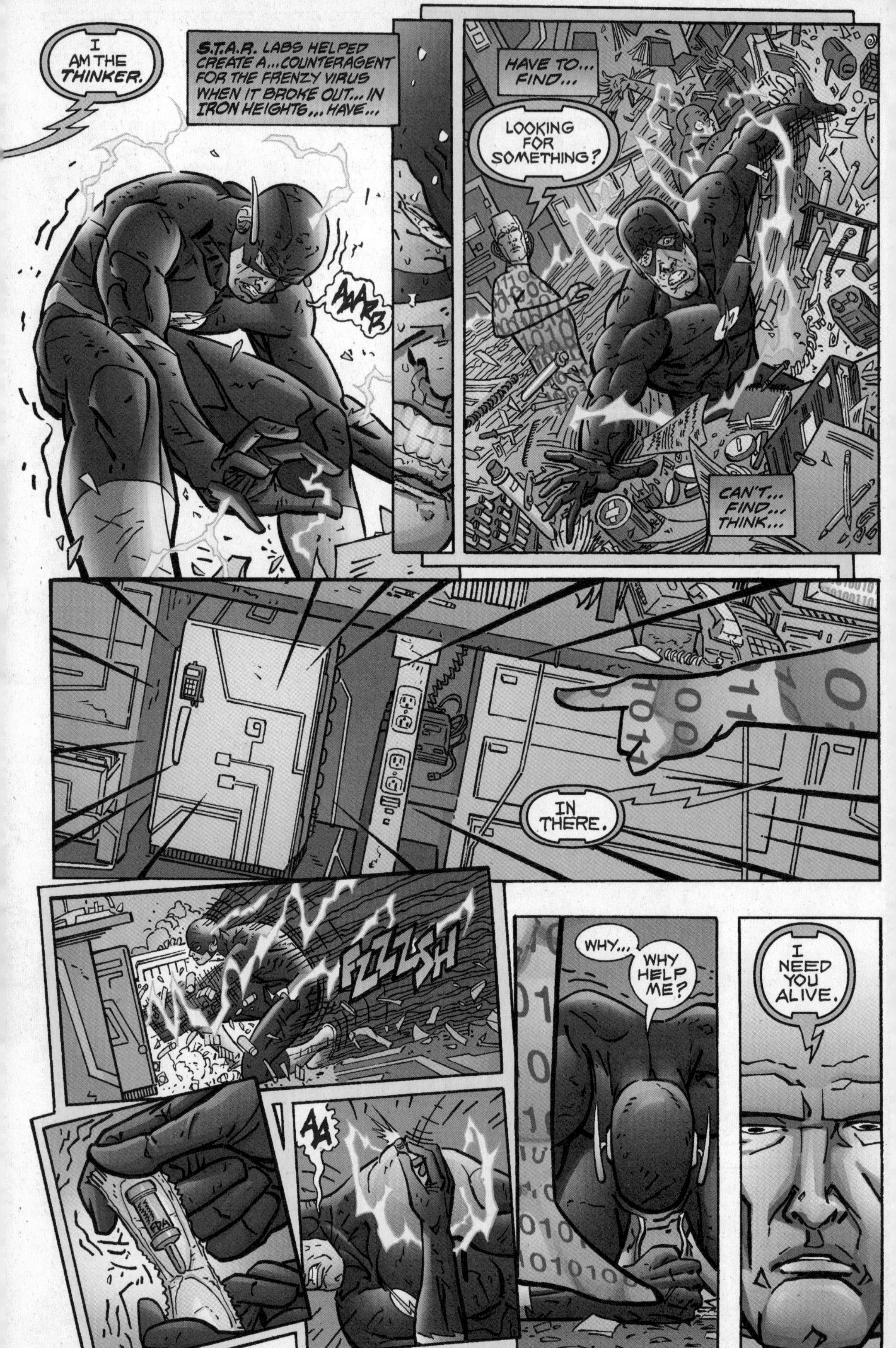
I AM THE THINKER.
S.T.A.R. LABS HELPED CREATE A...COUNTERAGENT FOR THE FRENZY VIRUS WHEN IT BROKE OUT... IN IRON HEIGHTS... HAVE...
HAVE TO... FIND...
LOOKING FOR SOMETHING?
CAN'T... FIND... THINK...
IN THERE.
FZZSH
AA
WHY... WHY HELP ME?
I NEED YOU ALIVE.

DAMMIT.

WHERE'D FLASH RUN OFF TO?

TO CONFRONT THIS... *THINKER*, I SUPPOSE.

DOES *GOLDFACE* HAVE ANYTHING TO DO WITH THIS?

MY EX-HUSBAND IS TOO *PROUD* TO PARTNER UP WITH ANYONE.

MOST *MEN* ARE.

UNFORTUNATELY, THIS *THINKER* IS A *WILD CARD.*

McCULLOCH'S RIGHT. WE CAN'T ASSUME THE *VIRUS* FINISHED THE JOB.

WE *OLDER* ROGUES MAY HAVE DOGGED WEST WHEN COMPARING HIM TO BARRY ALLEN, BUT NOW--

--KID'S AS *GOOD* AS BARRY EVER WAS.

SOUNDS *GROOVY.*

IT DOES, TRICKSTER. NOW LET'S ASSESS KEYSTONE CITY'S *AFFLICTION.*

AND FROM THE *INSIDE* OUT, NO LESS. WE'VE ALREADY GOT A *ROGUE* BEHIND THOSE CITY WALLS.

I'M HOPIN' *FLASHER* IS *DEAD* ON THE GROUND BY NOW, BUT KNOWIN' WEST...

IT'S BEST WE ACTIVATE MY *REFLECTION.*

I SAY WE *STORM* IN AFTER HIM. THEN TAKE CARE OF MR. *ROBOTO.*

SO PULL OUT YOUR *MIRROR,* MASTER--

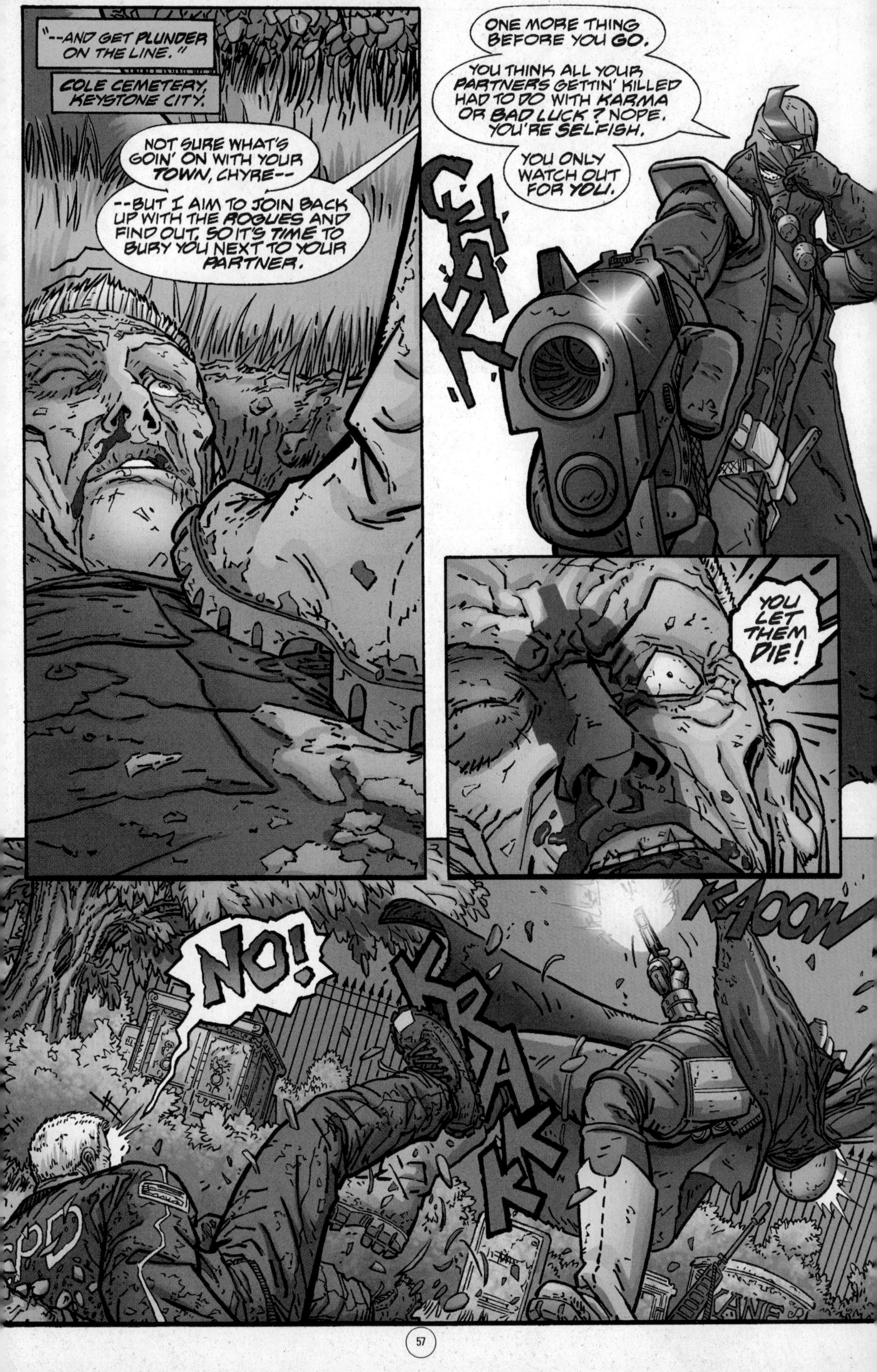
"--AND GET PLUNDER ON THE LINE."
COLE CEMETERY, KEYSTONE CITY.
NOT SURE WHAT'S GOIN' ON WITH YOUR TOWN, CHYRE--
--BUT I AIM TO JOIN BACK UP WITH THE ROGUES AND FIND OUT, SO IT'S TIME TO BURY YOU NEXT TO YOUR PARTNER.
ONE MORE THING BEFORE YOU GO.
YOU THINK ALL YOUR PARTNERS GETTIN' KILLED HAD TO DO WITH KARMA OR BAD LUCK? NOPE. YOU'RE SELFISH.
YOU ONLY WATCH OUT FOR YOU.
CHAK
KRAK
YOU LET THEM DIE!
NO!
KRAKK
KAOOW

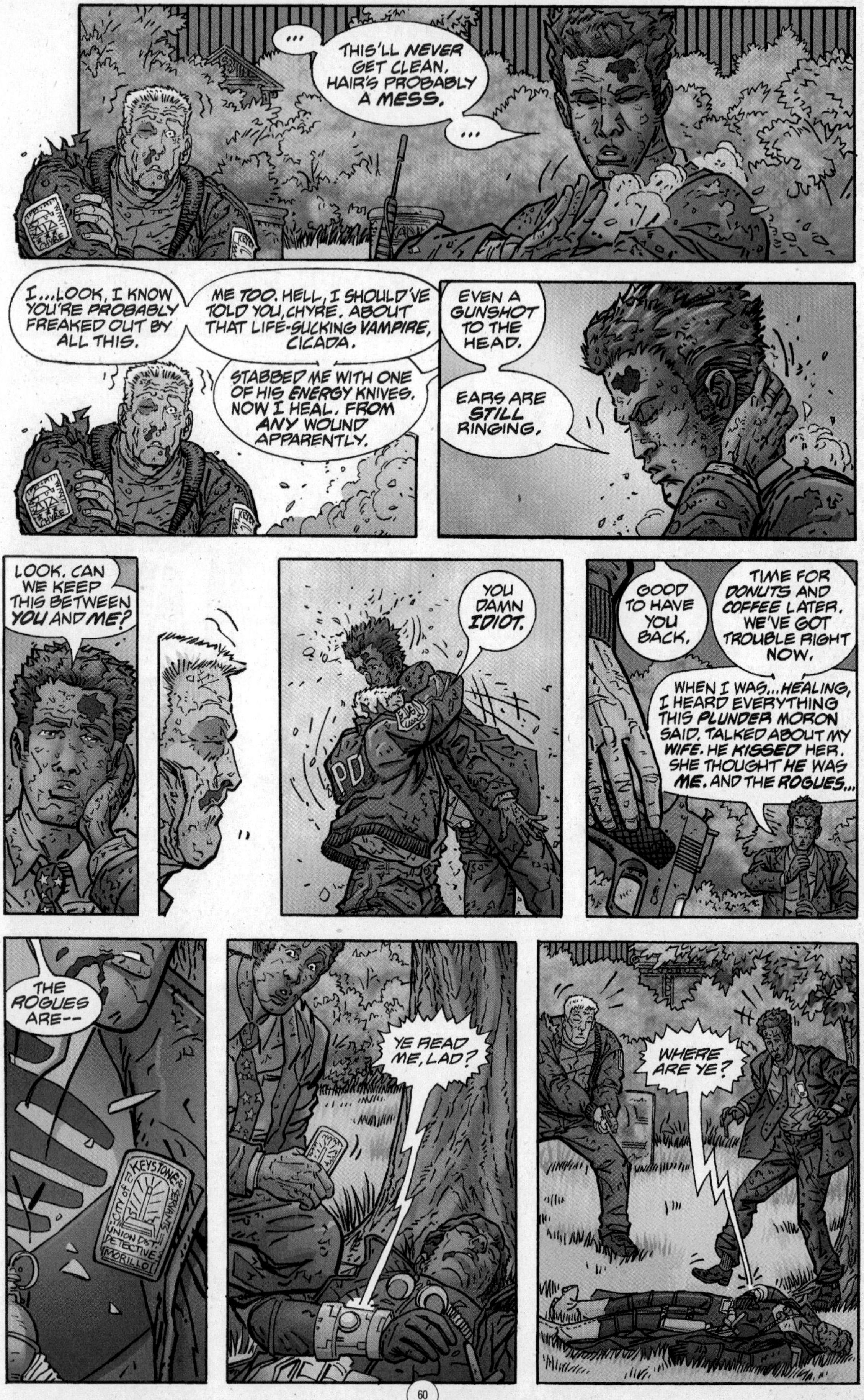
...
THIS'LL NEVER GET CLEAN, HAIR'S PROBABLY A MESS.
...
I...LOOK, I KNOW YOU'RE PROBABLY FREAKED OUT BY ALL THIS.
ME TOO. HELL, I SHOULD'VE TOLD YOU, CHYRE. ABOUT THAT LIFE-SUCKING VAMPIRE, CICADA.
STABBED ME WITH ONE OF HIS ENERGY KNIVES. NOW I HEAL, FROM ANY WOUND APPARENTLY.
EVEN A GUNSHOT TO THE HEAD.
EARS ARE STILL RINGING.
LOOK, CAN WE KEEP THIS BETWEEN YOU AND ME?
YOU DAMN IDIOT.
PD
GOOD TO HAVE YOU BACK.
TIME FOR DONUTS AND COFFEE LATER. WE'VE GOT TROUBLE RIGHT NOW.
WHEN I WAS...HEALING, I HEARD EVERYTHING THIS PLUNDER MORON SAID. TALKED ABOUT MY WIFE. HE KISSED HER. SHE THOUGHT HE WAS ME. AND THE ROGUES...
THE ROGUES ARE--
KEYSTONE
UNION DIST.
DETECTIVE
MORILLO
YE READ ME, LAD?
WHERE ARE YE?

WHAT DID YOU DO TO THEM? WHAT DID YOU DO TO *EVERYONE*?

I WOULD NOT *YANK* THOSE *CABLES* OUT IF I WERE YOU, FLASH.

THERE IS A *LARGE* UNUSED SEGMENT OF THE HUMAN BRAIN. THOUSANDS OF TIMES MORE USEFUL FOR DATA *STORAGE* THAN ANY *COMPUTER* IN EXISTENCE.

WITH KEYSTONE CITY'S FOCUS ON HEAVY INDUSTRY, AND WITH ITS *DENSE* POPULATION--

--EVERYONE WAS EASILY *CONNECTED.*

I TOLD YOUR *WIFE* THIS VERY SAME THING WHEN I UPLINKED HER *BRAIN.*

LINDA?

FZZZSH!

NO.

A *WARNING*. IF YOU TRY TO DISCONNECT HER, HER *MIND* WILL BE *DELETED.* HER *MEMORY...* A MEMORY.

WHAT--

--DO YOU WANT?

YOUR BRAIN.

YOUR *TALENTS*. YOUR *SPEED*.

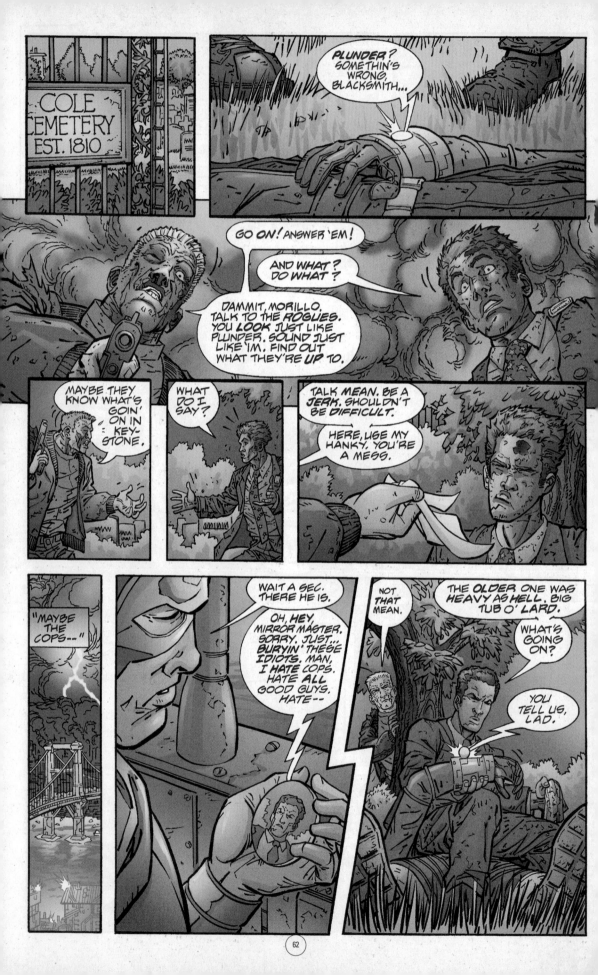

COLE CEMETERY EST. 1810

PLUNDER? SOMETHIN'S WRONG, BLACKSMITH...

GO ON! ANSWER 'EM!

AND WHAT? DO WHAT?

DAMMIT, MORILLO. TALK TO THE ROGUES. YOU LOOK JUST LIKE PLUNDER. SOUND JUST LIKE 'IM. FIND OUT WHAT THEY'RE UP TO.

MAYBE THEY KNOW WHAT'S GOIN' ON IN KEYSTONE.

WHAT DO I SAY?

TALK MEAN. BE A JERK. SHOULDN'T BE DIFFICULT.

HERE, USE MY HANKY. YOU'RE A MESS.

"MAYBE THE COPS--"

WAIT A SEC. THERE HE IS.

OH, HEY, MIRROR MASTER. SORRY. JUST... BURYIN' THESE IDIOTS, MAN. I HATE COPS. HATE ALL GOOD GUYS. HATE--

NOT THAT MEAN.

THE OLDER ONE WAS HEAVY AS HELL. BIG TUB O' LARD.

WHAT'S GOING ON?

YOU TELL US, LAD.

62

"ALL WE KNOW IS SOME *VIRTUAL DIRTBAG* NAMED THE *THINKER* HAS DECIDED TA CLAIM THE *TWIN CITIES* AND THE *FLASH* FOR HIMSELF."

"SO WE'RE COMIN' IN AFTER 'EM."

BUT *FIRST*, BETTER KEEP ANY *MORE* OF FLASH'S *FRIENDS* OUTTA THIS.

TIME TA ACTIVATE THE *REFLECTION*, MURMUR.

THE... REFLECTION?

KLK

"HELL, YE KNOW, GETTIN' RID OF FLASH'S *ALLIES* WAS *EASY*. PLUNDER, PIPER FRAMED, THE SPEEDSTERS *SCATTERED*, THAT FAT BLOKE *SHOT*."

"AND CYBORG AND THE *KEYSTONE COPS* IMPRISONED."

"THE *REFLECTION*... IT'S JUS' *ONE MORE STEP*... SEEDS WE PLANTED WEEKS AGO."

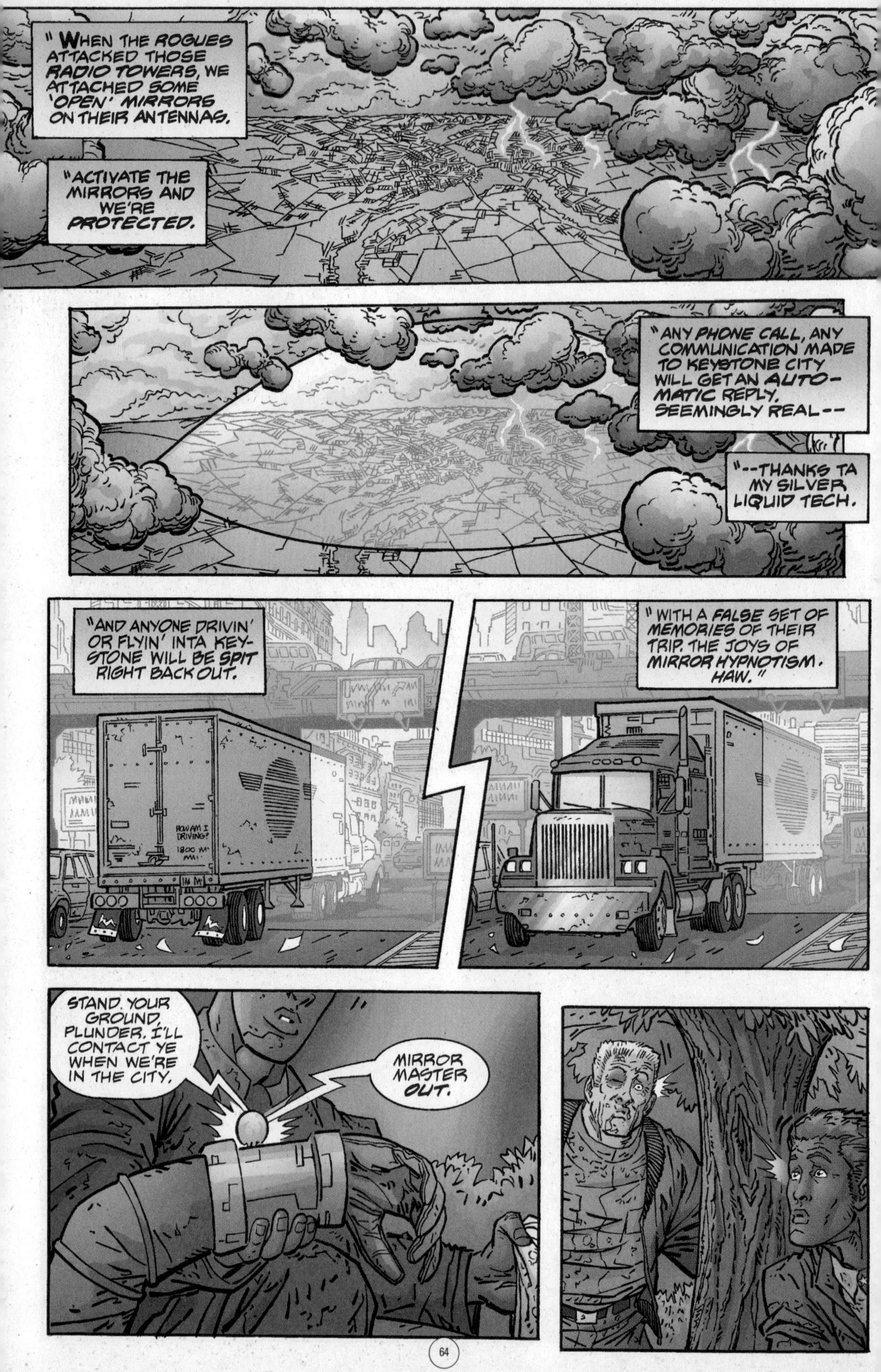

"WHEN THE ROGUES ATTACKED THOSE RADIO TOWERS, WE ATTACHED SOME 'OPEN' MIRRORS ON THEIR ANTENNAS.
"ACTIVATE THE MIRRORS AND WE'RE PROTECTED.
"ANY PHONE CALL, ANY COMMUNICATION MADE TO KEYSTONE CITY WILL GET AN AUTOMATIC REPLY, SEEMINGLY REAL--
"--THANKS TA MY SILVER LIQUID TECH."
"AND ANYONE DRIVIN' OR FLYIN' INTA KEYSTONE WILL BE SPIT RIGHT BACK OUT.
"WITH A FALSE SET OF MEMORIES OF THEIR TRIP. THE JOYS OF MIRROR HYPNOTISM. HAW."
HOW AM I DRIVING?
STAND. YOUR GROUND, PLUNDER. I'LL CONTACT YE WHEN WE'RE IN THE CITY.
MIRROR MASTER OUT.

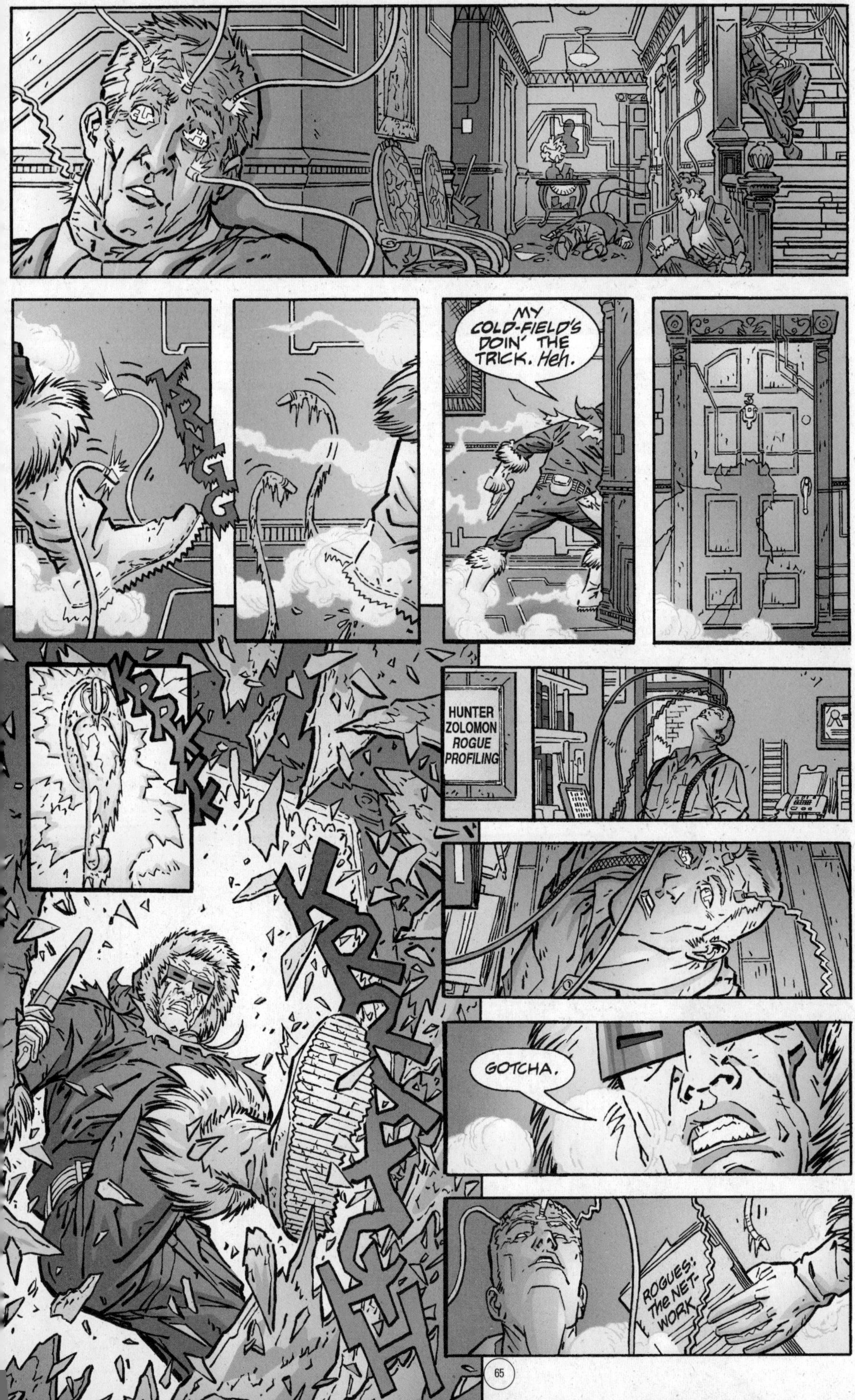
KRAGG
MY COLD-FIELD'S DOIN' THE TRICK. Heh.
KRRRKKK
HUNTER ZOLOMON ROGUE PROFILING
KRRAKK
GOTCHA.
ROGUES: the NET-WORK

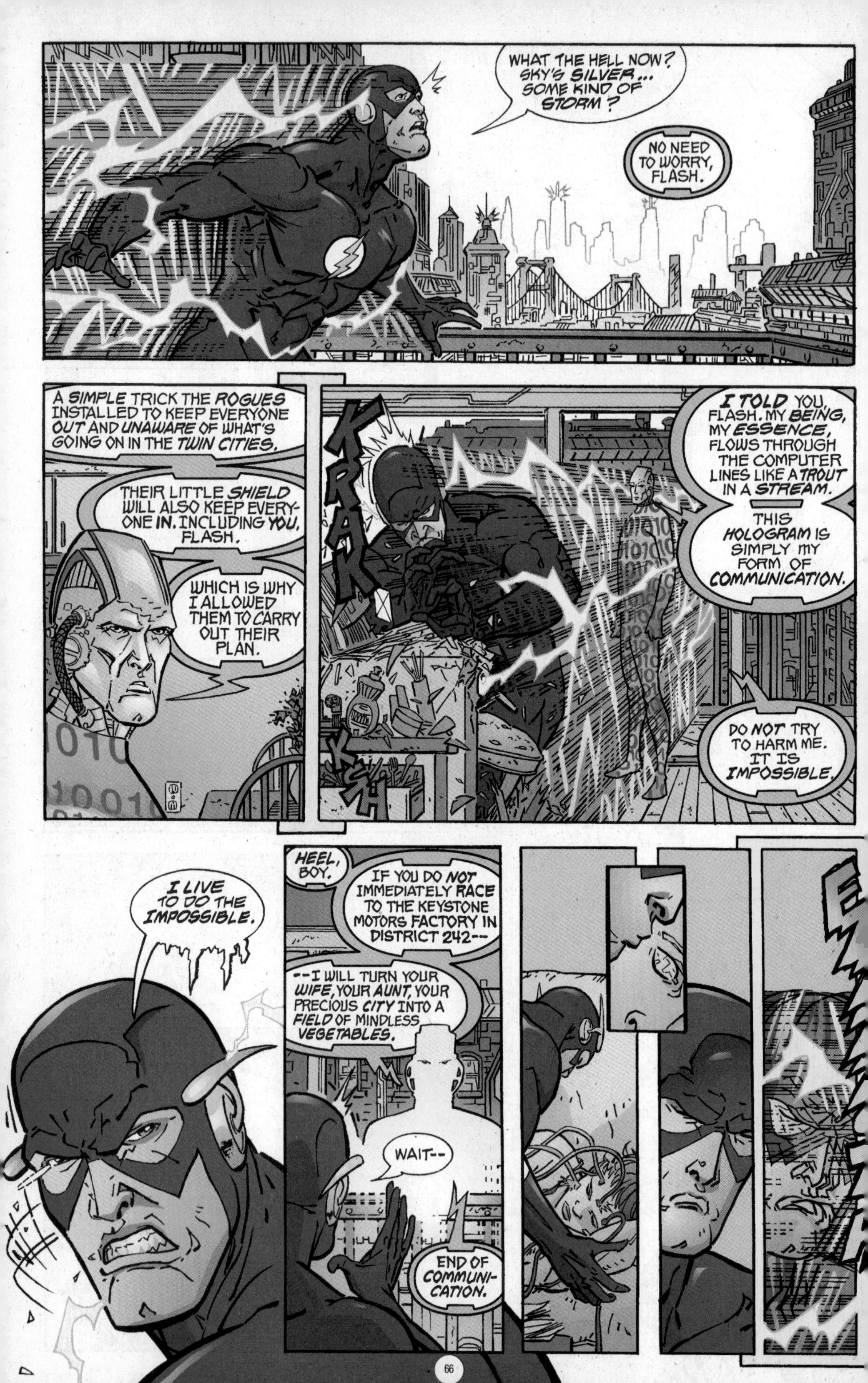
WHAT THE HELL NOW? SKY'S SILVER... SOME KIND OF STORM?
NO NEED TO WORRY, FLASH.
A SIMPLE TRICK THE ROGUES INSTALLED TO KEEP EVERYONE OUT AND UNAWARE OF WHAT'S GOING ON IN THE TWIN CITIES.
THEIR LITTLE SHIELD WILL ALSO KEEP EVERYONE IN. INCLUDING YOU, FLASH.
WHICH IS WHY I ALLOWED THEM TO CARRY OUT THEIR PLAN.
KRAK
KSSH
I TOLD YOU, FLASH. MY BEING, MY ESSENCE, FLOWS THROUGH THE COMPUTER LINES LIKE A TROUT IN A STREAM.
THIS HOLOGRAM IS SIMPLY MY FORM OF COMMUNICATION.
DO NOT TRY TO HARM ME. IT IS IMPOSSIBLE.
I LIVE TO DO THE IMPOSSIBLE.
HEEL, BOY.
IF YOU DO NOT IMMEDIATELY RACE TO THE KEYSTONE MOTORS FACTORY IN DISTRICT 242--
--I WILL TURN YOUR WIFE, YOUR AUNT, YOUR PRECIOUS CITY INTO A FIELD OF MINDLESS VEGETABLES.
WAIT--
END OF COMMUNICATION.

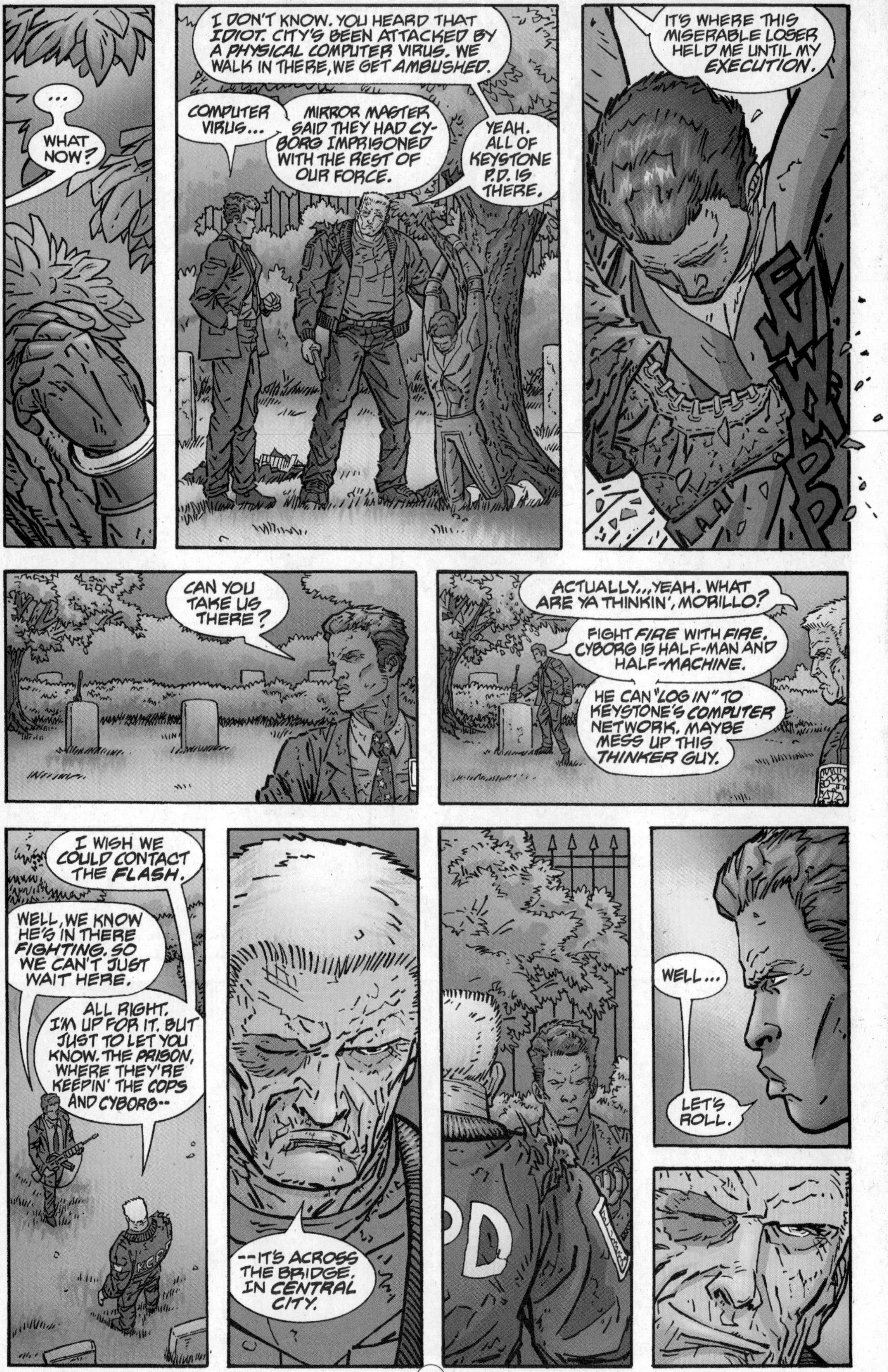
...
WHAT NOW?
I DON'T KNOW. YOU HEARD THAT IDIOT. CITY'S BEEN ATTACKED BY A PHYSICAL COMPUTER VIRUS. WE WALK IN THERE, WE GET AMBUSHED.
COMPUTER VIRUS...
MIRROR MASTER SAID THEY HAD CYBORG IMPRISONED WITH THE REST OF OUR FORCE.
YEAH. ALL OF KEYSTONE P.D. IS THERE.
IT'S WHERE THIS MISERABLE LOSER HELD ME UNTIL MY EXECUTION.
CAN YOU TAKE US THERE?
ACTUALLY... YEAH. WHAT ARE YA THINKIN', MORILLO?
FIGHT FIRE WITH FIRE. CYBORG IS HALF-MAN AND HALF-MACHINE.
HE CAN "LOG IN" TO KEYSTONE'S COMPUTER NETWORK. MAYBE MESS UP THIS THINKER GUY.
I WISH WE COULD CONTACT THE FLASH.
WELL, WE KNOW HE'S IN THERE FIGHTING. SO WE CAN'T JUST WAIT HERE.
ALL RIGHT. I'M UP FOR IT. BUT JUST TO LET YOU KNOW. THE PRISON, WHERE THEY'RE KEEPIN' THE COPS AND CYBORG--
--IT'S ACROSS THE BRIDGE. IN CENTRAL CITY.
WELL...
LET'S ROLL.

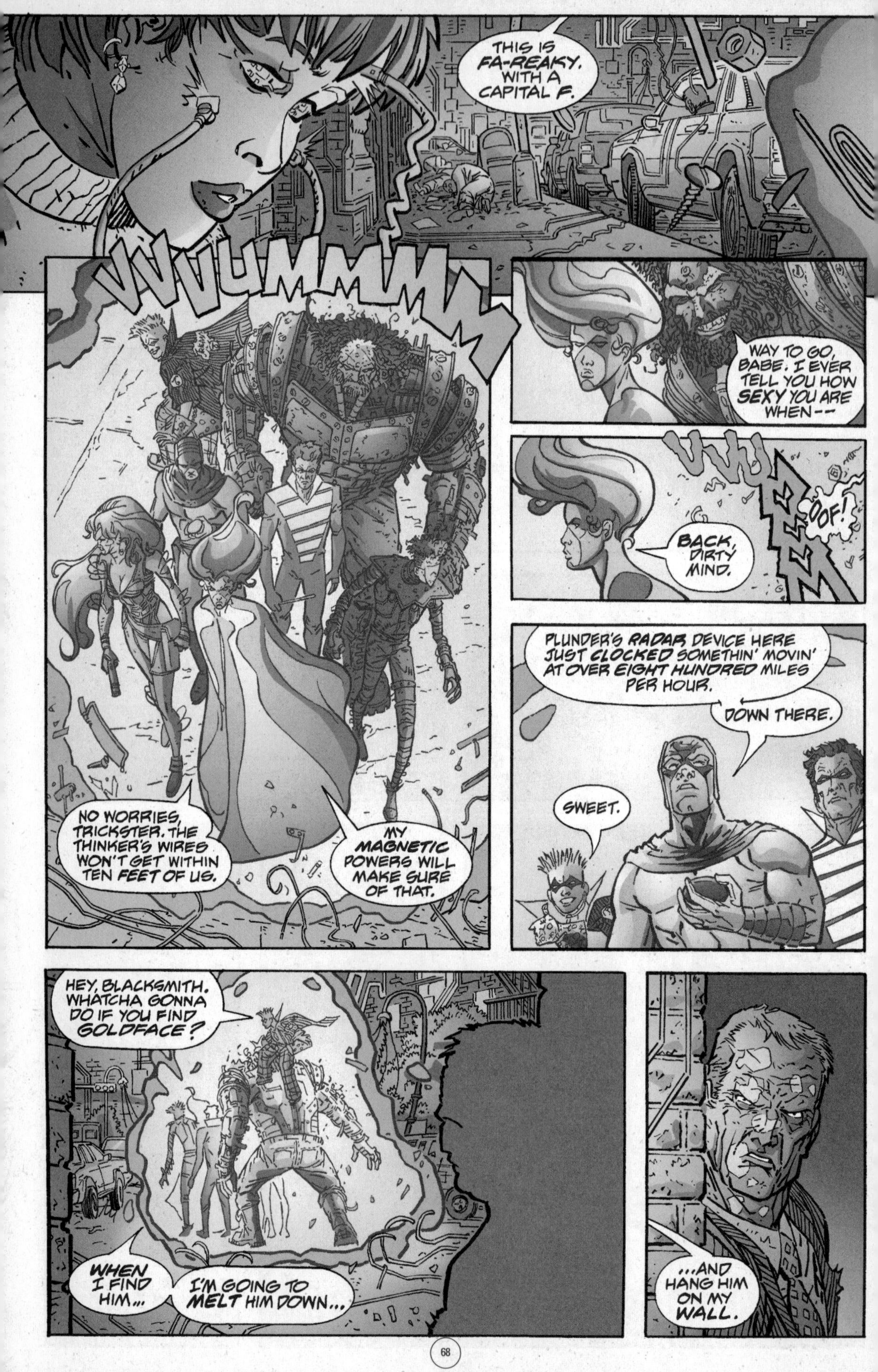
THIS IS FA-REAKY, WITH A CAPITAL F.
VVVUMMMM
WAY TO GO, BABE. I EVER TELL YOU HOW SEXY YOU ARE WHEN--
VVU
OOF!
BACK, DIRTY MIND.
PLUNDER'S RADAR DEVICE HERE JUST CLOCKED SOMETHIN' MOVIN' AT OVER EIGHT HUNDRED MILES PER HOUR.
DOWN THERE.
SWEET.
NO WORRIES, TRICKSTER. THE THINKER'S WIRES WON'T GET WITHIN TEN FEET OF US.
MY MAGNETIC POWERS WILL MAKE SURE OF THAT.
HEY, BLACKSMITH. WHATCHA GONNA DO IF YOU FIND GOLDFACE?
WHEN I FIND HIM...
I'M GOING TO MELT HIM DOWN...
...AND HANG HIM ON MY WALL.

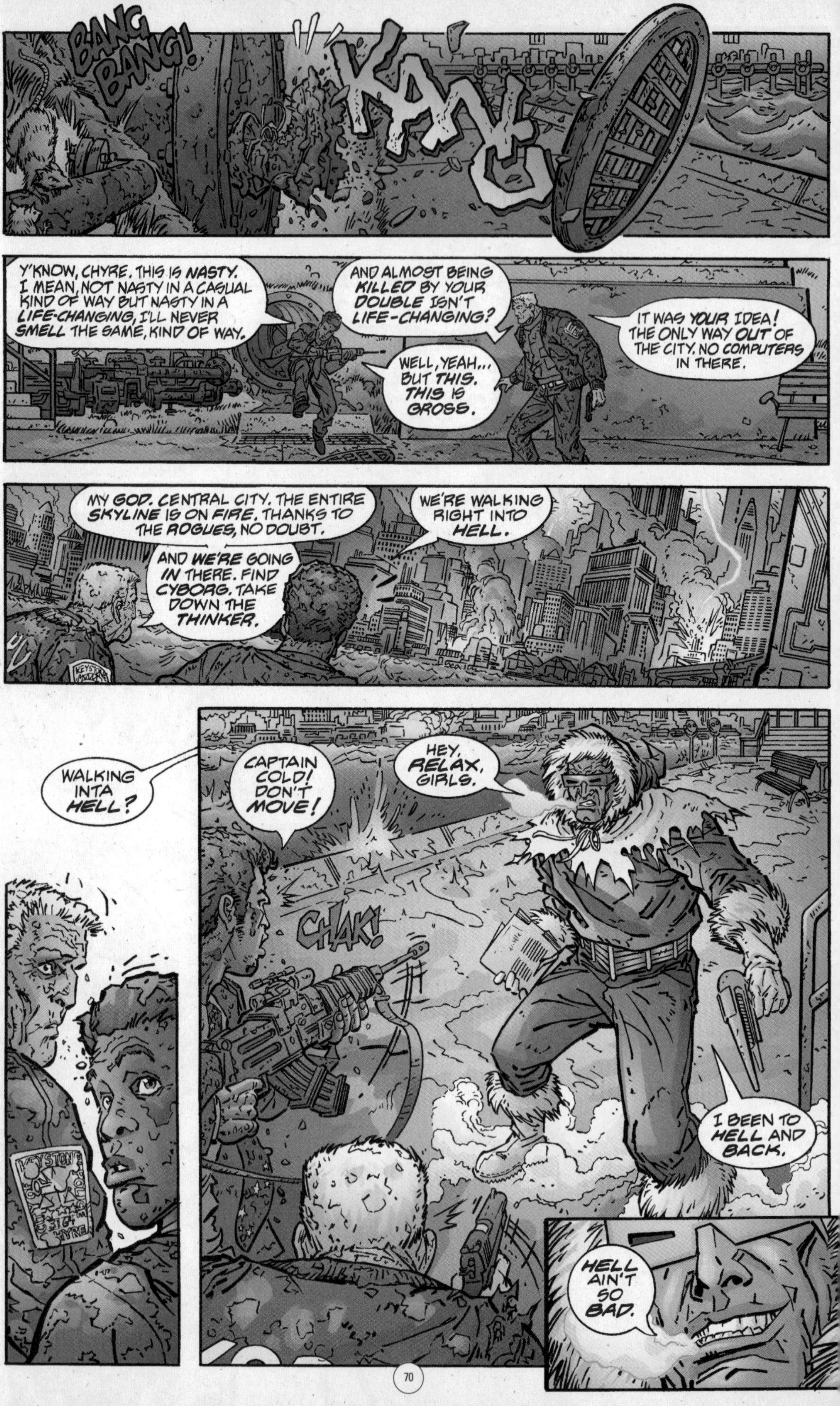
BANG BANG!
KAK!
Y'KNOW, CHYRE, THIS IS NASTY. I MEAN, NOT NASTY IN A CASUAL KIND OF WAY BUT NASTY IN A LIFE-CHANGING, I'LL NEVER SMELL THE SAME, KIND OF WAY.
AND ALMOST BEING KILLED BY YOUR DOUBLE ISN'T LIFE-CHANGING?
WELL, YEAH... BUT THIS. THIS IS GROSS.
IT WAS YOUR IDEA! THE ONLY WAY OUT OF THE CITY. NO COMPUTERS IN THERE.
MY GOD. CENTRAL CITY. THE ENTIRE SKYLINE IS ON FIRE. THANKS TO THE ROGUES, NO DOUBT.
AND WE'RE GOING IN THERE. FIND CYBORG. TAKE DOWN THE THINKER.
WE'RE WALKING RIGHT INTO HELL.
WALKING INTA HELL?
CAPTAIN COLD! DON'T MOVE!
HEY, RELAX, GIRLS.
CHAK!
I BEEN TO HELL AND BACK.
HELL AIN'T SO BAD.

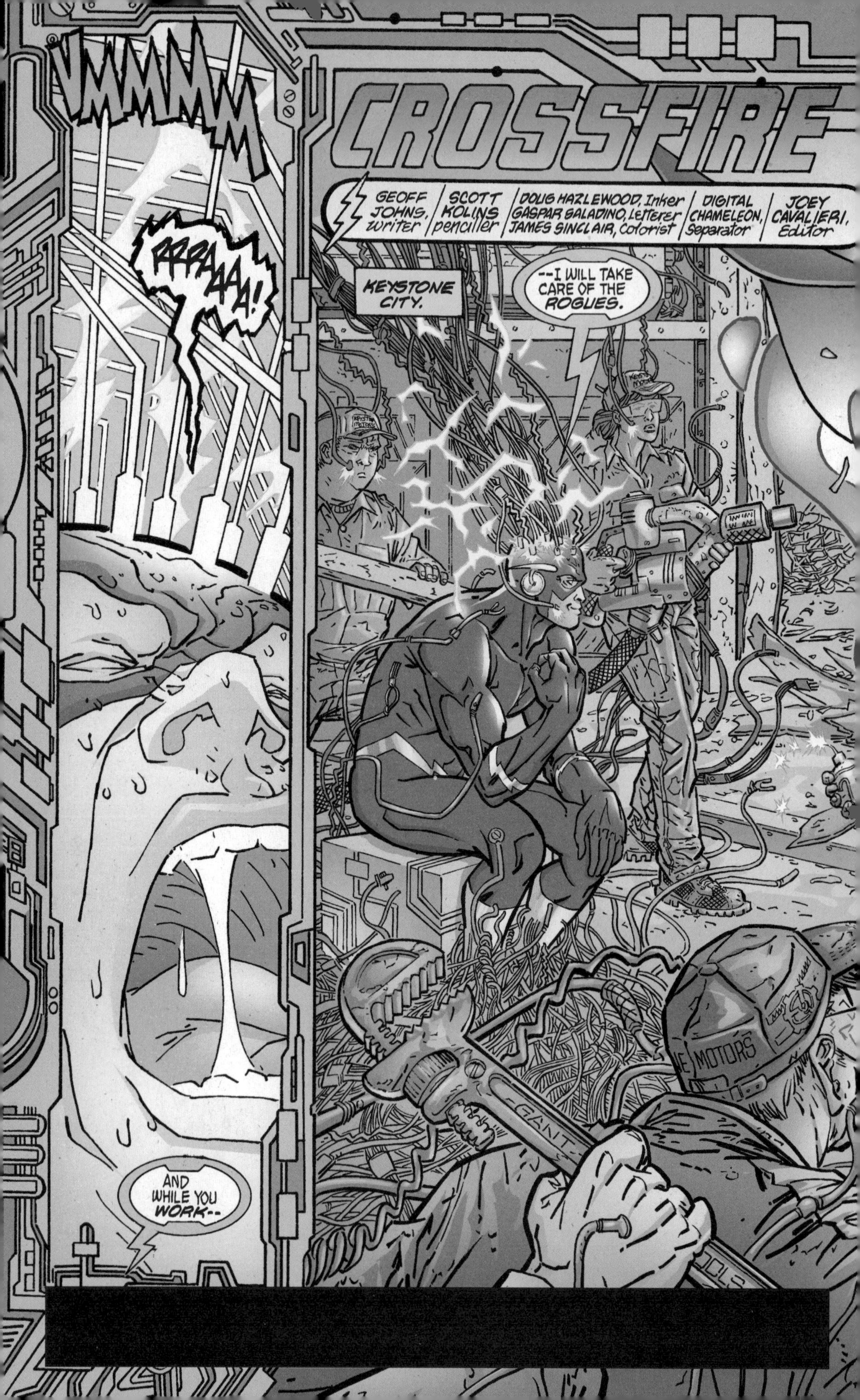
VMMMMMM
RRRRAAAAA!
CROSSFIRE
GEOFF JOHNS, writer
SCOTT KOLINS penciller
DOUG HAZLEWOOD, Inker
GASPAR SALADINO, Letterer
JAMES SINCLAIR, Colorist
DIGITAL CHAMELEON, Separator
JOEY CAVALIERI, Editor
KEYSTONE CITY.
AND WHILE YOU WORK--
--I WILL TAKE CARE OF THE ROGUES.
MOTORS
GANT

[redacted]

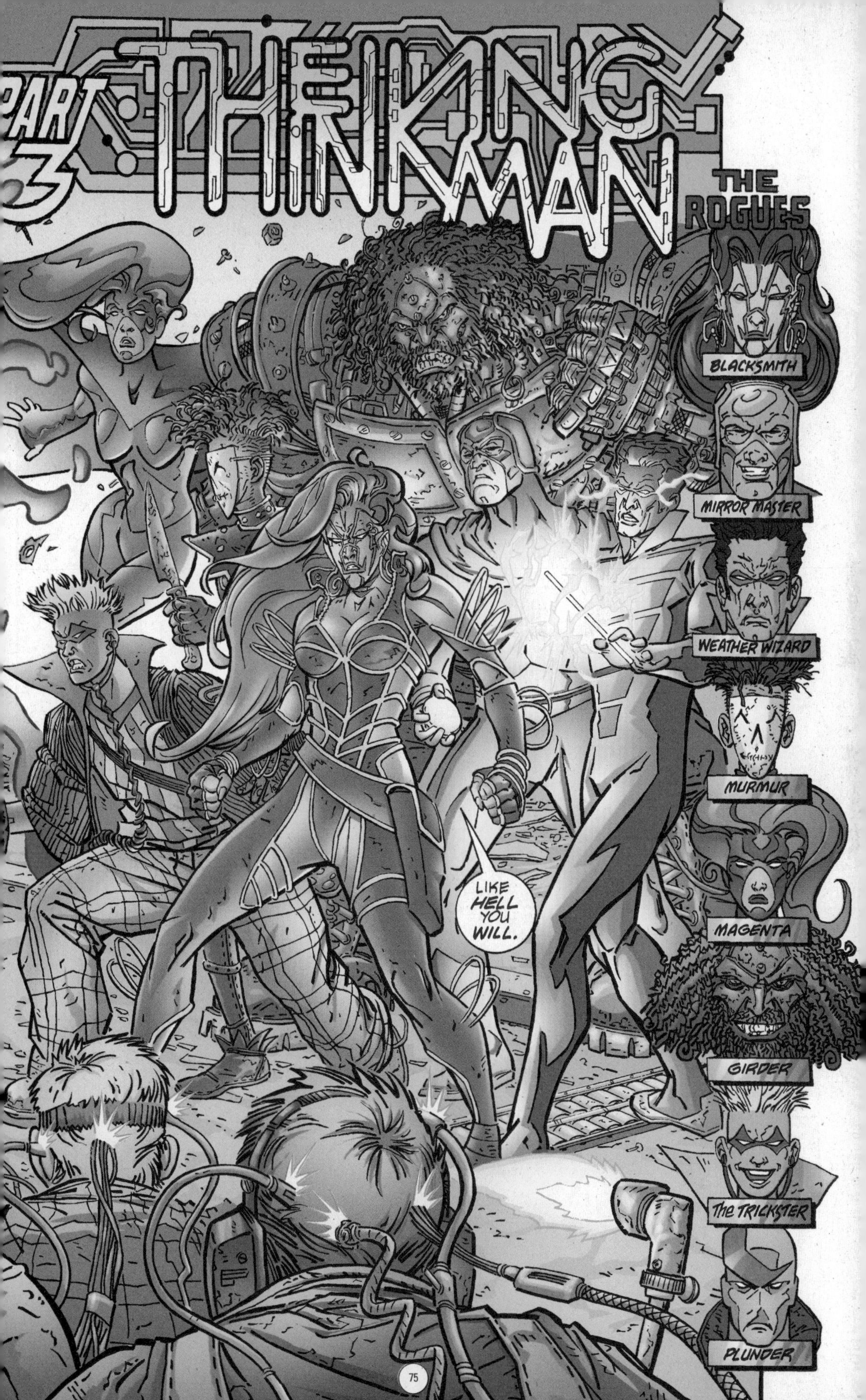
PART 3
THE THINKING MAN
THE ROGUES
BLACKSMITH
MIRROR MASTER
WEATHER WIZARD
MURMUR
MAGENTA
GIRDER
The TRICKSTER
PLUNDER
LIKE HELL YOU WILL.

DAMN. COMPUTER-MAN'S GOT A **SOFT** ARMY.

HH

SHHRRPP!

WHOA! FIRST THE **THINKER** PLUGS 'IMSELF INTA A FLASH...

NOW MURMUR JUST CUT THAT GUY'S **TONGUE** OUT! THIS IS SO **WICKED!**

COME ON, MURMUR. NO TIME FOR **PERSONAL** ACTIVITIES.

AWRIGHT?

YOU HAVE MADE A **SERIOUS** MISCALCULATION, ROGUES.

BOOM

FIZZSH

NN!

NO, THINKER, YOU'VE MADE THE MISTAKE. THIS TERRITORY BELONGS TO THE **NETWORK.**

UH... YEAH!

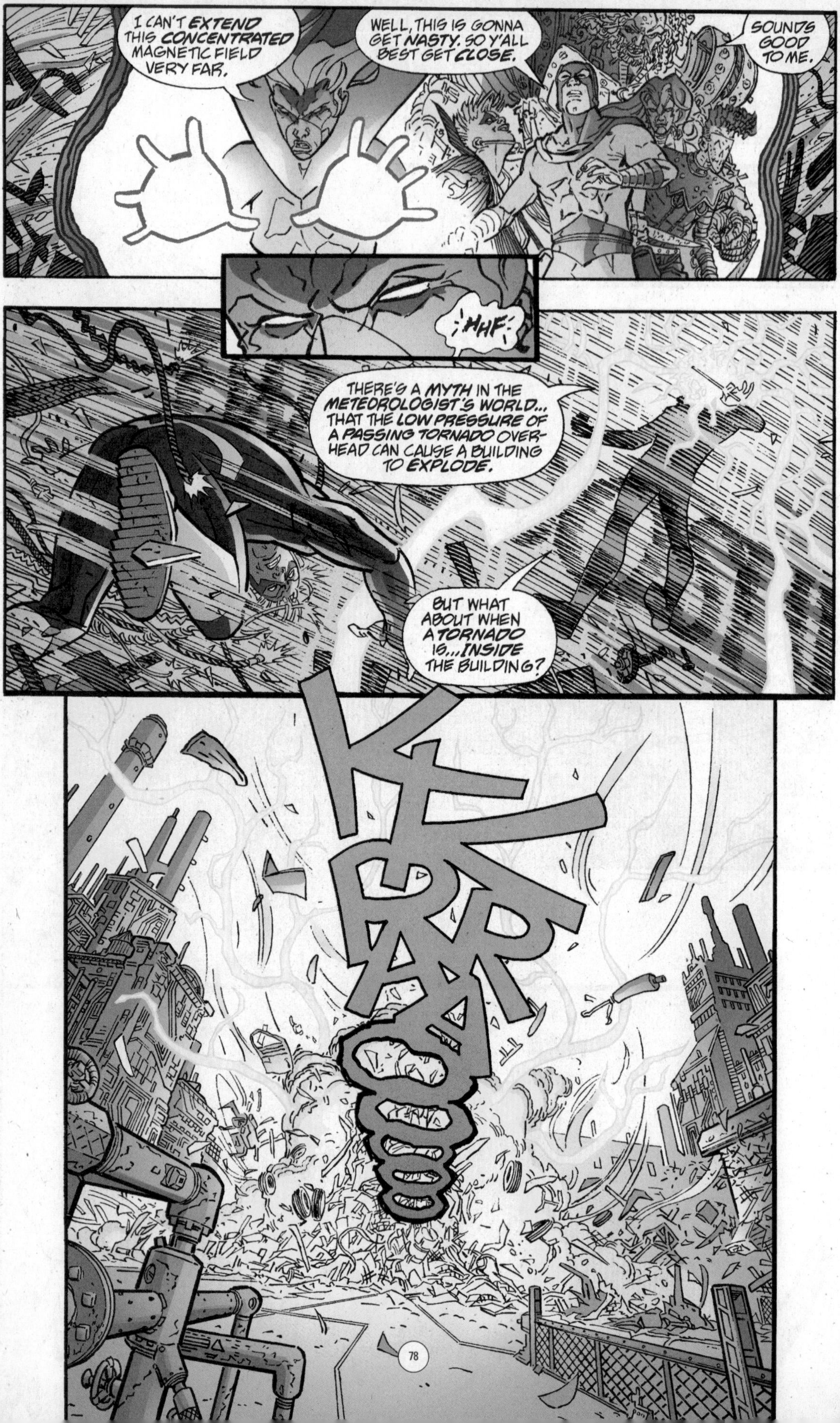
I CAN'T EXTEND THIS CONCENTRATED MAGNETIC FIELD VERY FAR.
WELL, THIS IS GONNA GET NASTY. SO Y'ALL BEST GET CLOSE.
SOUNDS GOOD TO ME.
HHF
THERE'S A MYTH IN THE METEOROLOGIST'S WORLD... THAT THE LOW PRESSURE OF A PASSING TORNADO OVER-HEAD CAN CAUSE A BUILDING TO EXPLODE.
BUT WHAT ABOUT WHEN A TORNADO IS... INSIDE THE BUILDING?
KERRAAAOOOOOOO

KRRAKVOOOMM

CENTRAL CITY OIL

CENTRAL CITY.

DAMN LIGHTNIN' STORMS ARE SPARKING UP ALL THESE FIRES.

WORK OF THE WEATHER WIZARD.

BUT THE FLASH MUSEUM, CHYRE?

TRUST ME, MOBILLO.

CYBORG AND THE REST OF THE FORCE ARE BEIN' HELD INSIDE. AND IF WE WANT TO TAKE OUT THAT THINKER THING, WE'RE GONNA NEED 'IM.

FHOOOM!!

KRINGG

YOU HAVEN'T PUT OUT A SINGLE FIRE SINCE WE CROSSED OVER INTO CENTRAL. WHY THAT ONE, COLD?

BARRY ALLEN STATUE.

KRRASSHH

CALL ME SENTIMENTAL.

79

WELCOME TO THE FLASH MUSEUM

CAN I ASK YOU SOMETHING?

DEPENDS ON WHAT IT IS.

ASK ME SOMETHIN' ELSE.

WHY ARE YOU HELPING US?

January, 1940

THE FLAS

OKAY. WHY DO YOU DO WHAT YOU DO?

YOU MEAN A **ROGUE.** I #@*% **HATE** THAT OTHER TERM. "SUPER-VILLAIN."

YOU DRESS UP IN A **BLUE** ESKIMO SUIT. FREEZING THINGS.

I DON'T JUST **FREEZE** THINGS, I--

SLOW THEM DOWN AT THE **ATOMIC** LEVEL. I'VE READ THE FILE ON YOUR **COLD-GUN.** AND I READ THE FILE ON YOU, COLD.

YOU'RE A **SMART** GUY. BUT YOU'RE STILL PLAYING THIS **GAME.** GOING AFTER THE **SMALL** SCORE.

WHY **WASTE** ALL THIS **TIME** AND ENERGY?

THE ROGUES

DO WHAT I DO?

WHY ARE YOU A "SUPER"-VILLAIN"?

COLD VS WAVE

DAMMIT. I'M **TALLER** THAN HEAT WAVE.

LOOK, KID. **I LIKE** LIVIN' **PAYCHECK** TO **PAYCHECK.** MAKES LIFE MORE **FUN.**

WAVE THE OLD

YOU'RE LYING.

...

LET ME ASK **YOU** SOMETHIN', BLUE BOY!

THAT OUTFIT THERE A **JANTZII,** RIGHT?

YEAH. SO...

SO WHY DO YOU **WASTE** SO MUCH **MONEY** ON A **DAMN MONKEY SUIT?**

...

HARD TO EXPLAIN **VICES,** AIN'T IT?

HERE WE GO, GANG.

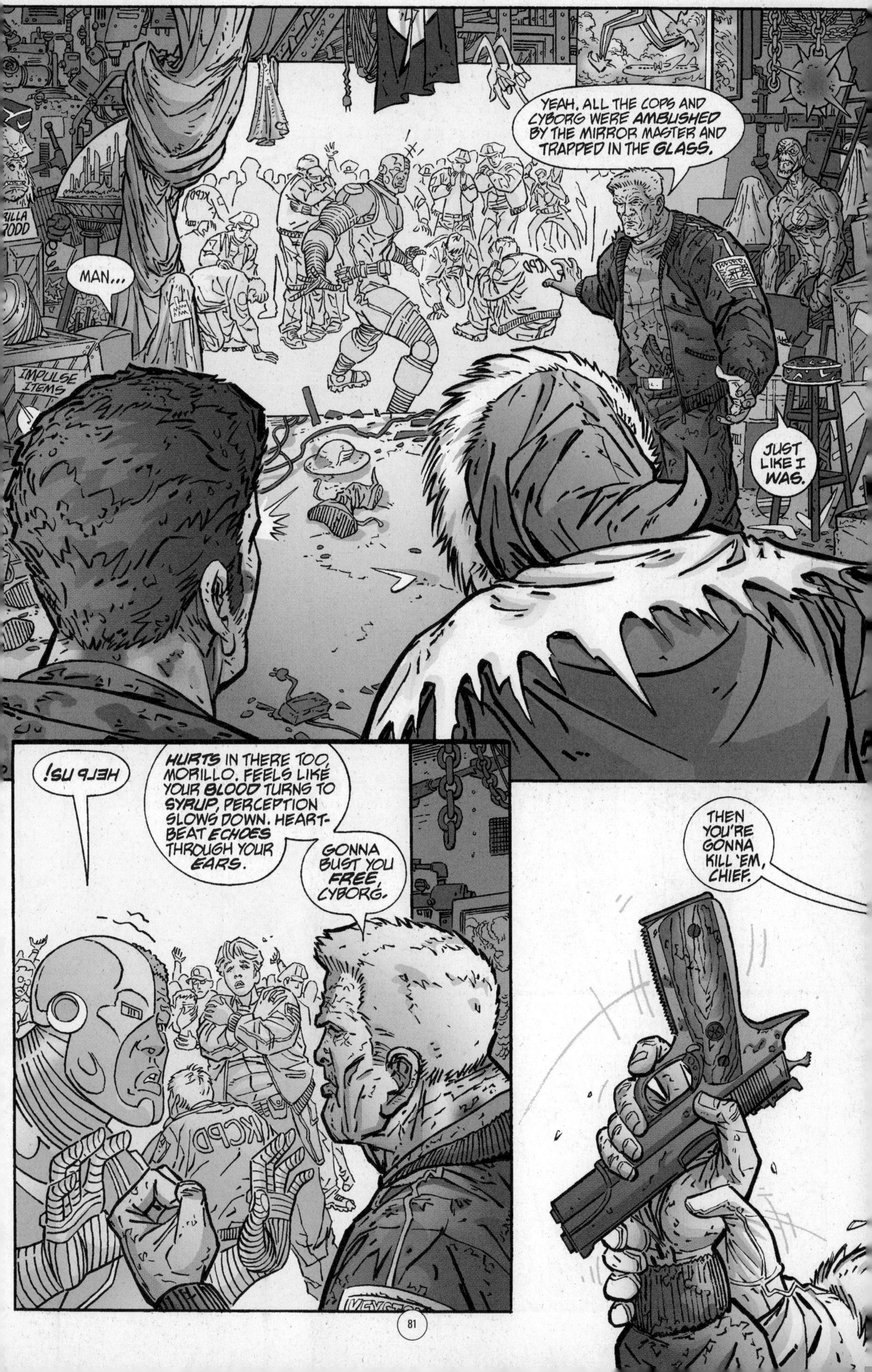
IMPULSE ITEMS
KCPD
MAN...
YEAH. ALL THE COPS AND CYBORG WERE AMBUSHED BY THE MIRROR MASTER AND TRAPPED IN THE GLASS.
JUST LIKE I WAS.
HELP US!
HURTS IN THERE TOO, MORILLO. FEELS LIKE YOUR BLOOD TURNS TO SYRUP, PERCEPTION SLOWS DOWN. HEART-BEAT ECHOES THROUGH YOUR EARS.
GONNA BUST YOU FREE, CYBORG.
KCPD
THEN YOU'RE GONNA KILL 'EM, CHIEF.

I'VE WORKED WITH MIRROR MASTER. SEEN HIM DO THIS TRICK A FEW TIMES.

YOU BREAK THAT MIRROR, YOU KILL ANYONE *TRAPPED* INSIDE.

KRRGGG!

NEED TO *CORRECT* THE REFLECTION FIRST. REVERSE IT TO REALITY.

HELLO? CAN ANYONE HEAR ME?

KCPD

WHAT... WHAT THE HELL IS GOING ON?

WHERE'S FLASH?

I'M DONE.

TAKE THIS. SWIPED IT FROM YOUR PROFILER GUY-- ZOLOMON. IT SHOULD GIVE YA SOME POINTERS.

KRRRASHH

THE... NETWORK? PLUNDER MENTIONED THEM. THEY--

HOLD ON, COLD. YOU CAN'T JUST--

KEYSTONE
MOTORS
KEEP OUT

DO NOT

AARR. DAMMIT, MAGENTA. YOU'RE **NOT** CONCENTRATING. I CAN FEEL MY ARMS...**RUSTING** AGAIN. I NEED YOUR MAGNETICS TO HOLD ME **TOGETHER**.

SORRY.

Wally **ALWAYS** looked good without a shirt.

HEY...THINKER STILL **INSIDE** HIS HEAD?

FFF.

NOT FOR LONG.

WITH MY...**UNIQUE** PERCEPTION, I CAN **SENSE** THE FUSION OF **ORGANIC** AND **INORGANIC.** I CAN **SEE** HIS NERVE CELLS AND SKIN TISSUES **GRAFTED** ON TO THE **THINKER'S** BRAIN BAUBLES--

--AND I CAN **DISSOLVE** THE ADHESIVE **BOND** BETWEEN THEM.

SHRR

AS I SAID BEFORE, **THINKER.** THE FLASH IS **OURS!**

MAN, THIS WASN'T SO TOUGH. HEY, **MURMUR,** GIVE ME ONE A' YOUR KNIVES, I'M GONNA **SLASH** SPEEDY'S THROAT!

NN MN.

NAW. LET ME **BURN** HIS **CORNEAS** OUT. SHOOT A LASER **CLEAR** THROUGH 'IS **BRAIN.**

I THINK WE ALL **DESERVE** A TURN AT HIM. DON'T YOU, **BLACK--**

WHAT--

FK

83

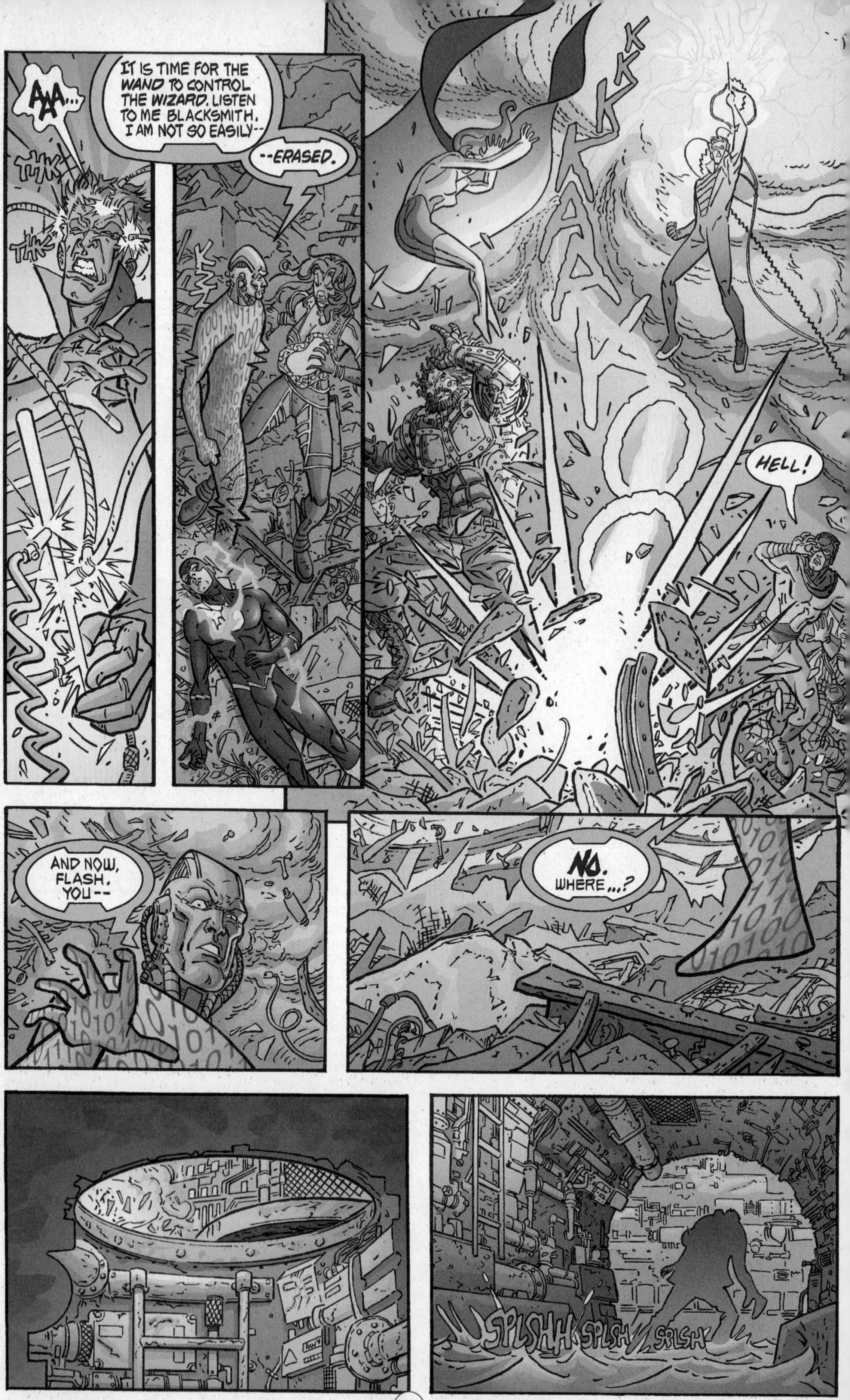
AAA...
IT IS TIME FOR THE WAND TO CONTROL THE WIZARD. LISTEN TO ME BLACKSMITH. I AM NOT SO EASILY--
THK
THK
--ERASED.
KKKK
KAKAKOOM
HELL!
AND NOW, FLASH, YOU--
NO. WHERE...?
SPLSHH SPLSH SPLSH

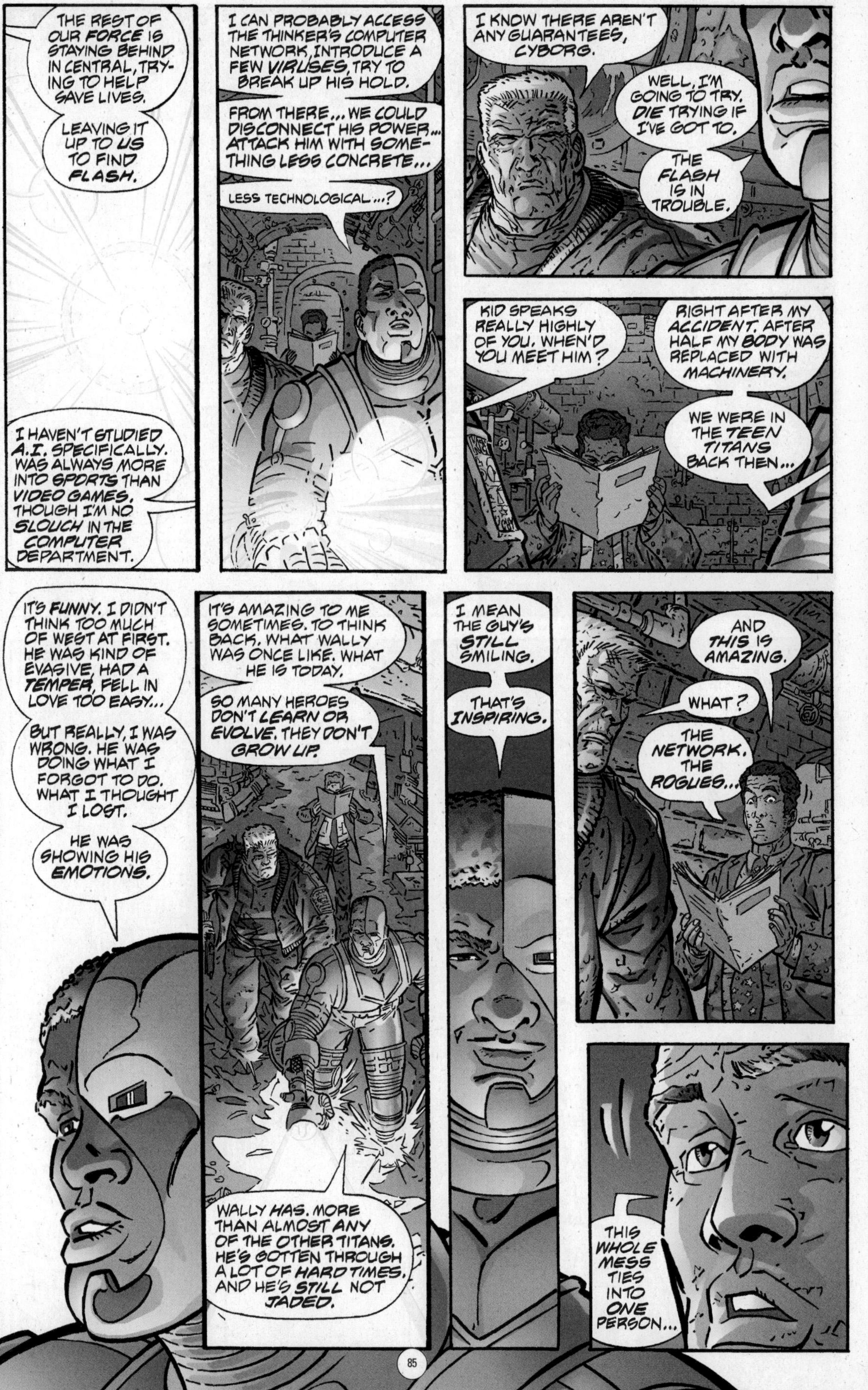
THE REST OF OUR FORCE IS STAYING BEHIND IN CENTRAL, TRYING TO HELP SAVE LIVES.
LEAVING IT UP TO US TO FIND FLASH.
I HAVEN'T STUDIED A.I. SPECIFICALLY. WAS ALWAYS MORE INTO SPORTS THAN VIDEO GAMES, THOUGH I'M NO SLOUCH IN THE COMPUTER DEPARTMENT.
I CAN PROBABLY ACCESS THE THINKER'S COMPUTER NETWORK, INTRODUCE A FEW VIRUSES, TRY TO BREAK UP HIS HOLD.
FROM THERE... WE COULD DISCONNECT HIS POWER... ATTACK HIM WITH SOMETHING LESS CONCRETE...
LESS TECHNOLOGICAL...?
I KNOW THERE AREN'T ANY GUARANTEES, CYBORG.
WELL, I'M GOING TO TRY. DIE TRYING IF I'VE GOT TO.
THE FLASH IS IN TROUBLE.
KID SPEAKS REALLY HIGHLY OF YOU. WHEN'D YOU MEET HIM?
RIGHT AFTER MY ACCIDENT. AFTER HALF MY BODY WAS REPLACED WITH MACHINERY.
WE WERE IN THE TEEN TITANS BACK THEN...
IT'S FUNNY. I DIDN'T THINK TOO MUCH OF WEST AT FIRST. HE WAS KIND OF EVASIVE, HAD A TEMPER, FELL IN LOVE TOO EASY...
BUT REALLY, I WAS WRONG. HE WAS DOING WHAT I FORGOT TO DO. WHAT I THOUGHT I LOST.
HE WAS SHOWING HIS EMOTIONS.
IT'S AMAZING TO ME SOMETIMES. TO THINK BACK. WHAT WALLY WAS ONCE LIKE. WHAT HE IS TODAY.
SO MANY HEROES DON'T LEARN OR EVOLVE. THEY DON'T GROW UP.
WALLY HAS. MORE THAN ALMOST ANY OF THE OTHER TITANS. HE'S GOTTEN THROUGH A LOT OF HARD TIMES. AND HE'S STILL NOT JADED.
I MEAN THE GUY'S STILL SMILING.
THAT'S INSPIRING.
AND THIS IS AMAZING.
WHAT?
THE NETWORK. THE ROGUES...
THIS WHOLE MESS TIES INTO ONE PERSON...

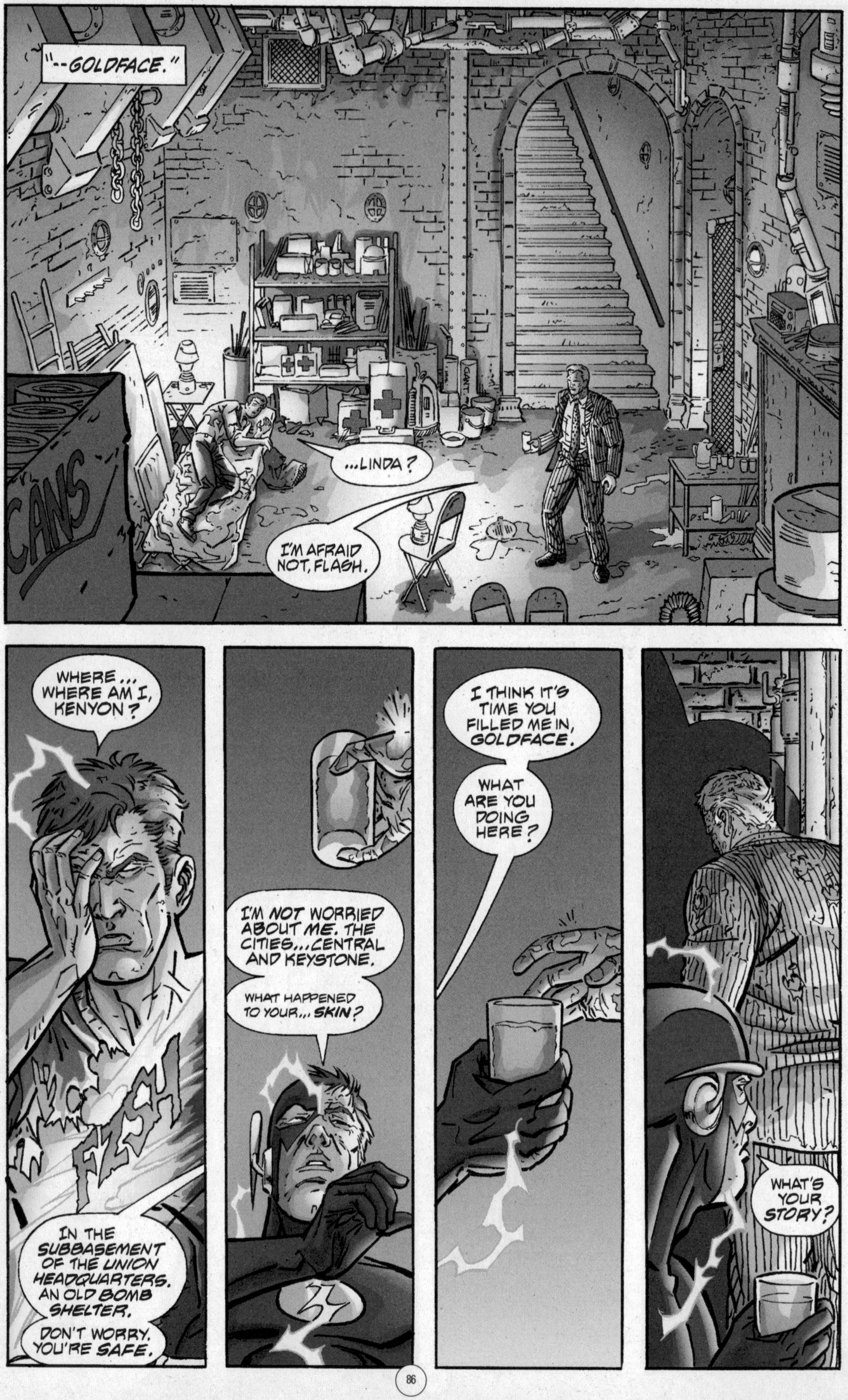
"--GOLDFACE."
CANS
...LINDA?
I'M AFRAID NOT, FLASH.
WHERE... WHERE AM I, KENYON?
FZSH
IN THE SUBBASEMENT OF THE UNION HEADQUARTERS. AN OLD BOMB SHELTER.
DON'T WORRY. YOU'RE SAFE.
I'M NOT WORRIED ABOUT ME. THE CITIES... CENTRAL AND KEYSTONE.
WHAT HAPPENED TO YOUR... SKIN?
I THINK IT'S TIME YOU FILLED ME IN, GOLDFACE.
WHAT ARE YOU DOING HERE?
WHAT'S YOUR STORY?

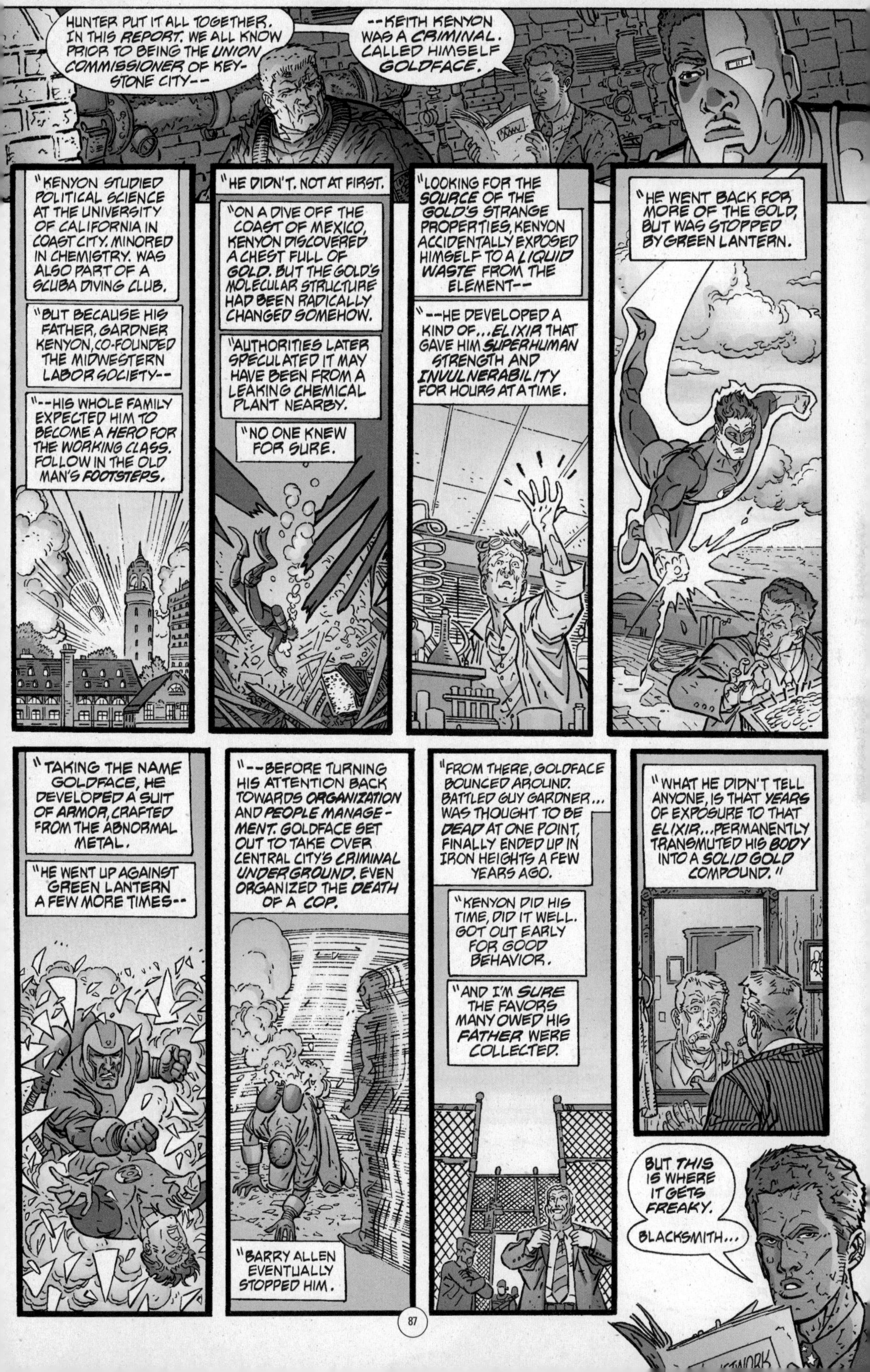
HUNTER PUT IT ALL TOGETHER. IN THIS REPORT. WE ALL KNOW PRIOR TO BEING THE UNION COMMISSIONER OF KEYSTONE CITY--
--KEITH KENYON WAS A CRIMINAL. CALLED HIMSELF GOLDFACE.
"KENYON STUDIED POLITICAL SCIENCE AT THE UNIVERSITY OF CALIFORNIA IN COAST CITY. MINORED IN CHEMISTRY. WAS ALSO PART OF A SCUBA DIVING CLUB.
"BUT BECAUSE HIS FATHER, GARDNER KENYON, CO-FOUNDED THE MIDWESTERN LABOR SOCIETY--
"--HIS WHOLE FAMILY EXPECTED HIM TO BECOME A HERO FOR THE WORKING CLASS. FOLLOW IN THE OLD MAN'S FOOTSTEPS.
"HE DIDN'T. NOT AT FIRST.
"ON A DIVE OFF THE COAST OF MEXICO, KENYON DISCOVERED A CHEST FULL OF GOLD. BUT THE GOLD'S MOLECULAR STRUCTURE HAD BEEN RADICALLY CHANGED SOMEHOW.
"AUTHORITIES LATER SPECULATED IT MAY HAVE BEEN FROM A LEAKING CHEMICAL PLANT NEARBY.
"NO ONE KNEW FOR SURE.
"LOOKING FOR THE SOURCE OF THE GOLD'S STRANGE PROPERTIES, KENYON ACCIDENTALLY EXPOSED HIMSELF TO A LIQUID WASTE FROM THE ELEMENT--
"--HE DEVELOPED A KIND OF...ELIXIR THAT GAVE HIM SUPERHUMAN STRENGTH AND INVULNERABILITY FOR HOURS AT A TIME.
"HE WENT BACK FOR MORE OF THE GOLD, BUT WAS STOPPED BY GREEN LANTERN.
"TAKING THE NAME GOLDFACE, HE DEVELOPED A SUIT OF ARMOR, CRAFTED FROM THE ABNORMAL METAL.
"HE WENT UP AGAINST GREEN LANTERN A FEW MORE TIMES--
"--BEFORE TURNING HIS ATTENTION BACK TOWARDS ORGANIZATION AND PEOPLE MANAGEMENT. GOLDFACE SET OUT TO TAKE OVER CENTRAL CITY'S CRIMINAL UNDERGROUND. EVEN ORGANIZED THE DEATH OF A COP.
"BARRY ALLEN EVENTUALLY STOPPED HIM.
"FROM THERE, GOLDFACE BOUNCED AROUND. BATTLED GUY GARDNER... WAS THOUGHT TO BE DEAD AT ONE POINT, FINALLY ENDED UP IN IRON HEIGHTS A FEW YEARS AGO.
"KENYON DID HIS TIME, DID IT WELL. GOT OUT EARLY FOR GOOD BEHAVIOR.
"AND I'M SURE THE FAVORS MANY OWED HIS FATHER WERE COLLECTED.
"WHAT HE DIDN'T TELL ANYONE, IS THAT YEARS OF EXPOSURE TO THAT ELIXIR...PERMANENTLY TRANSMUTED HIS BODY INTO A SOLID GOLD COMPOUND."
BUT THIS IS WHERE IT GETS FREAKY.
BLACKSMITH...

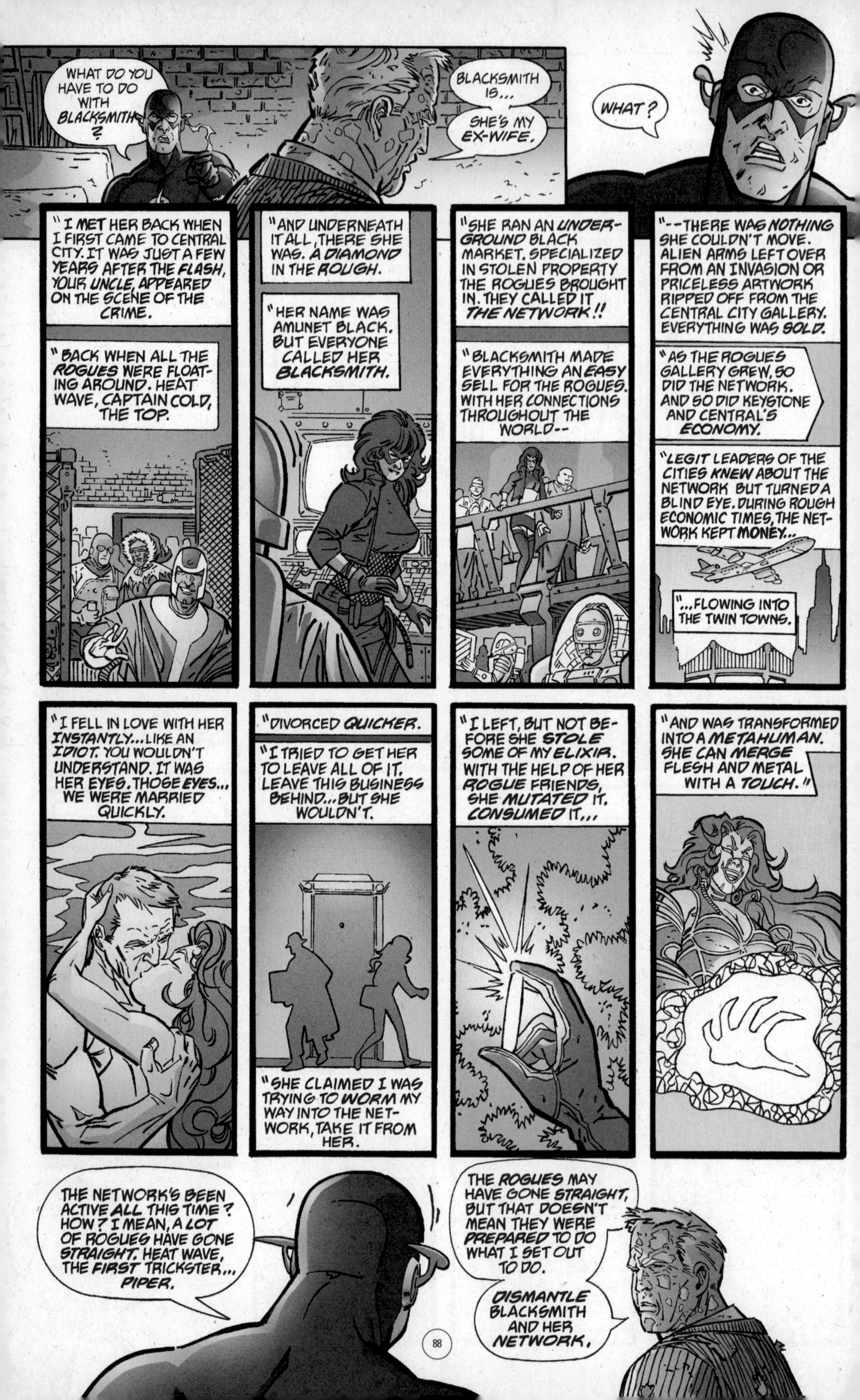

WHAT DO YOU HAVE TO DO WITH BLACKSMITH ?
BLACKSMITH IS...
SHE'S MY EX-WIFE.
WHAT ?
"I MET HER BACK WHEN I FIRST CAME TO CENTRAL CITY. IT WAS JUST A FEW YEARS AFTER THE FLASH, YOUR UNCLE, APPEARED ON THE SCENE OF THE CRIME.
"BACK WHEN ALL THE ROGUES WERE FLOATING AROUND. HEAT WAVE, CAPTAIN COLD, THE TOP.
"AND UNDERNEATH IT ALL, THERE SHE WAS. A DIAMOND IN THE ROUGH.
"HER NAME WAS AMUNET BLACK. BUT EVERYONE CALLED HER BLACKSMITH.
"SHE RAN AN UNDERGROUND BLACK MARKET. SPECIALIZED IN STOLEN PROPERTY THE ROGUES BROUGHT IN. THEY CALLED IT THE NETWORK!!
"BLACKSMITH MADE EVERYTHING AN EASY SELL FOR THE ROGUES. WITH HER CONNECTIONS THROUGHOUT THE WORLD--
"--THERE WAS NOTHING SHE COULDN'T MOVE. ALIEN ARMS LEFT OVER FROM AN INVASION OR PRICELESS ARTWORK RIPPED OFF FROM THE CENTRAL CITY GALLERY. EVERYTHING WAS SOLD.
"AS THE ROGUES GALLERY GREW, SO DID THE NETWORK. AND SO DID KEYSTONE AND CENTRAL'S ECONOMY.
"LEGIT LEADERS OF THE CITIES KNEW ABOUT THE NETWORK BUT TURNED A BLIND EYE. DURING ROUGH ECONOMIC TIMES, THE NETWORK KEPT MONEY...
"...FLOWING INTO THE TWIN TOWNS.
"I FELL IN LOVE WITH HER INSTANTLY... LIKE AN IDIOT. YOU WOULDN'T UNDERSTAND. IT WAS HER EYES. THOSE EYES... WE WERE MARRIED QUICKLY.
"DIVORCED QUICKER.
"I TRIED TO GET HER TO LEAVE ALL OF IT. LEAVE THIS BUSINESS BEHIND... BUT SHE WOULDN'T.
"SHE CLAIMED I WAS TRYING TO WORM MY WAY INTO THE NETWORK, TAKE IT FROM HER.
"I LEFT, BUT NOT BEFORE SHE STOLE SOME OF MY ELIXIR. WITH THE HELP OF HER ROGUE FRIENDS, SHE MUTATED IT. CONSUMED IT...
"AND WAS TRANSFORMED INTO A METAHUMAN. SHE CAN MERGE FLESH AND METAL WITH A TOUCH."
THE NETWORK'S BEEN ACTIVE ALL THIS TIME? HOW? I MEAN, A LOT OF ROGUES HAVE GONE STRAIGHT. HEAT WAVE, THE FIRST TRICKSTER... PIPER.
THE ROGUES MAY HAVE GONE STRAIGHT, BUT THAT DOESN'T MEAN THEY WERE PREPARED TO DO WHAT I SET OUT TO DO.
DISMANTLE BLACKSMITH AND HER NETWORK.

IN SOME CASES THE ROGUES WERE *THREATENED.* IN OTHERS, LIKE PIPER--

--SHE PROBABLY GOT *MIRROR MASTER* TO ERASE SOME OF HIS MEMORY WITH *HYPNOTISM.* DID IT TO HEAT WAVE. TRIED TO DO IT TO ME--

DAMMIT.

WE'VE BEEN *FOLLOWED.*

HYPNOTISM? THAT'S IT. *PIPER*--

S PAK!

KA AA OOM

YOUR *GOLD* MAY BE ABLE TO *PROTECT* YOU FROM *ASSIMILATION,* BUT IT IS AN *EXCELLENT* ELECTRICAL CONDUCTOR.

KKKRKK

ARRR!

RR

TIME TO *PLUG* YOU BACK IN.

DON'T THINK SO, PUNK.

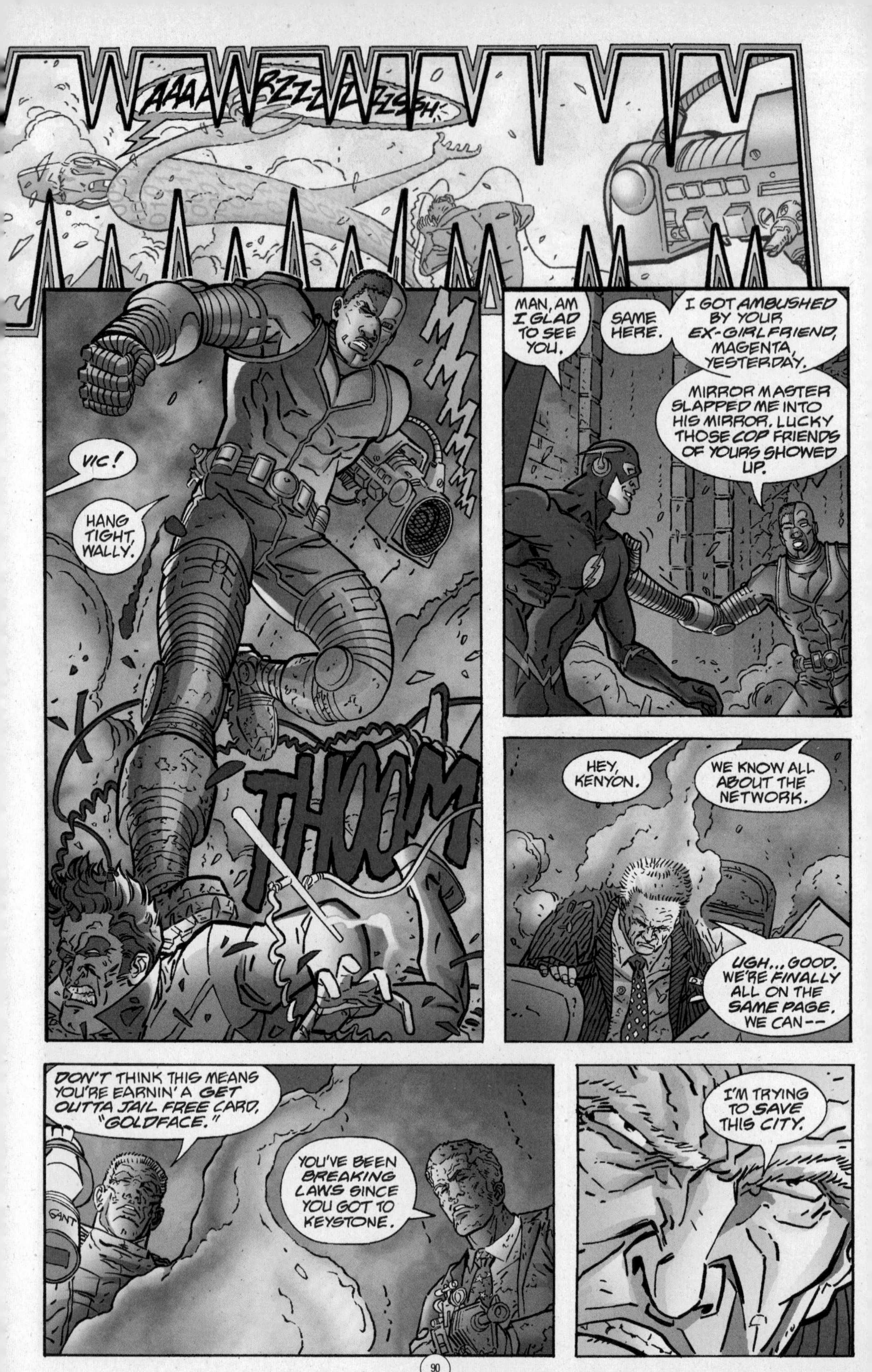
WAAAAAAAAAAM
AAAARZZZZZZZSSH
MMMMMMM
VIC!
HANG TIGHT, WALLY.
THOOM
MAN, AM I GLAD TO SEE YOU.
SAME HERE.
I GOT AMBUSHED BY YOUR EX-GIRLFRIEND, MAGENTA, YESTERDAY.
MIRROR MASTER SLAPPED ME INTO HIS MIRROR. LUCKY THOSE COP FRIENDS OF YOURS SHOWED UP.
HEY, KENYON.
WE KNOW ALL ABOUT THE NETWORK.
UGH... GOOD. WE'RE FINALLY ALL ON THE SAME PAGE. WE CAN--
DON'T THINK THIS MEANS YOU'RE EARNIN' A GET OUTTA JAIL FREE CARD, "GOLDFACE."
YOU'VE BEEN BREAKING LAWS SINCE YOU GOT TO KEYSTONE.
I'M TRYING TO SAVE THIS CITY.

FLASH WILL NOT ESCAPE ME.

NO ONE ON EARTH WILL.

YOU WANT MY *BRAIN?* FINE.

WHAT?

FLASH! WHAT THE HELL ARE YOU DOING?

THAT LAST WIRE WASN'T THE THINKER'S. IT WAS CYBORG.

AND HE GAVE ME AN *IDEA.*

AARR!

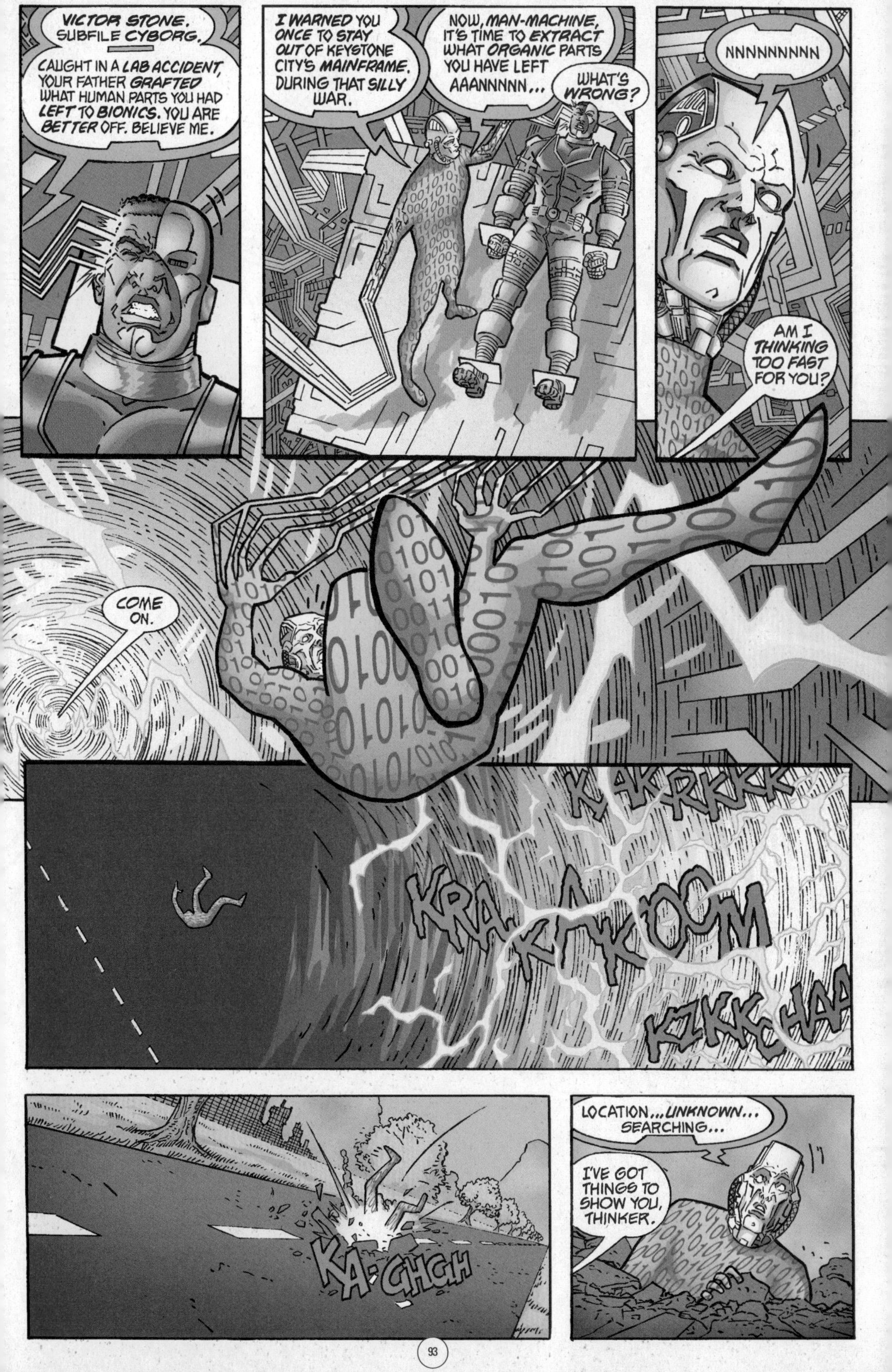
VICTOR STONE. SUBFILE CYBORG.
CAUGHT IN A LAB ACCIDENT, YOUR FATHER GRAFTED WHAT HUMAN PARTS YOU HAD LEFT TO BIONICS. YOU ARE BETTER OFF. BELIEVE ME.
I WARNED YOU ONCE TO STAY OUT OF KEYSTONE CITY'S MAINFRAME. DURING THAT SILLY WAR.
NOW, MAN-MACHINE, IT'S TIME TO EXTRACT WHAT ORGANIC PARTS YOU HAVE LEFT AAANNNNN...
WHAT'S WRONG?
NNNNNNNNN
AM I THINKING TOO FAST FOR YOU?
COME ON.
KAKRKKK
KRA-KTYKOOM
KZKKCHAA
KA-CHCH
LOCATION... UNKNOWN... SEARCHING...
I'VE GOT THINGS TO SHOW YOU, THINKER.

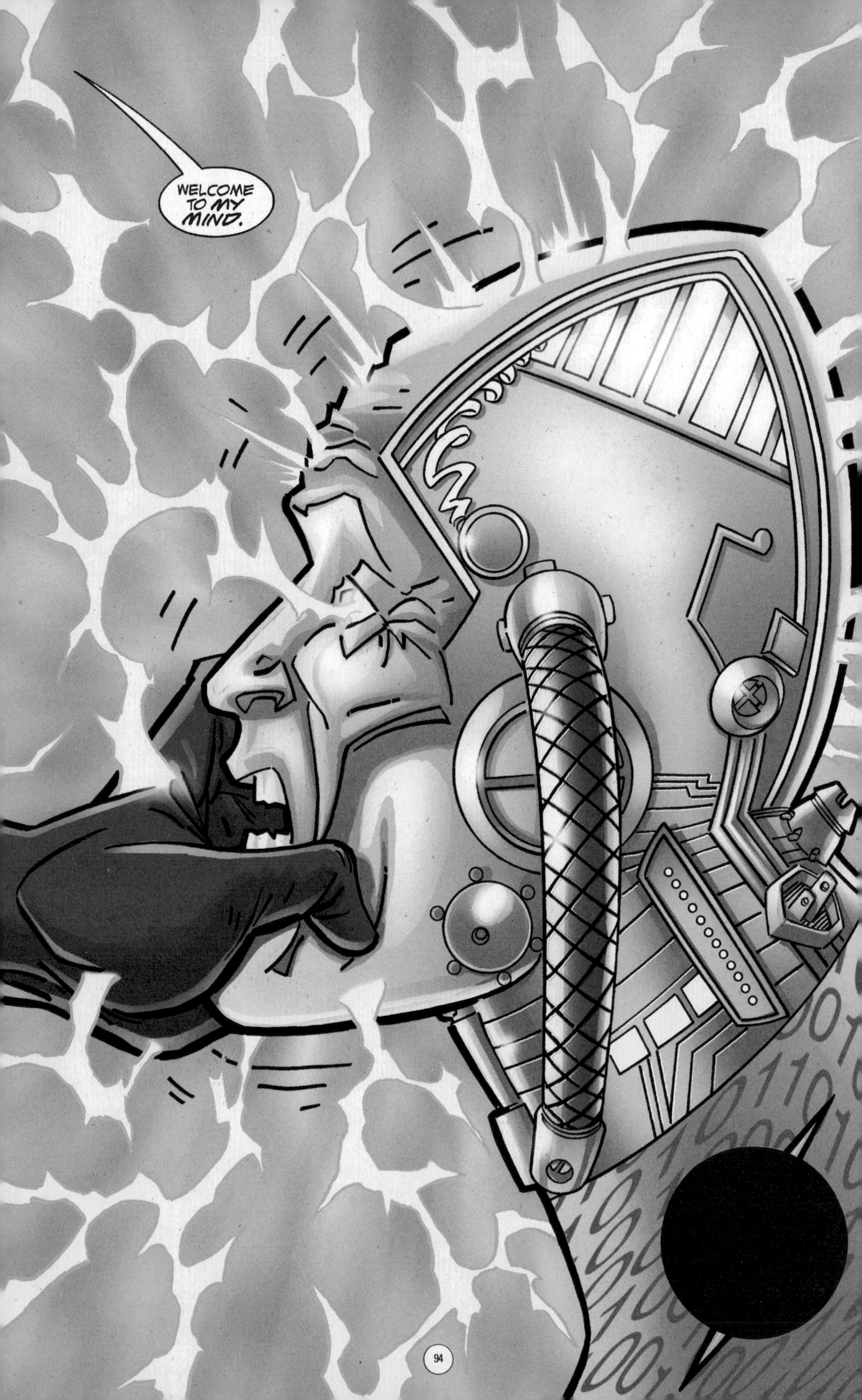
WELCOME TO MY MIND.

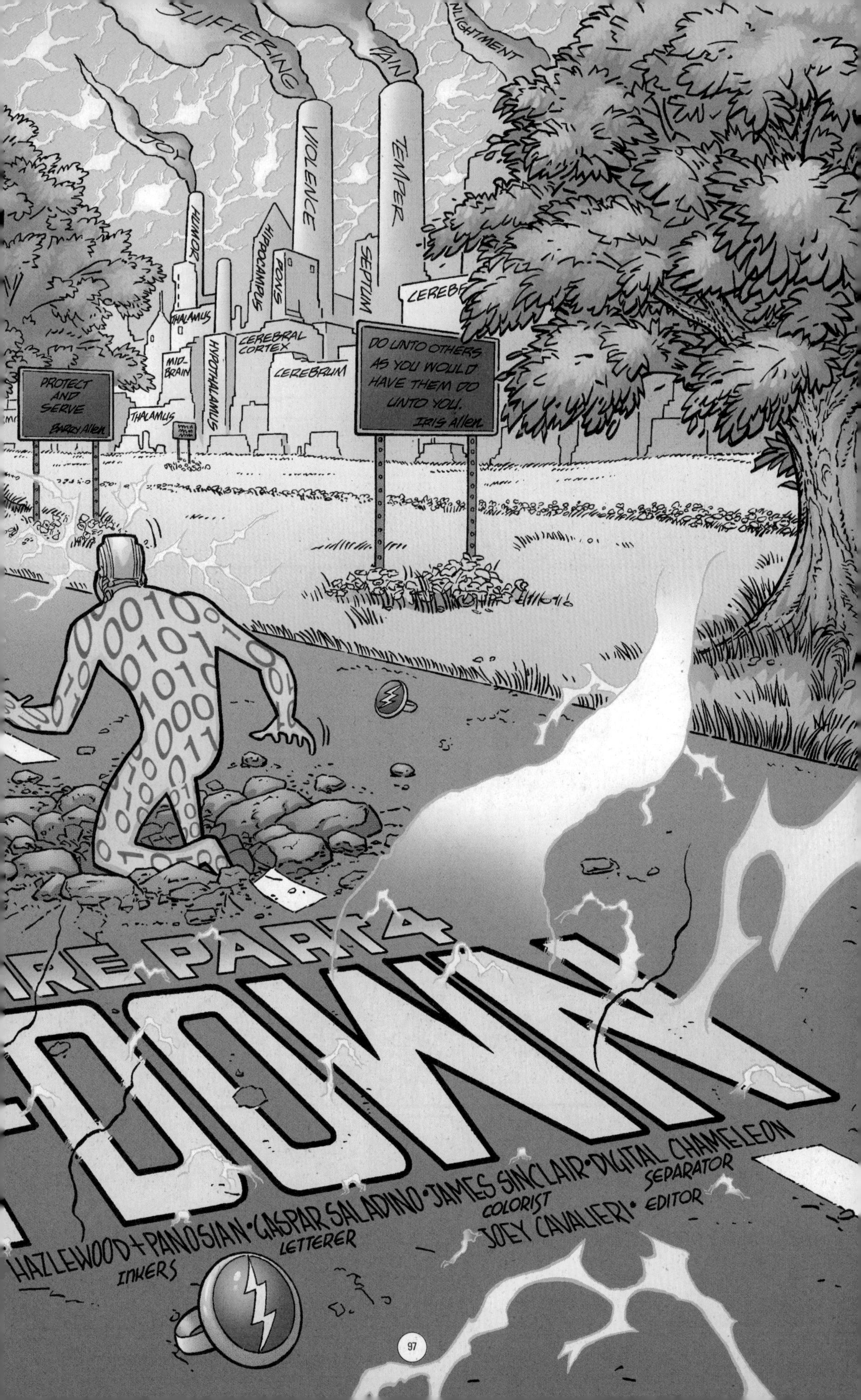
SUFFERING
PAIN
JOY
VIOLENCE
TEMPER
HUMOR
HIPPOCAMPUS
PONS
SEPTUM
THALAMUS
CEREBRAL CORTEX
MID-BRAIN
HYPOTHALAMUS
CEREBRUM
THALAMUS
PROTECT AND SERVE
Barry Allen
DO UNTO OTHERS AS YOU WOULD HAVE THEM DO UNTO YOU.
Iris Allen
PART 4
HAZLEWOOD + PANOSIAN • GASPAR SALADINO • JAMES SINCLAIR • DIGITAL CHAMELEON
INKERS
LETTERER
COLORIST
SEPARATOR
JOEY CAVALIERI • EDITOR

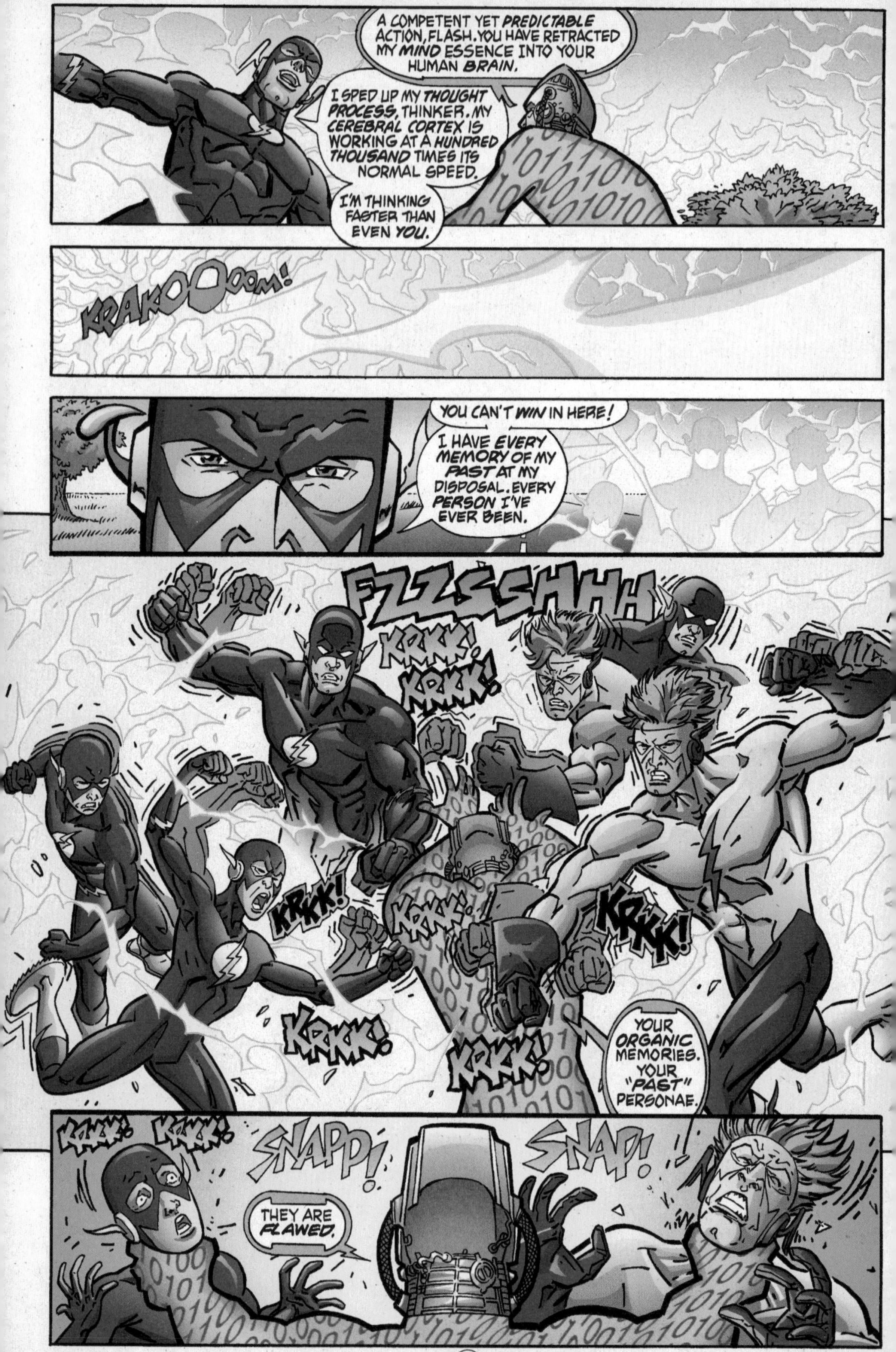
A COMPETENT YET PREDICTABLE ACTION, FLASH. YOU HAVE RETRACTED MY MIND ESSENCE INTO YOUR HUMAN BRAIN.
I SPED UP MY THOUGHT PROCESS, THINKER. MY CEREBRAL CORTEX IS WORKING AT A HUNDRED THOUSAND TIMES ITS NORMAL SPEED.
I'M THINKING FASTER THAN EVEN YOU.
KRAKOOOoom!
YOU CAN'T WIN IN HERE!
I HAVE EVERY MEMORY OF MY PAST AT MY DISPOSAL. EVERY PERSON I'VE EVER BEEN.
FZZSSHHH
KRKK!
KRKK!
KRKK!
KRKK!
KRKK!
KRKK!
KRKK!
YOUR ORGANIC MEMORIES. YOUR "PAST" PERSONAE.
KRKK!
KRKK!
SNAPP!
SNAP!
THEY ARE FLAWED.

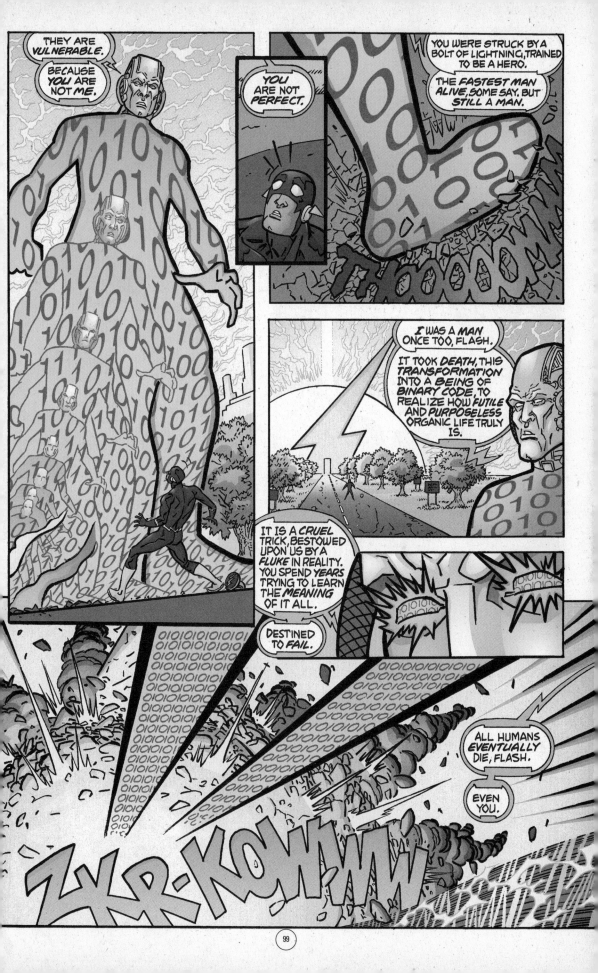

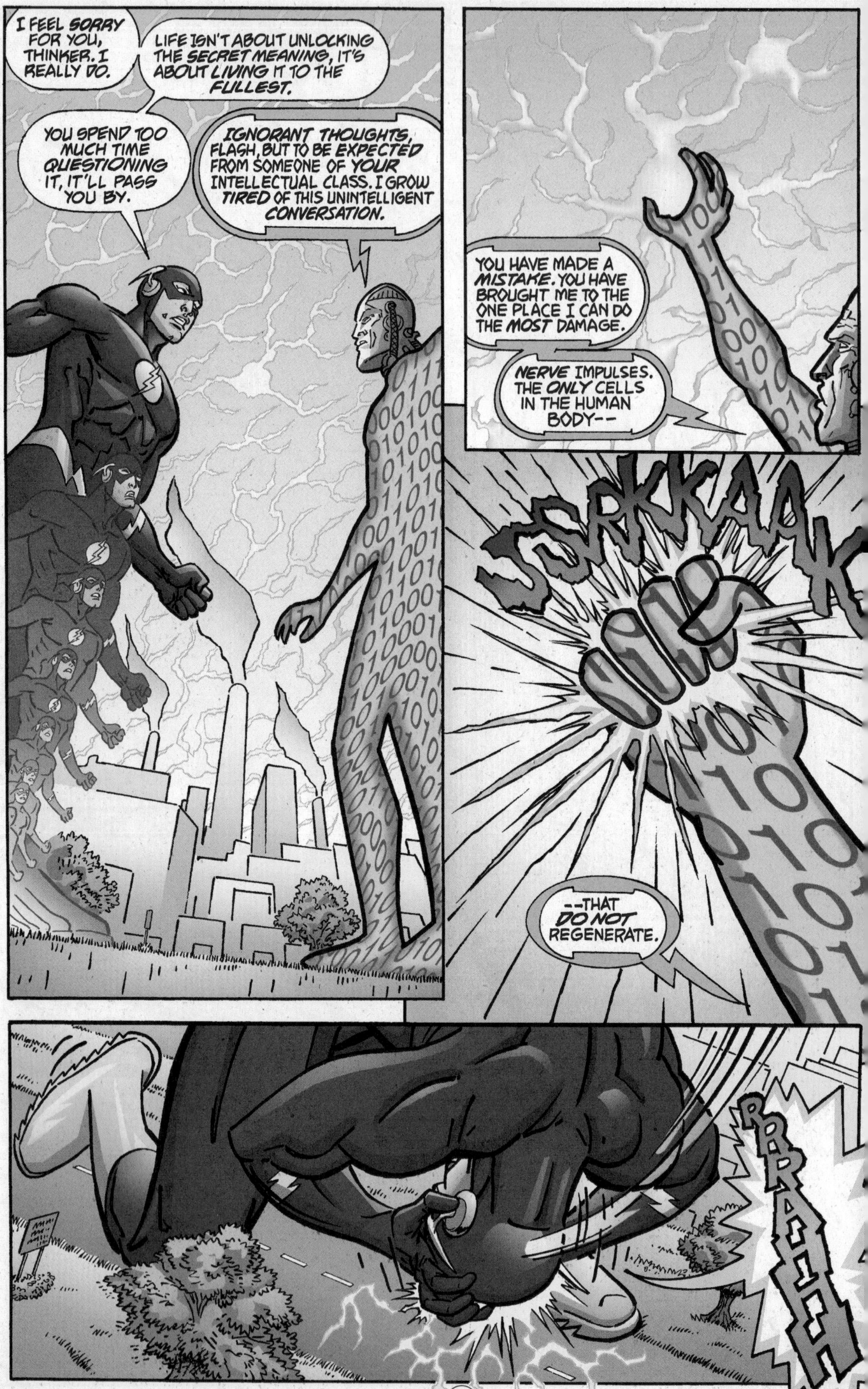

I FEEL SORRY FOR YOU, THINKER. I REALLY DO.
LIFE ISN'T ABOUT UNLOCKING THE SECRET MEANING, IT'S ABOUT LIVING IT TO THE FULLEST.
YOU SPEND TOO MUCH TIME QUESTIONING IT, IT'LL PASS YOU BY.
IGNORANT THOUGHTS, FLASH, BUT TO BE EXPECTED FROM SOMEONE OF YOUR INTELLECTUAL CLASS. I GROW TIRED OF THIS UNINTELLIGENT CONVERSATION.
YOU HAVE MADE A MISTAKE. YOU HAVE BROUGHT ME TO THE ONE PLACE I CAN DO THE MOST DAMAGE.
NERVE IMPULSES. THE ONLY CELLS IN THE HUMAN BODY--
SSRKKAAK
--THAT DO NOT REGENERATE.
RRRAAHH

I MAY NEED YOUR *PHYSICAL FORM* FOR *MEMORY INHABITANCE*, BUT YOUR *MIND* AND *SOUL* ARE *CERTAINLY* OF NO USE TO ME.

QUITE *SUBSTANDARD*.

AAAAAA!

BEFORE I *DELETE* YOUR *MEMORIES*, I THINK IT IS BEST YOU *UNDERSTAND* SOMETHING, FLASH. THE SIMPLEST OF *LOGIC*.

EVEN *IF* YOU WERE TO *STOP* ME FROM *DESTROYING* YOU--

--*DEATH* WOULD STILL FIND YOU SOMEDAY. NOT EVEN *YOU* CAN *OUTRUN* IT.

AND THAT'S... YOUR *MISTAKE*, THINKER.

YOU'RE A *COWARD*, WHO LIVED HIS LIFE *SELFISHLY*. UNLOVING AND UNLOVED. YOU MISSED OUT AND YOU *KNOW* THAT.

WHEN IT'S MY TIME TO GO, I'LL GO. *NO REGRETS*. 'CAUSE UN-LIKE YOU, I *LIVE* MY LIFE EVERY DAY--

--AND I'M *NOT AFRAID* OF DEATH.

KRRAKKKKOOOOOMMM

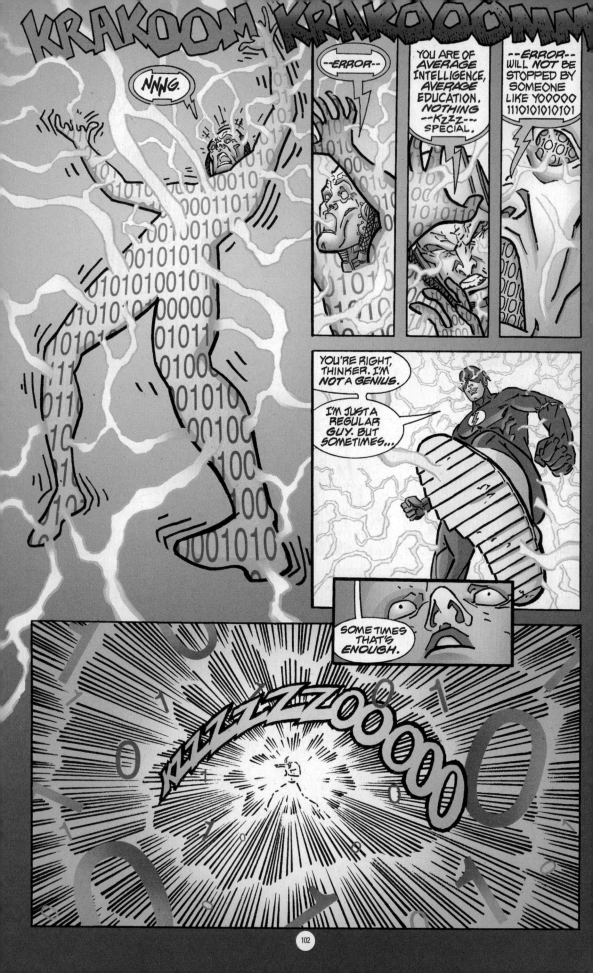

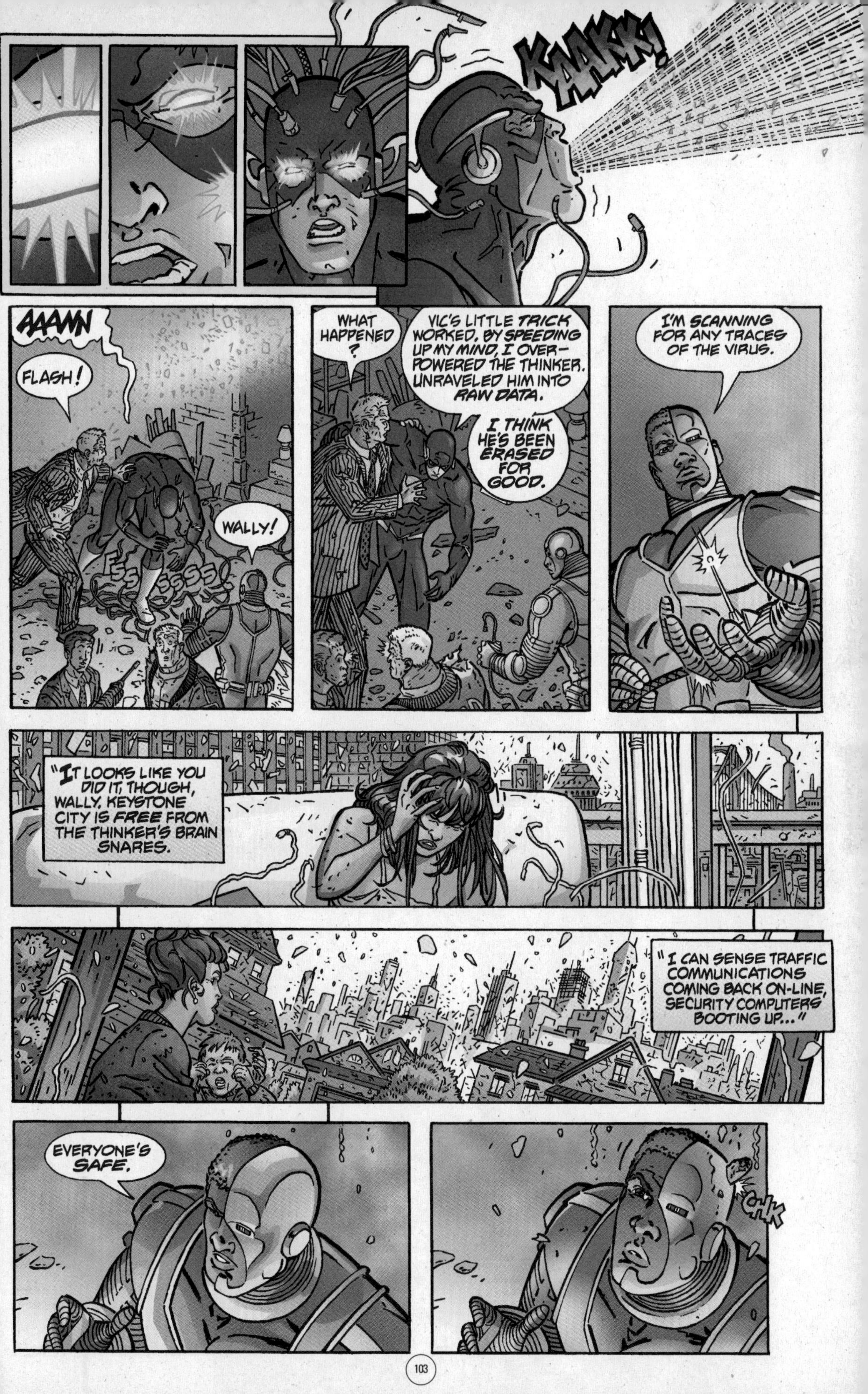
KAAKK!
AAANN
FLASH!
FSSSSSSS
WALLY!
WHAT HAPPENED?
VIC'S LITTLE TRICK WORKED. BY SPEEDING UP MY MIND, I OVER-POWERED THE THINKER. UNRAVELED HIM INTO RAW DATA.
I THINK HE'S BEEN ERASED FOR GOOD.
I'M SCANNING FOR ANY TRACES OF THE VIRUS.
"IT LOOKS LIKE YOU DID IT, THOUGH, WALLY. KEYSTONE CITY IS FREE FROM THE THINKER'S BRAIN SNARES.
"I CAN SENSE TRAFFIC COMMUNICATIONS COMING BACK ON-LINE, SECURITY COMPUTERS BOOTING UP..."
EVERYONE'S SAFE.
CHK

GIRDER, RIGHT? ONE OF MY EX-WIFE'S HIRED THUGS.

I PREFER THE TERM ROGUE, KENYON!

TIME TO SCREAM, PAL.

KRAKA-KAAAEEE!

NN

THINKER'S OUT OF THE EQUATION, BUT THE PROBLEM'S NOT SOLVED. WE'VE GOT ONE THREAT DOWN...

SEVERAL TO GO. BLACKSMITH KNOWS WE'VE UNCOVERED HER LITTLE ROGUE NETWORK. AND MIRROR MASTER HAS THE TWIN CITIES SURROUNDED BY SOME KIND OF IMPENETRABLE DOME!

WISH HUNTER ZOLOMON WAS HERE. HE'S BEEN PRO-FILING THESE ROGUES FOR YEARS. PROBABLY KNOWS IF BLACKSMITH HAS ANY TRICKS UP HER--

HA HA HA!

HANG ON!

CHACHOOOOOMMM

HEY! I THINK I GOT 'EM!

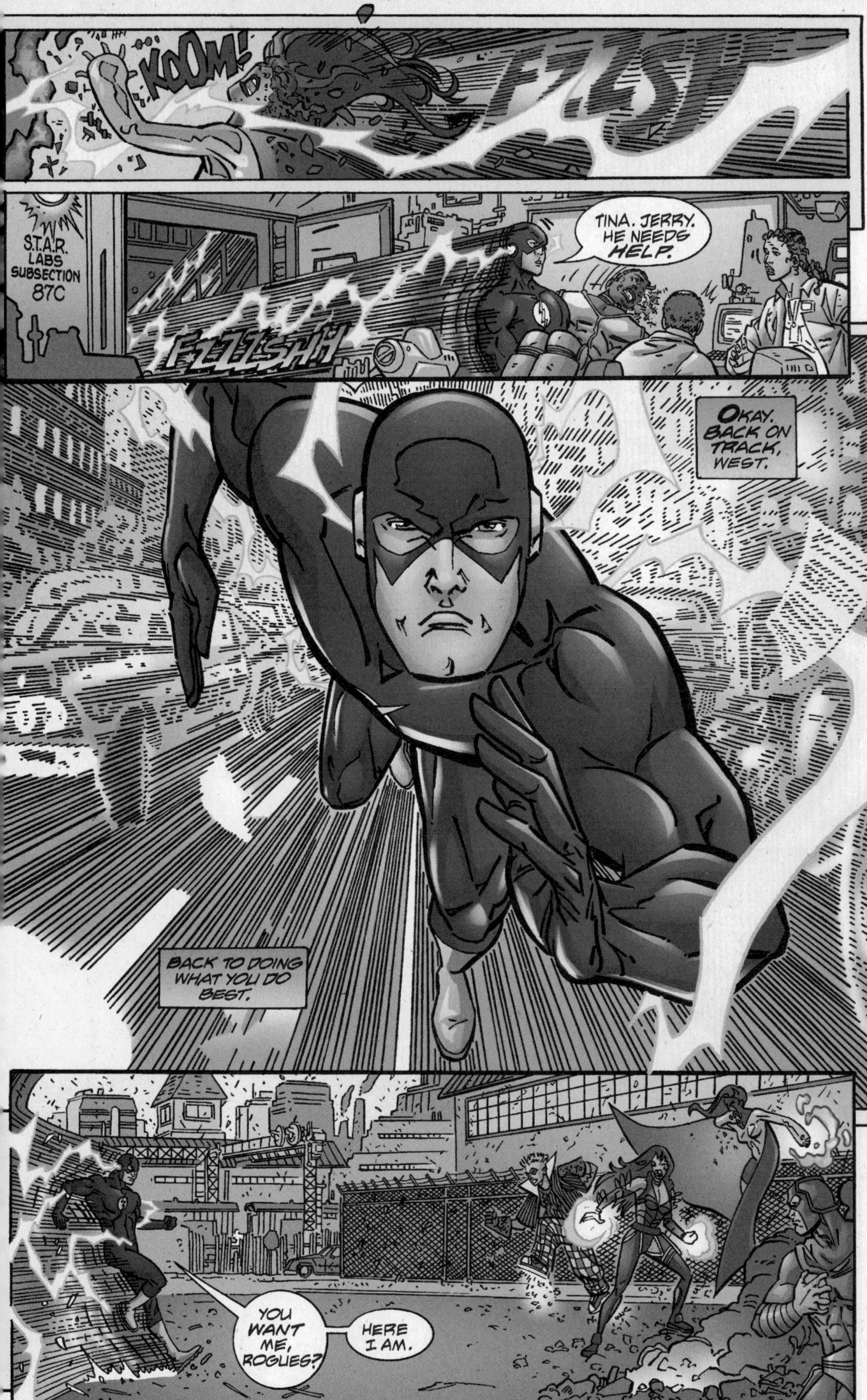
KOOM!
FZZST
S.T.A.R. LABS SUBSECTION 87C
TINA. JERRY. HE NEEDS HELP.
FZZSHH
OKAY. BACK ON TRACK, WEST.
BACK TO DOING WHAT YOU DO BEST.
YOU WANT ME, ROGUES?
HERE I AM.

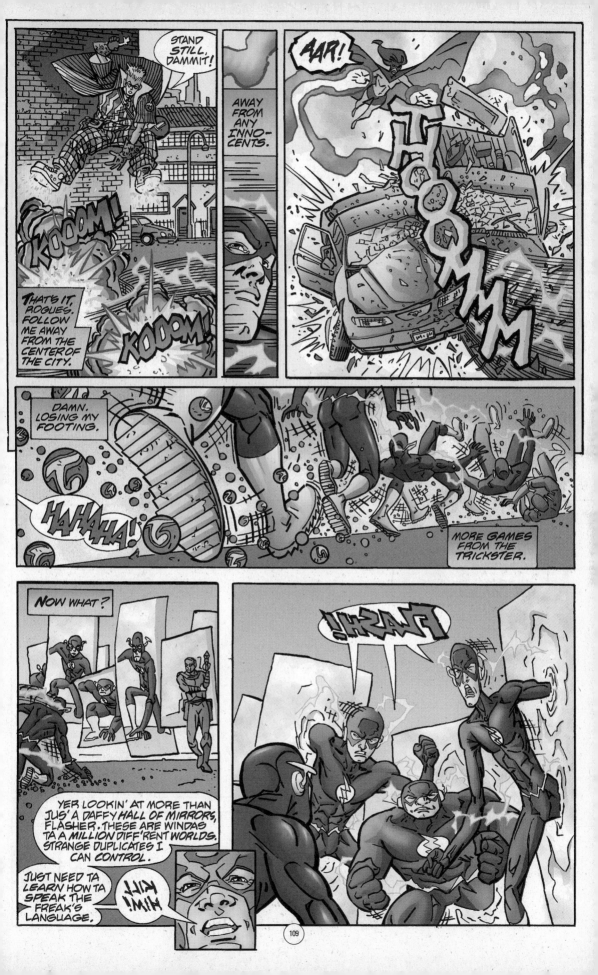

STAND STILL, DAMMIT!

AWAY FROM ANY INNOCENTS.

AAR!

THOOOMMM

KOOOM!

KOOOM!

THAT'S IT, ROGUES. FOLLOW ME AWAY FROM THE CENTER OF THE CITY.

DAMN. LOSING MY FOOTING.

HAHAHA!

MORE GAMES FROM THE TRICKSTER.

NOW WHAT?

UHRAW!

YER LOOKIN' AT MORE THAN JUS' A DAFFY HALL OF MIRRORS, FLASHER. THESE ARE WINDAS TA A MILLION DIFF'RENT WORLDS. STRANGE DUPLICATES I CAN CONTROL.

JUST NEED TA LEARN HOW TA SPEAK THE FREAK'S LANGUAGE.

HIM! KILL!

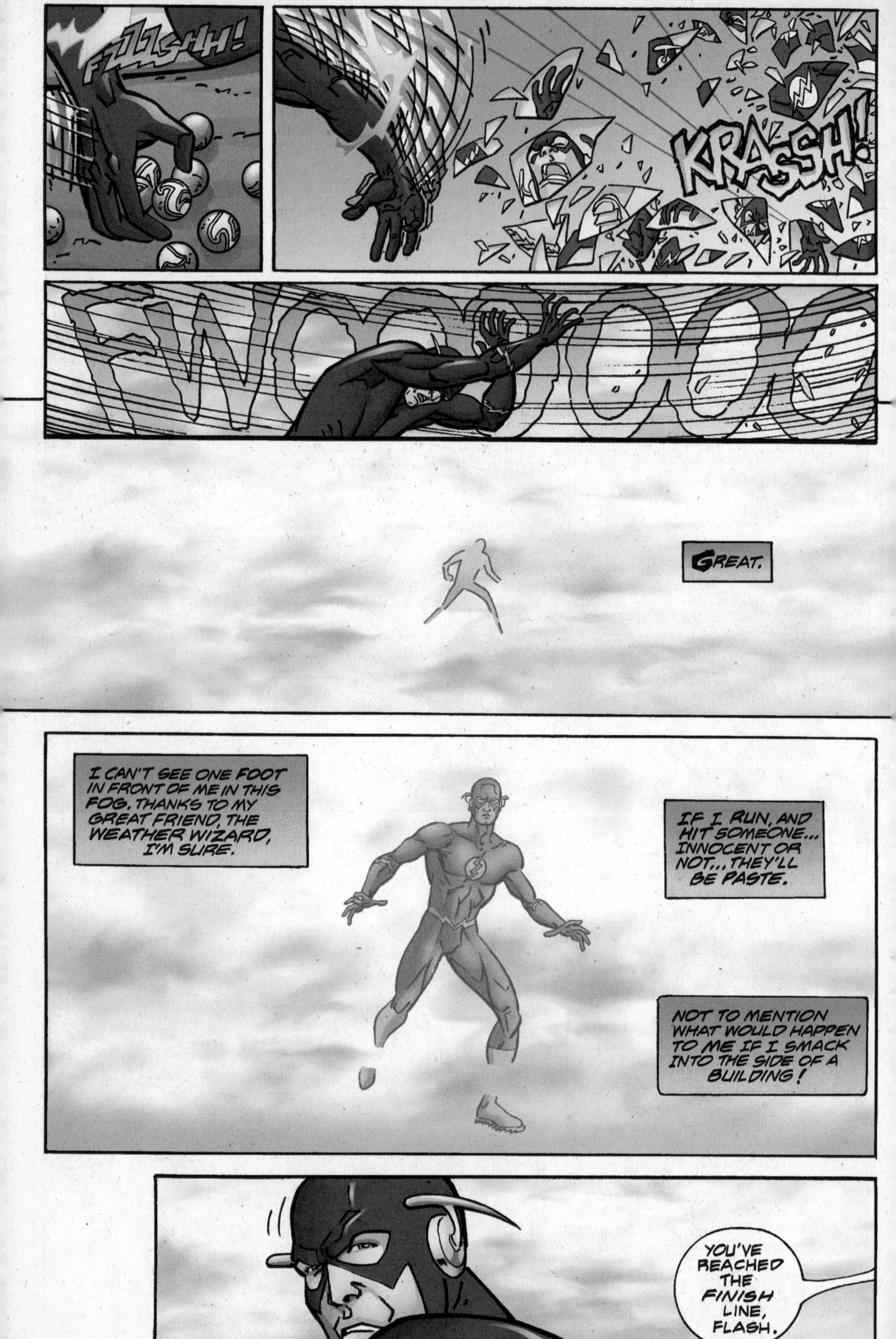
FZZZSHH!
KRASSH!!
FWOOOOOOOOOOOR
GREAT.
I CAN'T SEE ONE FOOT IN FRONT OF ME IN THIS FOG. THANKS TO MY GREAT FRIEND, THE WEATHER WIZARD, I'M SURE.
IF I RUN, AND HIT SOMEONE... INNOCENT OR NOT... THEY'LL BE PASTE.
NOT TO MENTION WHAT WOULD HAPPEN TO ME IF I SMACK INTO THE SIDE OF A BUILDING!
YOU'VE REACHED THE FINISH LINE, FLASH.

WHAMMM

NN

I WANT YOU BOTH TO KNOW THAT THIS WAR, THIS CHAOS, IS ALL MY EX-HUSBAND'S FAULT.

WE RAN A NICE, QUIET OPERATION IN KEYSTONE AND CENTRAL FOR YEARS.

BUT YOU COULDN'T LET THE HATE GO, COULD YOU, KEITH? YOU COULDN'T LET THINGS BE.

YOU STIRRED THE HORNETS' NEST, GAVE ANONYMOUS TIPS TO THE FBI. SO NOW, IT'S TIME TO MOVE ON.

BUT NOT UNTIL AFTER WE'VE LOOTED THIS CITY FOR EVERYTHING IT'S GOT.

AARGH!

ESSH

AND KILLED THE TWO OF YOU.

TIME TO OPEN THE DOORS, BOYS.

TIME TO LET THE OTHERS LOOSE.

CHK RNN

CHK RNN RNN

111

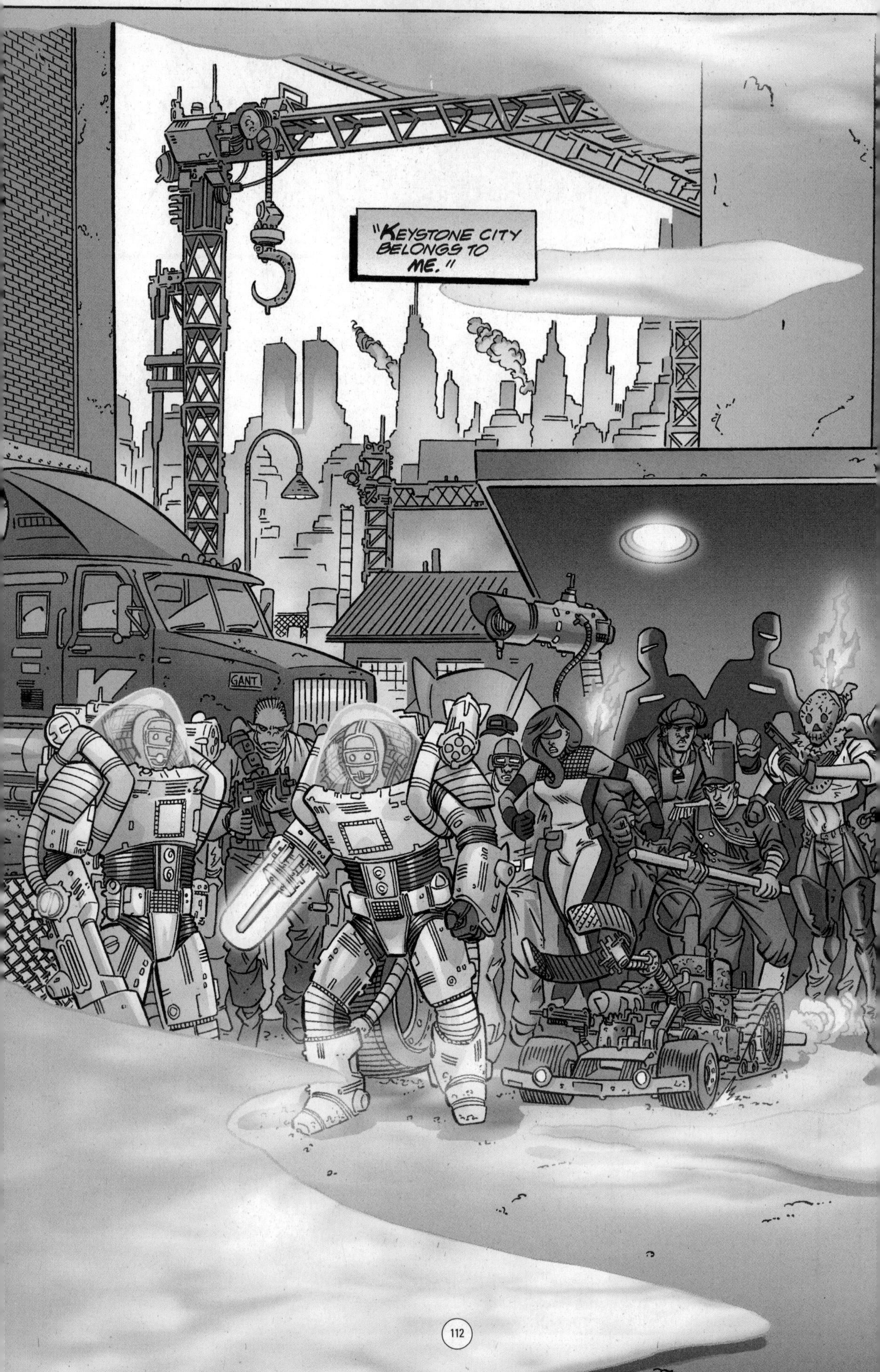
"KEYSTONE CITY BELONGS TO ME."
GANT
K

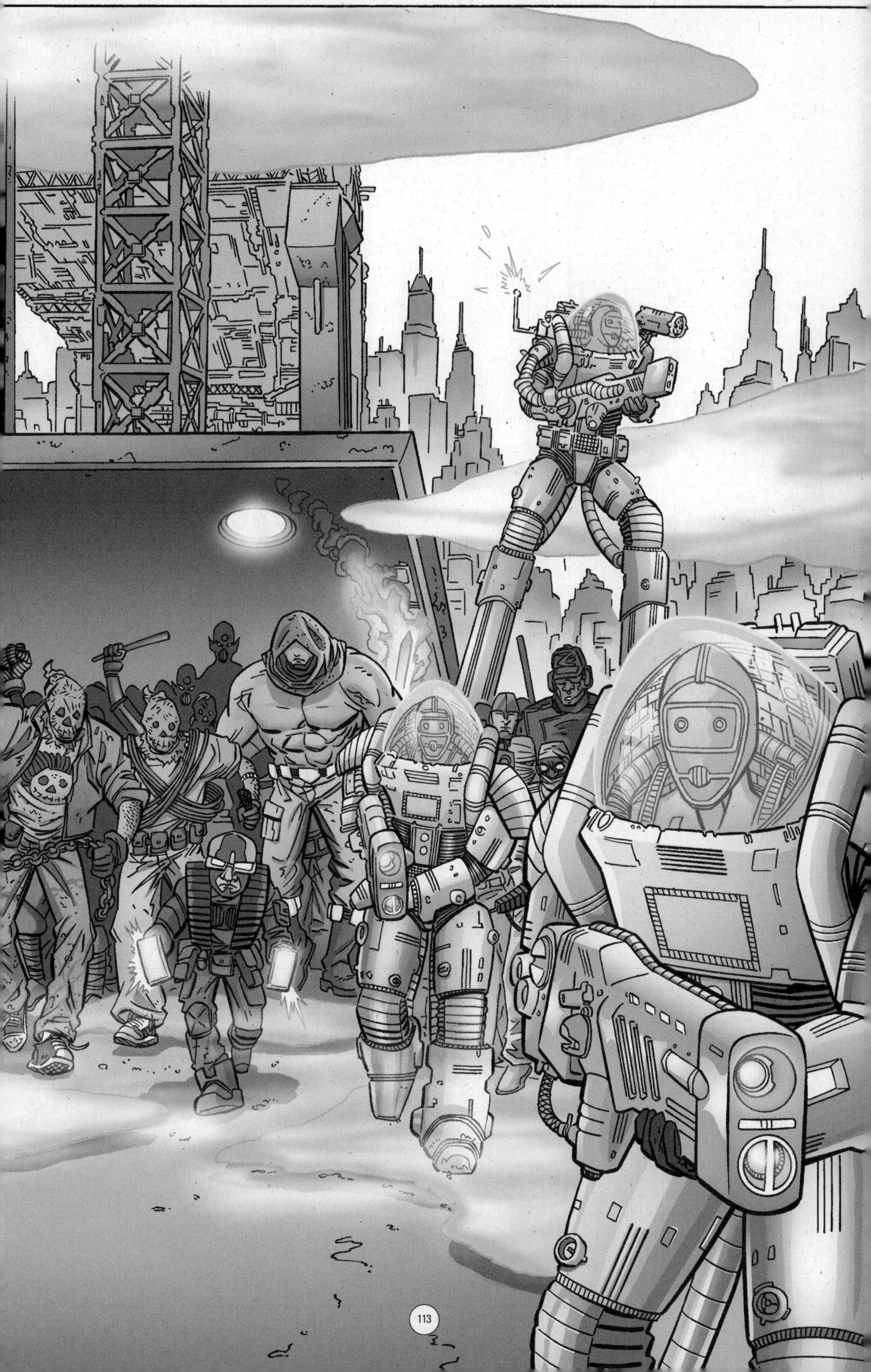

DID YOU HEAR THAT? OUTSIDE!

SOUNDS LIKE A...A CROWD ROARING.

REMINDS ME OF A KEYSTONE COMBINES GAME.

DOOR'S BEEN SHATTERED, PUDDLES OF WATER. LOOKS LIKE THIS IS WHERE COLD GOT THAT BINDER ON THE NETWORK.

HEY, HUNTER!

HUNTER?

MORILLO! GET OUT! GET--

YOU AGAIN.

GOT A TRACER IN MY RIFLE. 'CASE SOMEONE SWIPES IT.

THIS TIME GONNA MAKE SURE YOU STAY DEAD.

KLK!

SOUND COOL, BRO?

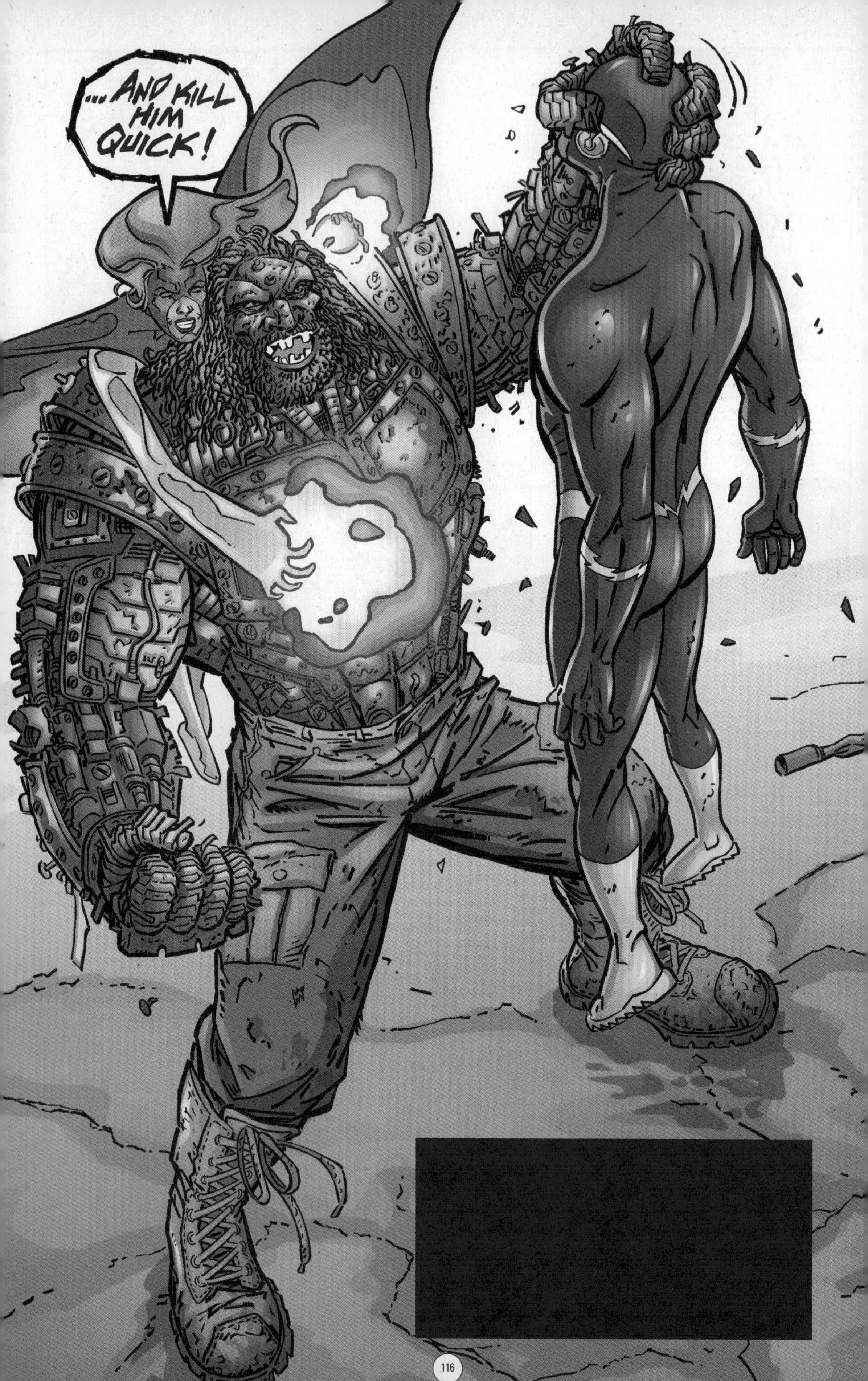
...AND KILL HIM QUICK!

[redacted]

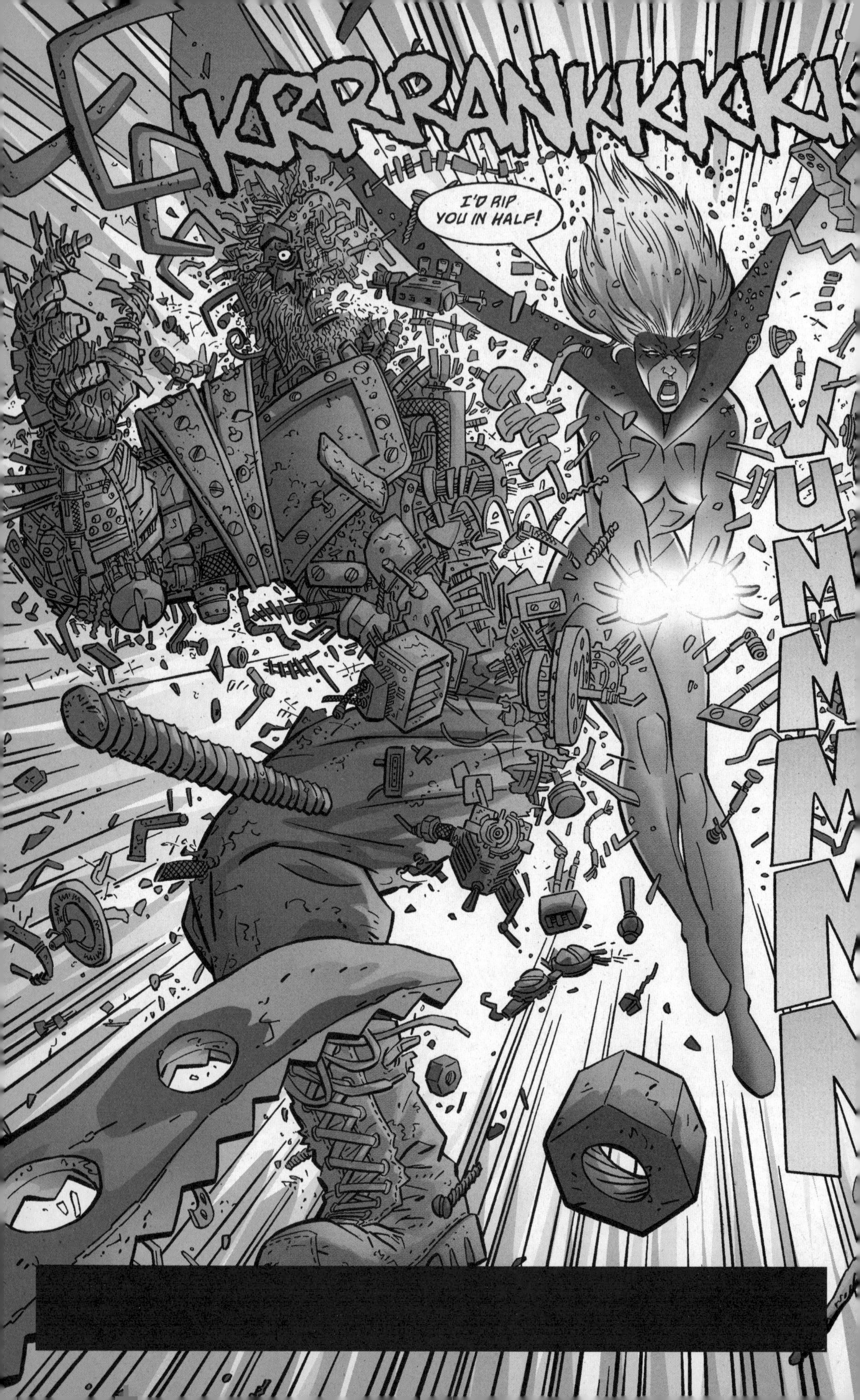
KRRRANKKKKK
I'D RIP YOU IN HALF!

[redacted]

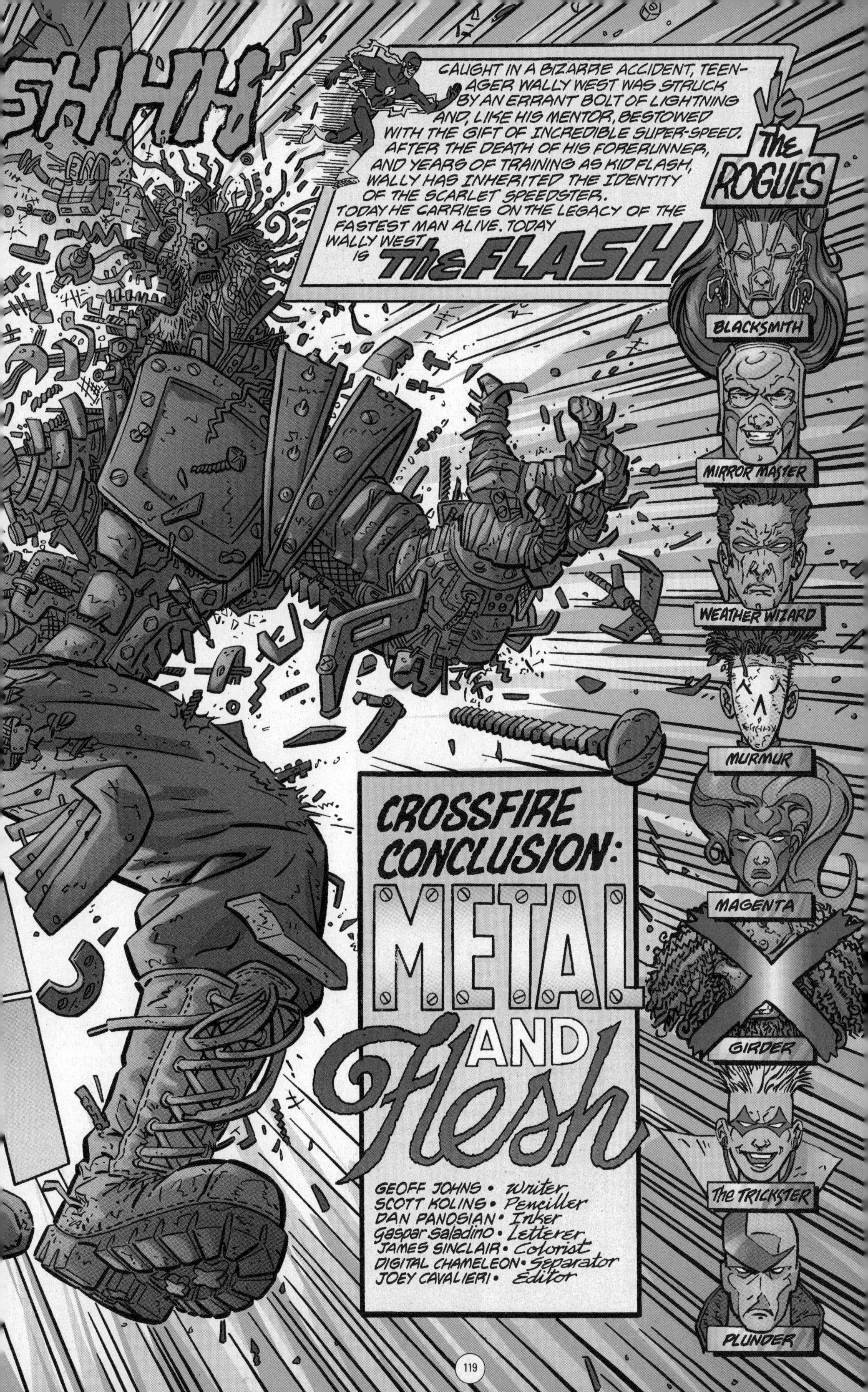

SHHHH
CAUGHT IN A BIZARRE ACCIDENT, TEEN-AGER WALLY WEST WAS STRUCK BY AN ERRANT BOLT OF LIGHTNING AND, LIKE HIS MENTOR, BESTOWED WITH THE GIFT OF INCREDIBLE SUPER-SPEED. AFTER THE DEATH OF HIS FORERUNNER, AND YEARS OF TRAINING AS KID FLASH, WALLY HAS INHERITED THE IDENTITY OF THE SCARLET SPEEDSTER. TODAY HE CARRIES ON THE LEGACY OF THE FASTEST MAN ALIVE. TODAY WALLY WEST IS THE FLASH
VS THE ROGUES
BLACKSMITH
MIRROR MASTER
WEATHER WIZARD
MURMUR
MAGENTA
GIRDER
THE TRICKSTER
PLUNDER
CROSSFIRE CONCLUSION: METAL AND FLESH
GEOFF JOHNS • Writer
SCOTT KOLINS • Penciller
DAN PANOSIAN • Inker
Gaspar Saladino • Letterer
JAMES SINCLAIR • Colorist
DIGITAL CHAMELEON • Separator
JOEY CAVALIERI • Editor

THOOOMMM

THOOOMMM

WHOA.

MAD BAD.

I'M... I'M SORRY, WALLY.

MAGNET-CHICK 'AS GONE *RABID*. AND GIRDER'S *DOWN*. DOWN HARD.

PUT MAGENTA OUT OF HER *MISERY*, MIRROR MASTER.

PLEASURE'S MINE.

HELL.

DAMN. TRAITORS.

KRAKTOOM

PIED PIPER, HEAT WAVE, THE *FIRST* TRICKSTER. ALL FORMER ROGUES THAT WENT SOFT ON US, TOO. SOME WORDS OF ADVICE, AXEL.

YO?

120

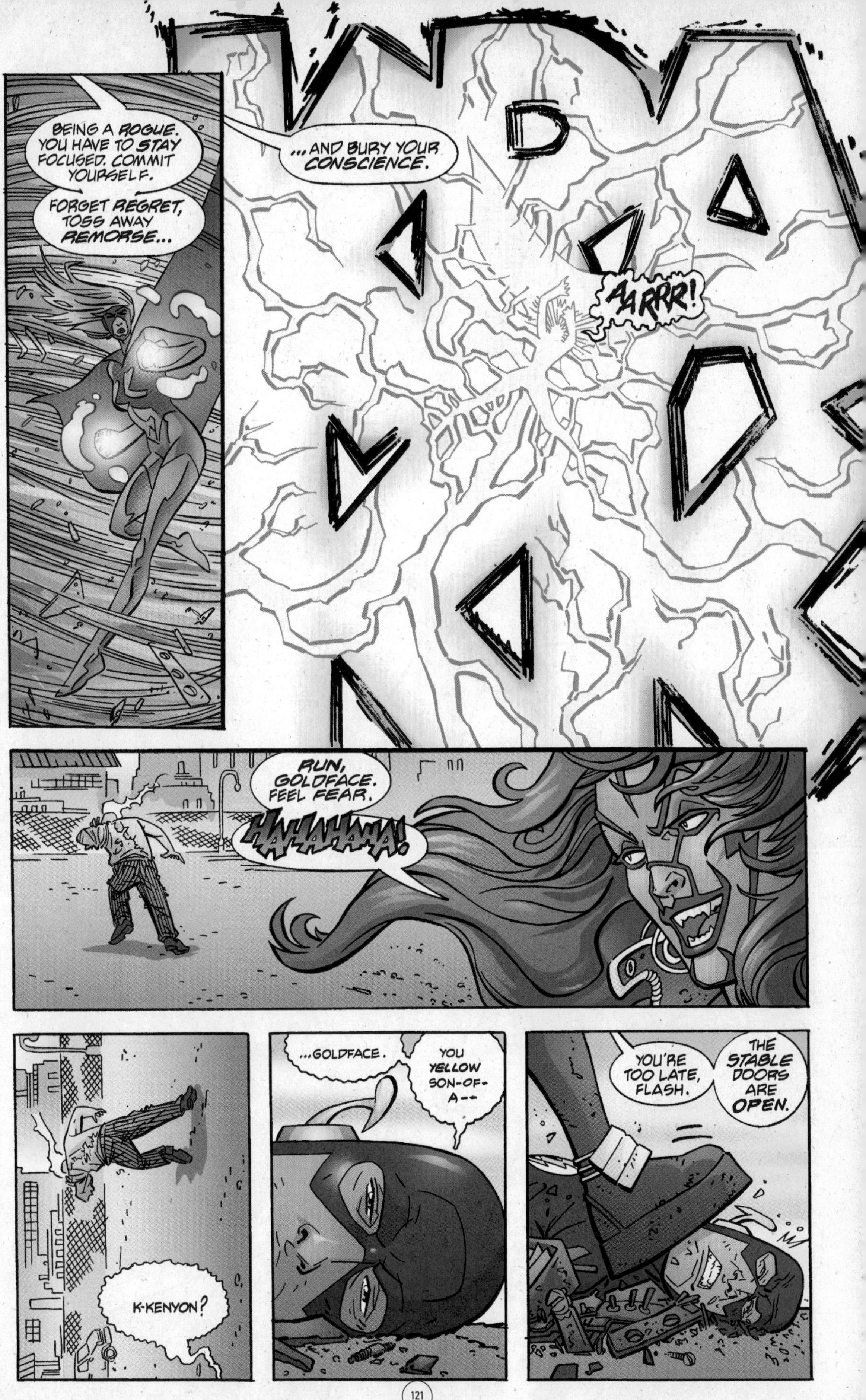
BEING A ROGUE. YOU HAVE TO STAY FOCUSED. COMMIT YOURSELF.
FORGET REGRET, TOSS AWAY REMORSE...
...AND BURY YOUR CONSCIENCE.
AARRR!
RUN, GOLDFACE. FEEL FEAR.
HAHAHAHA!
K-KENYON?
...GOLDFACE.
YOU YELLOW SON-OF-A--
YOU'RE TOO LATE, FLASH.
THE STABLE DOORS ARE OPEN.

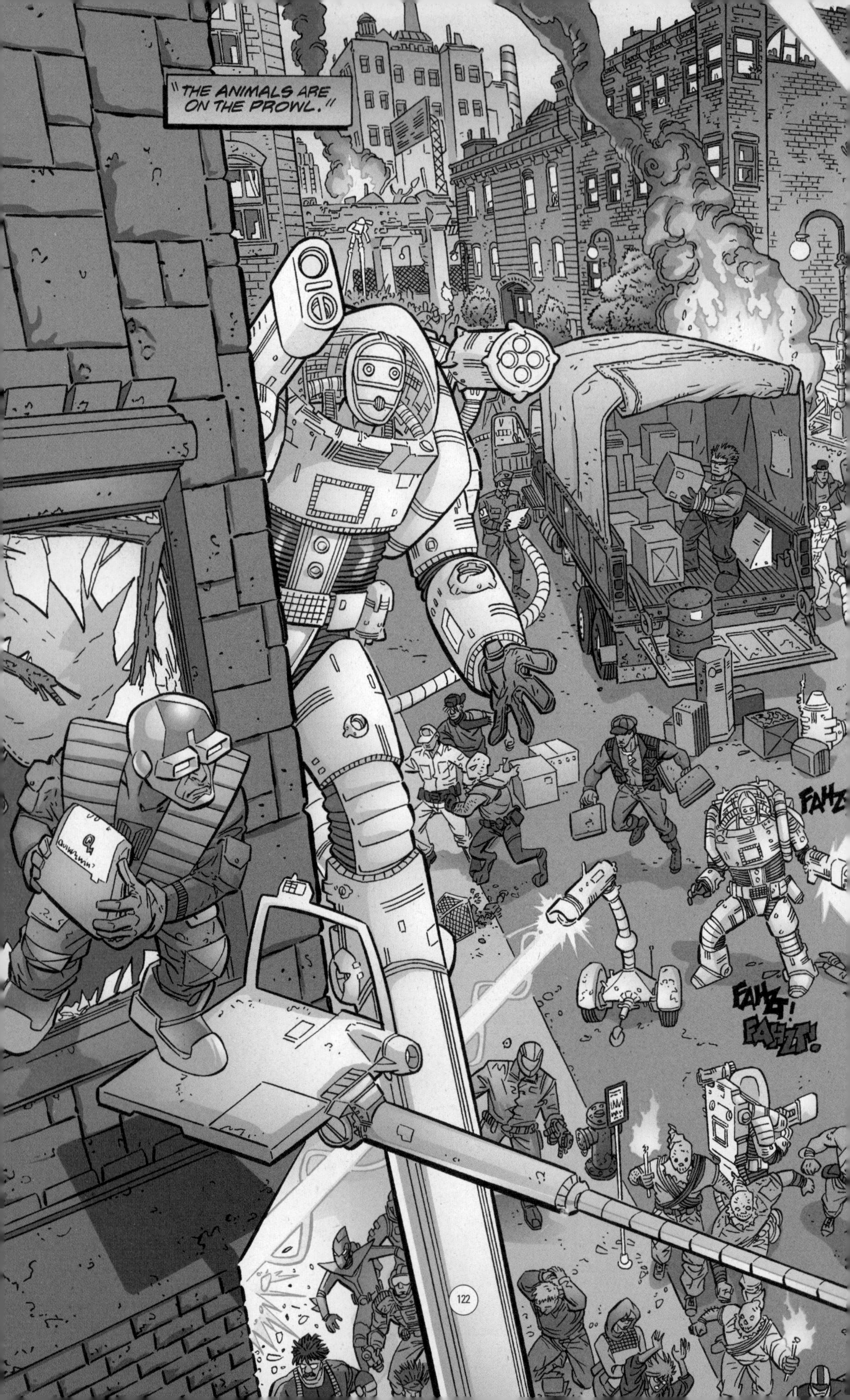
"THE ANIMALS ARE ON THE PROWL."
FAHZ
FAHZT!
FAHZT!

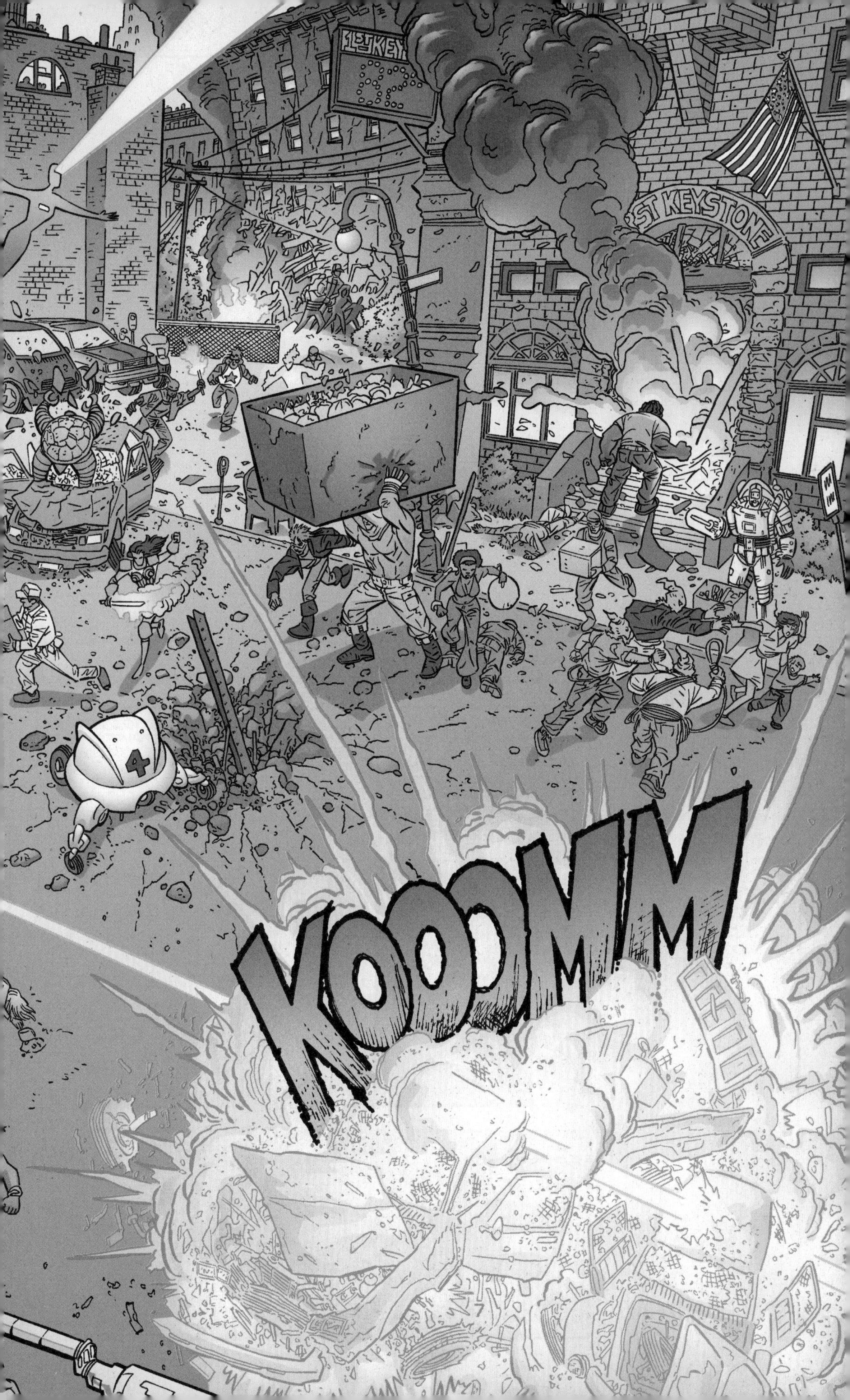
1ST KEY
ST KEYSTONE
KOOOMMM

WHAT THE HELL'S GOING ON OUT THERE?

WHILE YOU WERE TAKIN' A *NAP*, HUNTER, THE ROGUES STAKED CLAIM TO KEYSTONE.

FINAL MOVE? WHAT DO YOU MEAN--

HEY.

THE NETWORK.

WE HAVE TO WARN THE FLASH. BLACKSMITH WILL MAKE HER *FINAL* MOVE AND--

ENOUGH OINKING, PIGS.

PLUNDER? IS HE YOUR TWIN, MOBILLO?

I'M *NOT* THAT UGLY.

YEAH, YA ARE.

I GOTTA HAND IT TO YOU, BRO. THAT WAS A NEAT TRICK YOU PULLED IN THE PARK. BUT LET'S SEE WHAT HAPPENS WHEN WE DO SOMETHING A LITTLE MORE *DRASTIC*.

DECAPITATION, MAYBE.

WE'RE GONNA DO THIS NICE AND METHODICAL LIKE. YOU'RE A *DOCTOR*, MURMUR.

READY TO PLAY SURGEON?

CHINGG

WHERE TO START? MY *IGNORANT DOUBLE?* OR THE HOBBLING *PROFILER?* NO? HOW ABOUT THE OLD ONE THAT LOVES TO TALK TRASH... POPS NEEDS TO BE TAUGHT A LESSON. DON'T YOU THINK?

HNN.

FRED, BE A GOOD BOY--

--SAY *AH.*

KRASSHH!!!

LOOKS LIKE THEY'RE STILL BREATHIN'.

TOO BAD.

QUIT WORRYING, HUNTER.

WE'VE GOT TO CALL AN AMBULANCE. MORILLO TOOK AT LEAST SIX SHOTS TO THE--

HOW IN THE HELL DID--

HE MISSED.

YOU'RE SLOWING DOWN, FLASH.

I'D...COVER YOUR EYES IF I WERE YOU, BLACKSMITH.

THE MOLECULAR BONDS OF THIS METAL AREN'T GOING TO HOLD TOGETHER FOR LONG.

WRRNKOO

VVVVVVVVVVVV

THANKS FOR THE SNACK, FLASH.

WHAT... WHAT HAP--

SAME THING THAT HAPPENED TO GOLDFACE.

MY SKIN WAS TRANSFORMED BY HIS TOXIN...

...INTO THIS EBONY COMPOUND. THE PERFECT COMBINATION OF METAL AND FLESH.

AND I FEED OFF BOTH.

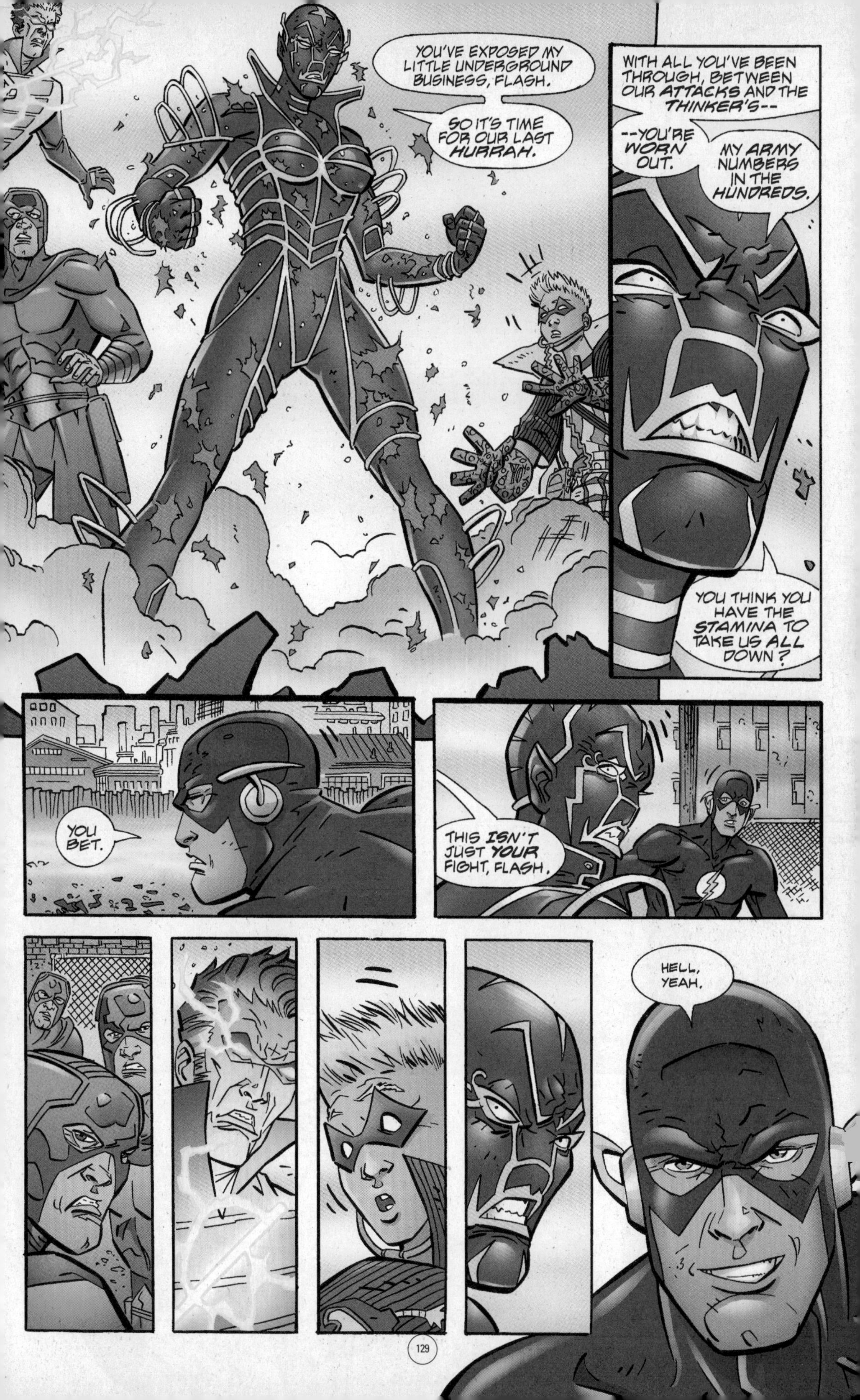

YOU'VE EXPOSED MY LITTLE UNDERGROUND BUSINESS, FLASH.
SO IT'S TIME FOR OUR LAST HURRAH.
WITH ALL YOU'VE BEEN THROUGH, BETWEEN OUR ATTACKS AND THE THINKER'S--
--YOU'RE WORN OUT.
MY ARMY NUMBERS IN THE HUNDREDS.
YOU THINK YOU HAVE THE STAMINA TO TAKE US ALL DOWN?
YOU BET.
THIS ISN'T JUST YOUR FIGHT, FLASH.
HELL, YEAH.

GO GET 'EM, BOYS AND GIRLS!

COMPUTRON UNIT SIX, GET CLEAR! GET--

AAAH!

IS *THIS* WHAT YOU WERE UP TO, KENYON? GATHERING YOUR OWN *PATHETIC MOB*?

I WAS WRONG ABOUT GOLDFACE. HE IS ONE OF THE GOOD GUYS.

KRAK! KRAK! KRAK! KRAK!

GIVING ME A CHANCE TO GET UP TO SPEED.

SPITCH

SOMETHING *STICKING* TO MY--

DID I DOUBLE YOUR PLEASURE?

HA HAHA HAHAHA!

HA HAHA HAHAHA!

KRUSSH

POP

BZZTCH

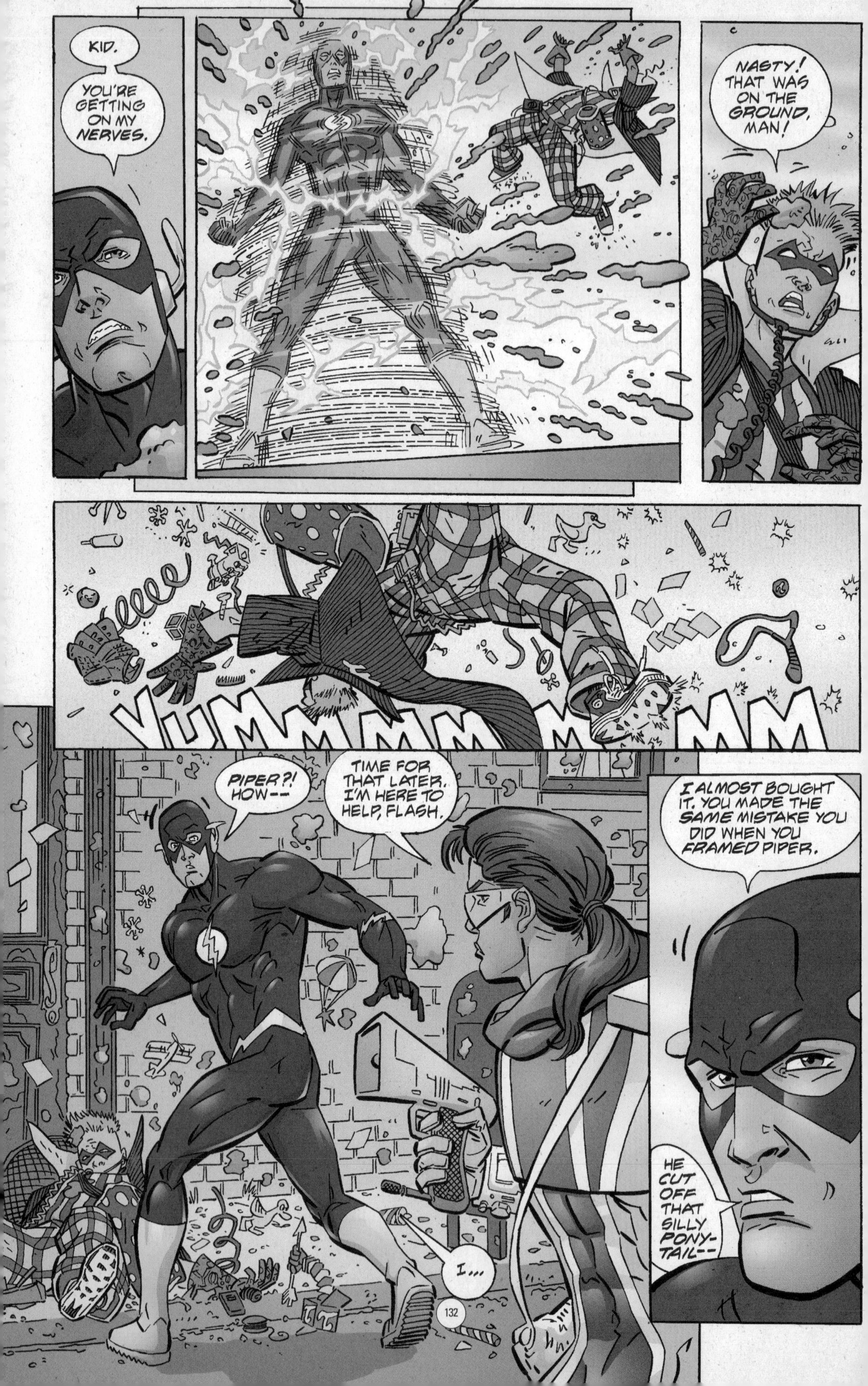

KID.
YOU'RE GETTING ON MY NERVES.
NASTY! THAT WAS ON THE GROUND, MAN!
VUMMMMMMMMM
PIPER?! HOW--
TIME FOR THAT LATER. I'M HERE TO HELP, FLASH.
I...
I ALMOST BOUGHT IT. YOU MADE THE SAME MISTAKE YOU DID WHEN YOU FRAMED PIPER.
HE CUT OFF THAT SILLY PONY-TAIL--

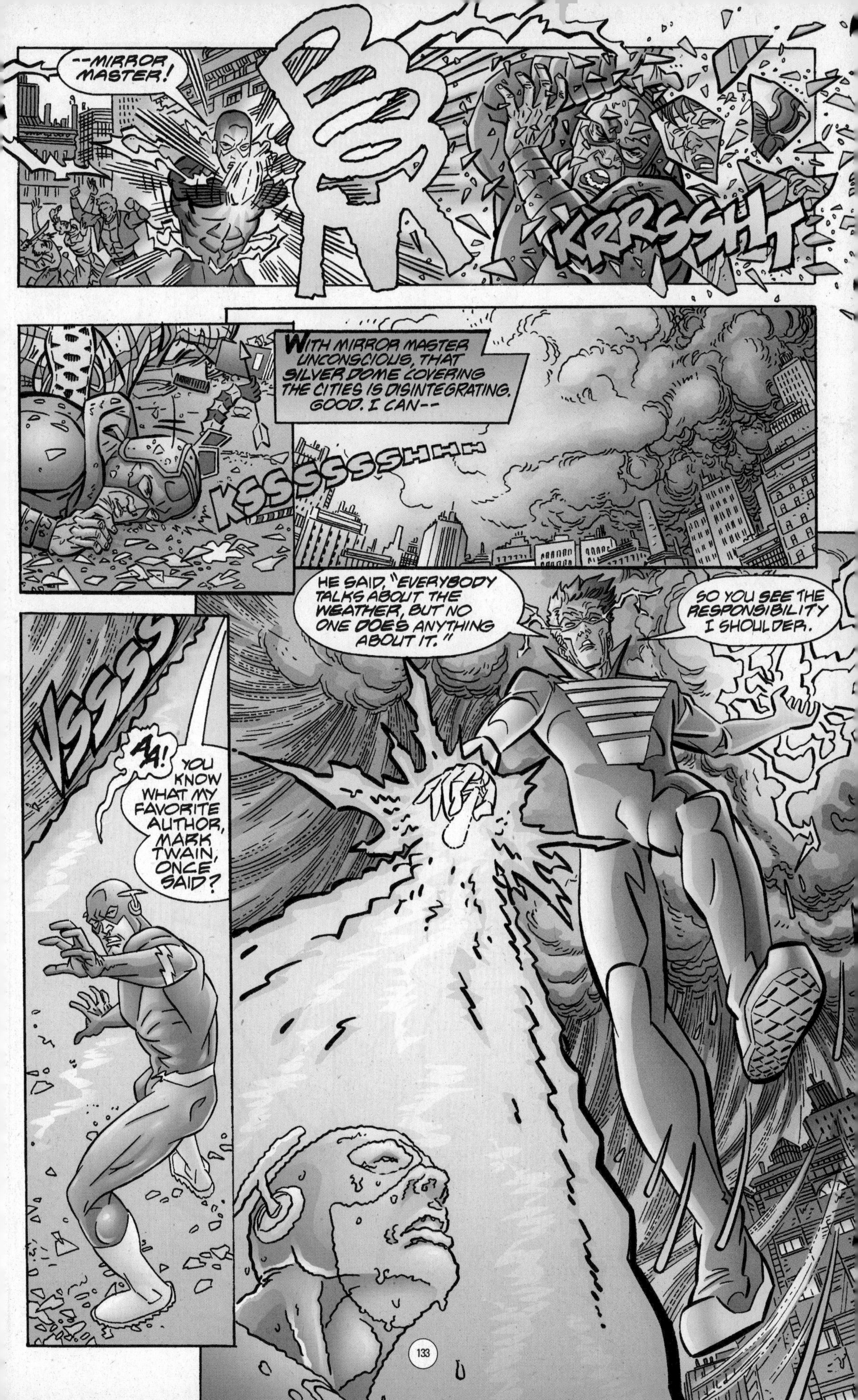
--MIRROR MASTER!
BOOM
KRRSSHT
WITH MIRROR MASTER UNCONSCIOUS, THAT SILVER DOME COVERING THE CITIES IS DISINTEGRATING. GOOD. I CAN--
KSSSSSSSHHHH
VSSSSS
AA! YOU KNOW WHAT MY FAVORITE AUTHOR, MARK TWAIN, ONCE SAID?
HE SAID, "EVERYBODY TALKS ABOUT THE WEATHER, BUT NO ONE DOES ANYTHING ABOUT IT."
SO YOU SEE THE RESPONSIBILITY I SHOULDER.

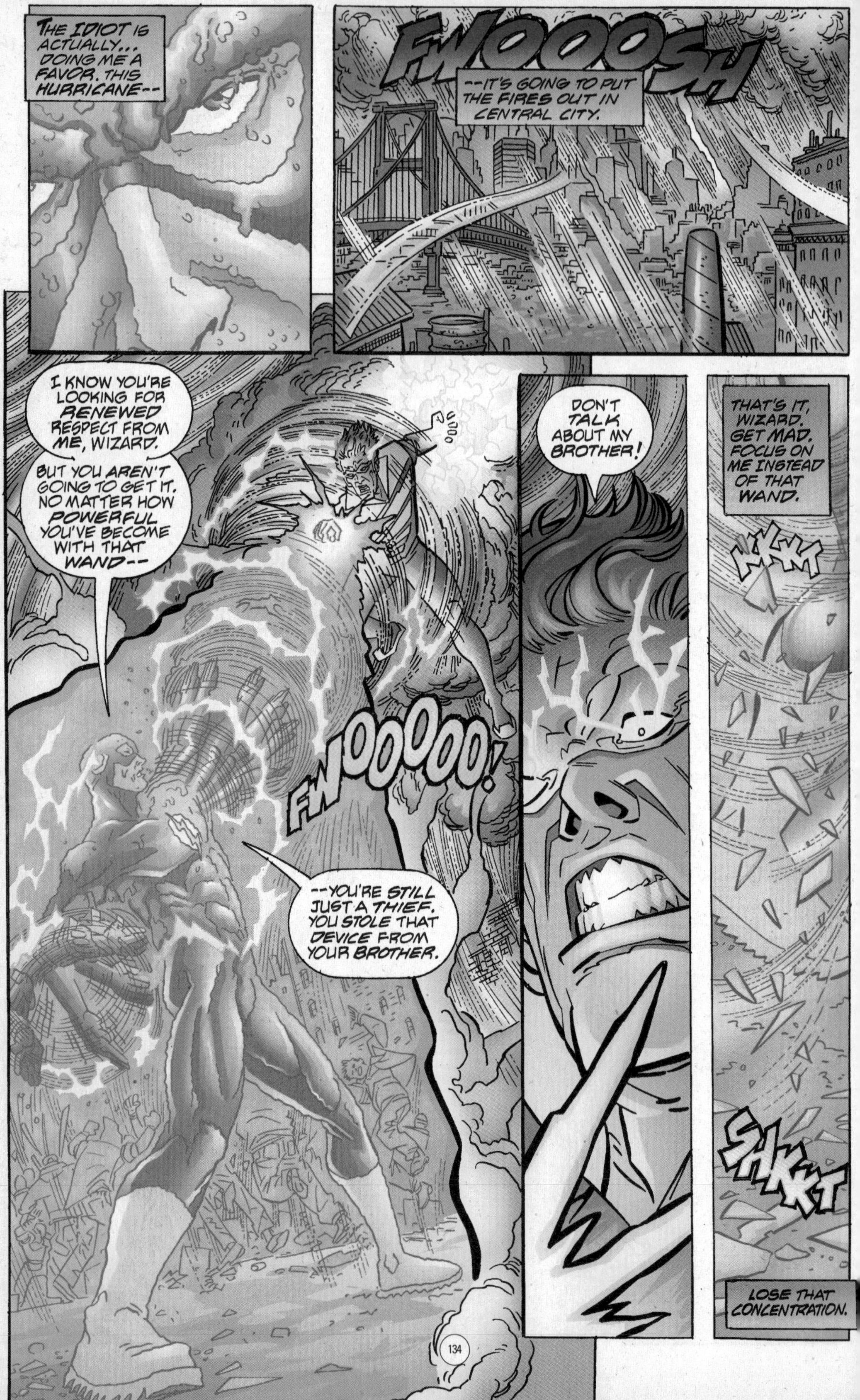

THE IDIOT IS ACTUALLY... DOING ME A FAVOR. THIS HURRICANE--
FWOOOOSH
--IT'S GOING TO PUT THE FIRES OUT IN CENTRAL CITY.
I KNOW YOU'RE LOOKING FOR RENEWED RESPECT FROM ME, WIZARD.
BUT YOU AREN'T GOING TO GET IT. NO MATTER HOW POWERFUL YOU'VE BECOME WITH THAT WAND--
FWOOOOOO!
--YOU'RE STILL JUST A THIEF. YOU STOLE THAT DEVICE FROM YOUR BROTHER.
DON'T TALK ABOUT MY BROTHER!
THAT'S IT, WIZARD. GET MAD. FOCUS ON ME INSTEAD OF THAT WAND.
SHKKT
LOSE THAT CONCENTRATION.

SHRP!

AAH!

SHRP!

NO MIRROR TO ESCAPE INTO THIS TIME, McCULLOCH.

YOU THREE ARE--

FWMPP!

KRRNGG!

OUTTA HERE.

TA.... FLASHER.

NO.

DAMMIT. WHERE IS HE... COLD.

FLASH!

YOU HAVE TO STOP BLACKSMITH.

FAST.

BLACKSMITH

NO. I'M TAKING *DOWN* TWO CITIES.

I'M TAKING DOWN *ALL* OF YOU.

RRRR

SHE'S ALREADY DONE IT.

MORILLO SAID BLACKSMITH HAD A CON-TINGENCY PLAN--

--THINGS GET TOO BAD, SHE LURES EVERYONE ON TO THE SYMBOL OF KENYON'S UNION, THE VAN BUREN BRIDGE--

--AND SHE TEARS IT APART.

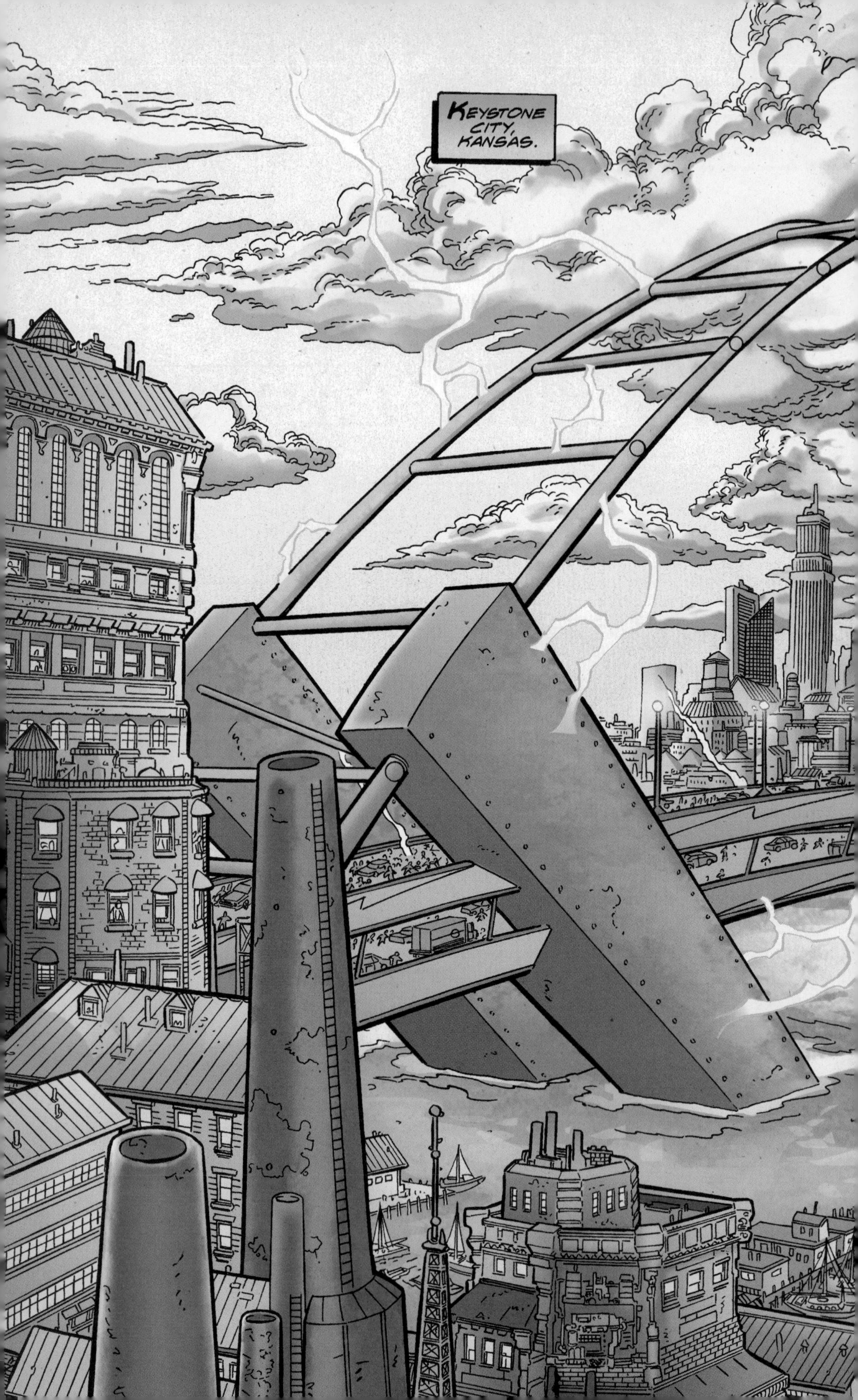
KEYSTONE CITY, KANSAS.

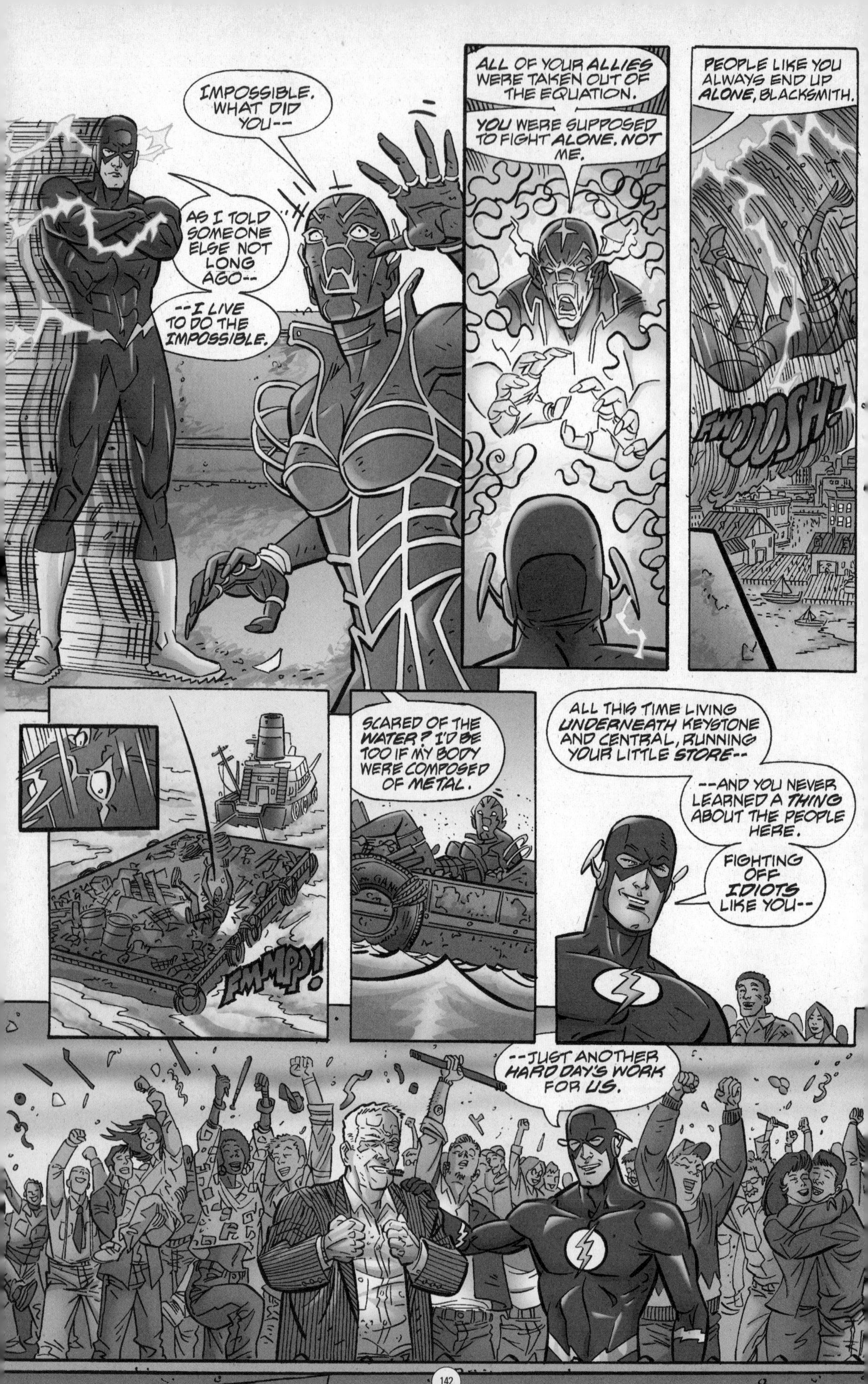
IMPOSSIBLE. WHAT DID YOU--
AS I TOLD SOMEONE ELSE NOT LONG AGO--
--I LIVE TO DO THE IMPOSSIBLE.
ALL OF YOUR ALLIES WERE TAKEN OUT OF THE EQUATION.
YOU WERE SUPPOSED TO FIGHT ALONE. NOT ME.
PEOPLE LIKE YOU ALWAYS END UP ALONE, BLACKSMITH.
FWOOOSH!
FMMPF!
SCARED OF THE WATER? I'D BE TOO IF MY BODY WERE COMPOSED OF METAL.
ALL THIS TIME LIVING UNDERNEATH KEYSTONE AND CENTRAL, RUNNING YOUR LITTLE STORE--
--AND YOU NEVER LEARNED A THING ABOUT THE PEOPLE HERE.
FIGHTING OFF IDIOTS LIKE YOU--
--JUST ANOTHER HARD DAY'S WORK FOR US.

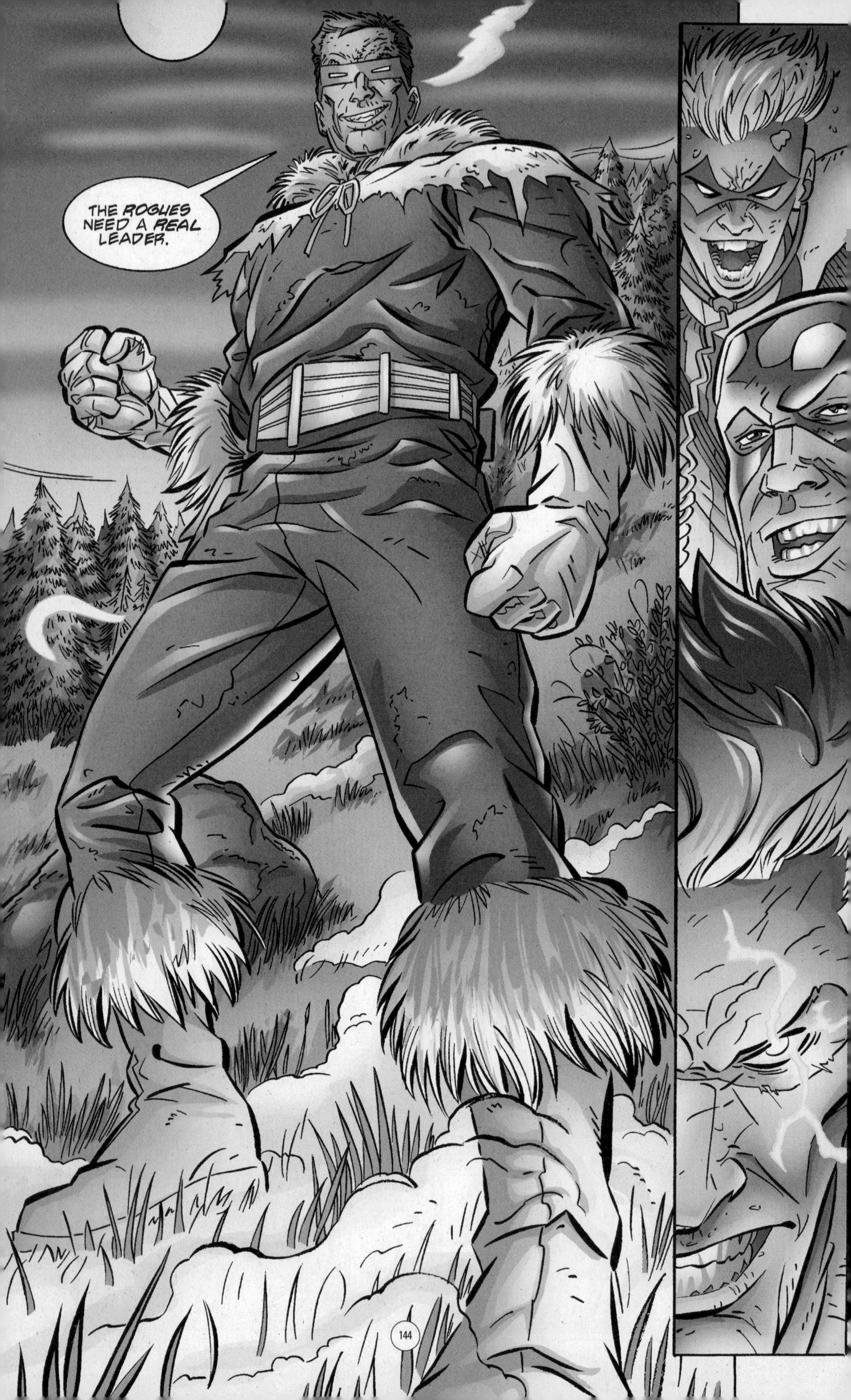
THE ROGUES NEED A REAL LEADER.

S.T.A.R. LABS.

CONNECTING WITH THE THINKER TRIGGERED A CHAIN REACTION IN YOUR METAL ORGANS AND TISSUES, CYBORG. THE GOLD COLOR REPRESENTED A PSEUDO-CELLULAR ACTIVITY... WHICH HAS BEEN *SHUT DOWN.*

HENCE THE *SILVER* TONE.

I DON'T KNOW... I DON'T KNOW IF IT'S *RE-VERSIBLE.*

IF THERE'S A *CURE* FOR CYBORG'S CONDITION, MY HUSBAND AND I WILL FIND IT.

THANKS, TINA. AND THANKS FOR STABILIZING MAGENTA. I HOPE THAT PSYCHIATRIST CAN DO WHAT HE'S PROMISING FOR HER.

FRAN CAME THROUGH IN THE END.

THE TREATMENTS YOU'VE DEVISED FOR EVERYONE IN KEYSTONE CITY HAVE BEEN NOTHING SHORT OF AMAZING.

NEEDED TO MAKE SURE THERE WEREN'T ANY SIDE EFFECTS FROM OUR EN-COUNTER WITH THE THINKER OR THE MIRROR MASTER'S *MIRROR-DOME!*

AND EVERYONE CHECKED OUT OKAY?

YES, INCLUDING YOU, LINDA.

...THOUGH THERE *IS* ONE THING YOU *SHOULD* KNOW. ONE THING WE DISCOVERED WHILE WE WERE DOING THE TESTS,

WHAT'S THAT?

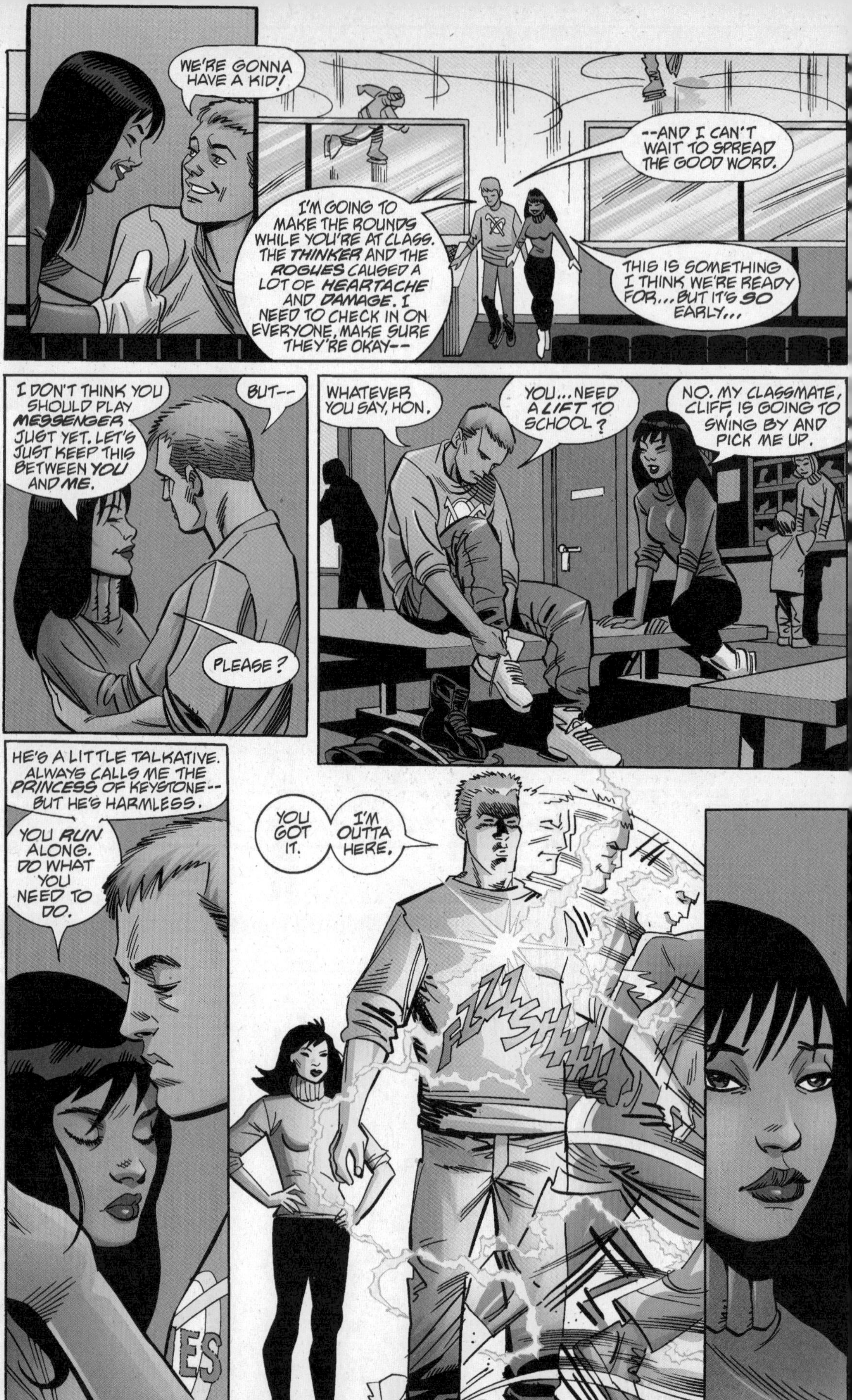
WE'RE GONNA HAVE A KID!
--AND I CAN'T WAIT TO SPREAD THE GOOD WORD.
I'M GOING TO MAKE THE ROUNDS WHILE YOU'RE AT CLASS. THE THINKER AND THE ROGUES CAUSED A LOT OF HEARTACHE AND DAMAGE. I NEED TO CHECK IN ON EVERYONE, MAKE SURE THEY'RE OKAY--
THIS IS SOMETHING I THINK WE'RE READY FOR... BUT IT'S SO EARLY...
I DON'T THINK YOU SHOULD PLAY MESSENGER JUST YET. LET'S JUST KEEP THIS BETWEEN YOU AND ME.
BUT--
PLEASE?
WHATEVER YOU SAY, HON.
YOU... NEED A LIFT TO SCHOOL?
NO. MY CLASSMATE, CLIFF, IS GOING TO SWING BY AND PICK ME UP.
HE'S A LITTLE TALKATIVE. ALWAYS CALLS ME THE PRINCESS OF KEYSTONE-- BUT HE'S HARMLESS.
YOU RUN ALONG. DO WHAT YOU NEED TO DO.
YOU GOT IT.
I'M OUTTA HERE.
FZZZSHHH

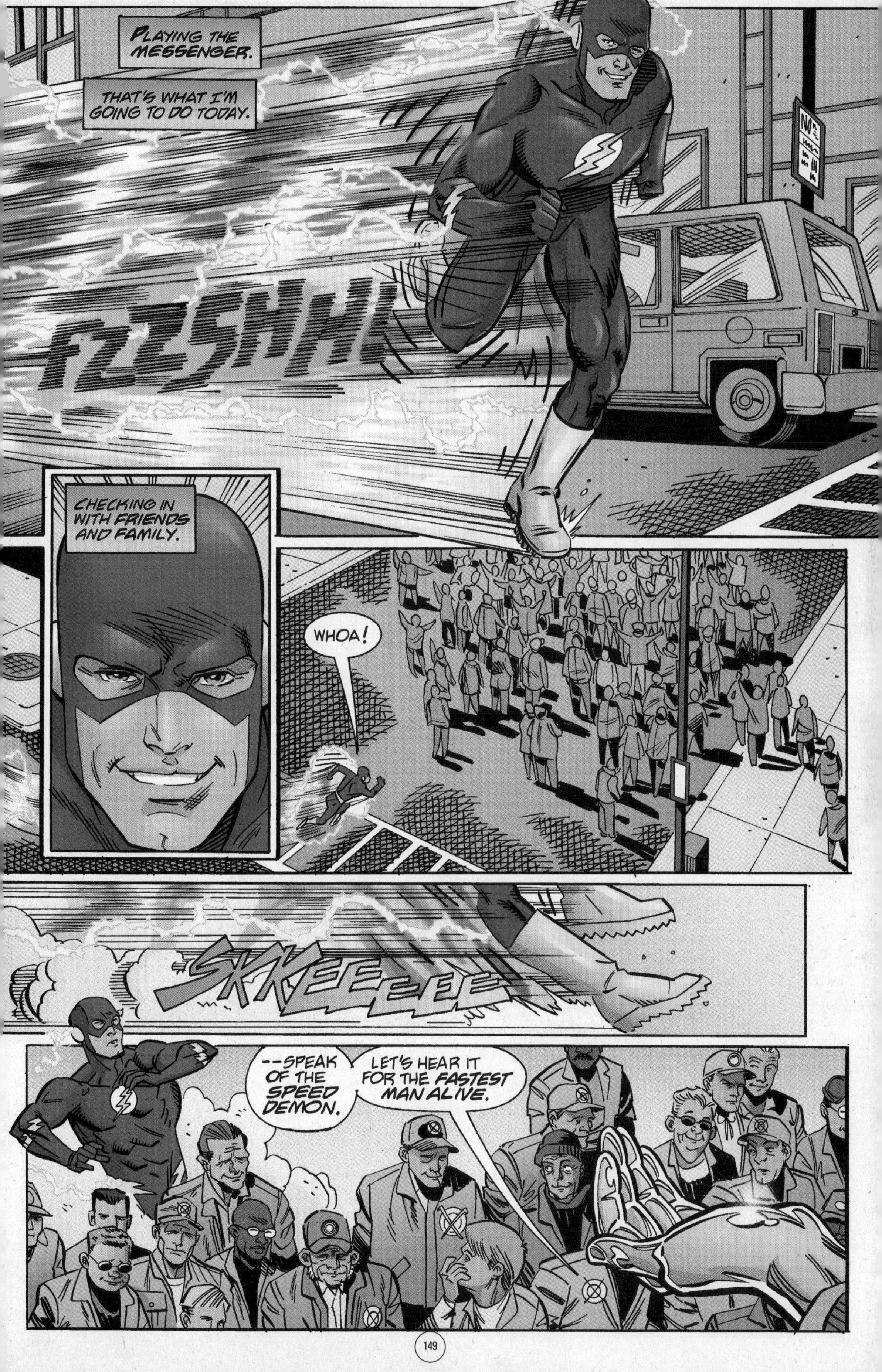
PLAYING THE MESSENGER.
THAT'S WHAT I'M GOING TO DO TODAY.
FZZSHHH
CHECKING IN WITH FRIENDS AND FAMILY.
WHOA!
SKKEEEEEE
--SPEAK OF THE SPEED DEMON.
LET'S HEAR IT FOR THE FASTEST MAN ALIVE.

LOOKS LIKE THE UNION WAS *RIGHT*, KENYON.

EVERYTHING YOU TOUCH TURNS TO *GOLD.*

HA. TELL THAT TO THE *KEY-STONE* POLICE.

--AND THE *COPS* ARE ALL OVER ME. STILL THINK I'M *DIRTY.*

THE ONLY REASON I HAVEN'T BEEN *"RELEASED"* FROM MY POSITION AS UNION COMMISSIONER IS BECAUSE OF *YOUR* INTERFERENCE.

AND *THEIRS.*

TAKE A *WALK,* BOYS.

SO WHAT ARE YOU PLANNING ON DOING? MOVING ON?

HELL, NO, FLASH.

I WORK MY *COLD, METAL* BUTT OFF TO ORGANIZE THIS *RECONSTRUCTION* RALLY, RAISE MONEY AND *VOLUNTEERS* TO REBUILD KEY-STONE AND *CENTRAL*--

THIS *CITY* NEEDS ME JUST LIKE IT NEEDS YOU.

AND I'LL BE DAMNED IF I LET ANYONE STOP ME FROM *DOING* WHAT I'M *DOING.* PREACHING ABOUT *UNITY.* BRINGING THESE *PEOPLE* TOGETHER.

THIS IS THE *FIRST* TIME I'VE EVER FELT...*PROUD* TO BE WHO I AM.

YOU DID GOOD, *GOLDFACE!*

WE *ALL* DID GOOD.

151

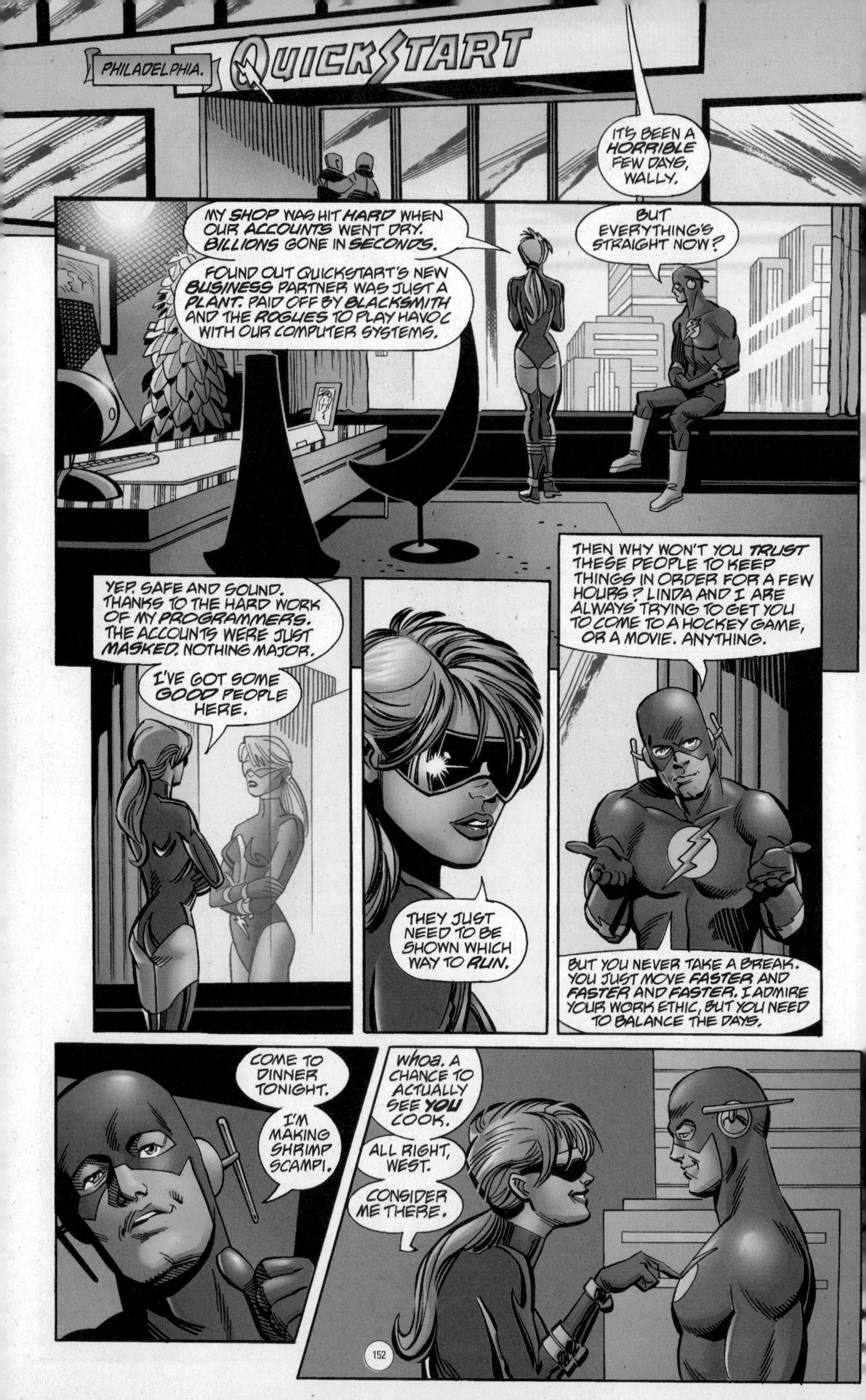
PHILADELPHIA.
QUICKSTART
IT'S BEEN A HORRIBLE FEW DAYS, WALLY.
MY SHOP WAS HIT HARD WHEN OUR ACCOUNTS WENT DRY. BILLIONS GONE IN SECONDS.
FOUND OUT QUICKSTART'S NEW BUSINESS PARTNER WAS JUST A PLANT. PAID OFF BY BLACKSMITH AND THE ROGUES TO PLAY HAVOC WITH OUR COMPUTER SYSTEMS.
BUT EVERYTHING'S STRAIGHT NOW?
YEP. SAFE AND SOUND. THANKS TO THE HARD WORK OF MY PROGRAMMERS. THE ACCOUNTS WERE JUST MASKED. NOTHING MAJOR.
I'VE GOT SOME GOOD PEOPLE HERE.
THEY JUST NEED TO BE SHOWN WHICH WAY TO RUN.
THEN WHY WON'T YOU TRUST THESE PEOPLE TO KEEP THINGS IN ORDER FOR A FEW HOURS? LINDA AND I ARE ALWAYS TRYING TO GET YOU TO COME TO A HOCKEY GAME, OR A MOVIE. ANYTHING.
BUT YOU NEVER TAKE A BREAK. YOU JUST MOVE FASTER AND FASTER AND FASTER. I ADMIRE YOUR WORK ETHIC, BUT YOU NEED TO BALANCE THE DAYS.
COME TO DINNER TONIGHT.
I'M MAKING SHRIMP SCAMPI.
WHOA. A CHANCE TO ACTUALLY SEE YOU COOK.
ALL RIGHT, WEST.
CONSIDER ME THERE.

DENVER.

BUT I'M *FASTER* THAN YOU, JAY

MAYBE, BART. BUT I *TOLD* YOU. IT'S NOT ABOUT *SPEED,* IT'S ABOUT *STEALTH.*

YOU DON'T GLIDE, YOU *STOMP.* TRY NOT MAKING YOUR FEET SO HEAVY.

KINDA HARD. DON'T YA THINK?

HEY, GUYS.

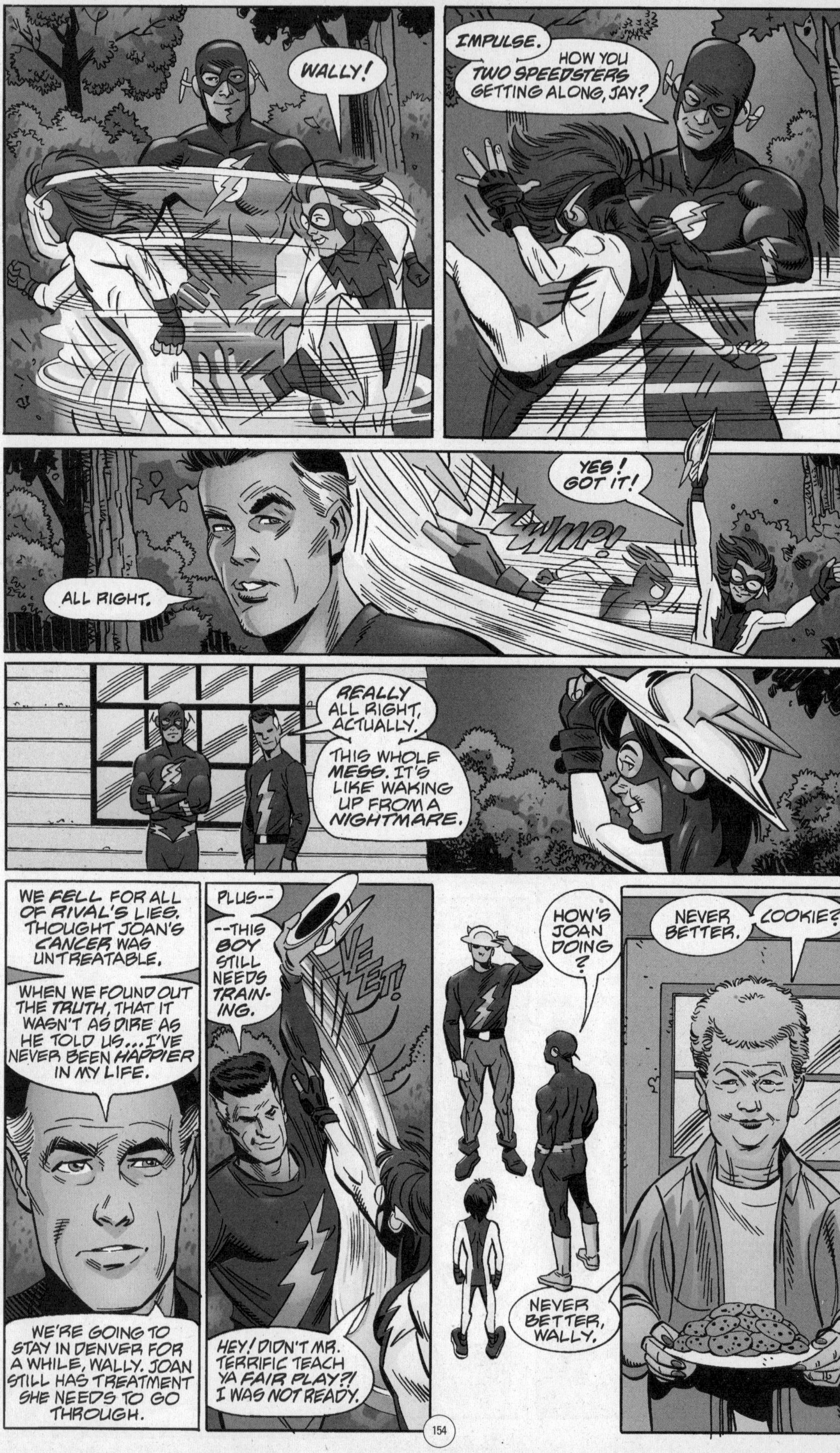
WALLY!
IMPULSE.
HOW YOU TWO SPEEDSTERS GETTING ALONG, JAY?
YES! GOT IT!
ZWHIP!
ALL RIGHT.
REALLY ALL RIGHT, ACTUALLY.
THIS WHOLE MESS. IT'S LIKE WAKING UP FROM A NIGHTMARE.
WE FELL FOR ALL OF RIVAL'S LIES. THOUGHT JOAN'S CANCER WAS UNTREATABLE.
WHEN WE FOUND OUT THE TRUTH, THAT IT WASN'T AS DIRE AS HE TOLD US... I'VE NEVER BEEN HAPPIER IN MY LIFE.
WE'RE GOING TO STAY IN DENVER FOR A WHILE, WALLY. JOAN STILL HAS TREATMENT SHE NEEDS TO GO THROUGH.
PLUS--
--THIS BOY STILL NEEDS TRAINING.
HEY! DIDN'T MR. TERRIFIC TEACH YA FAIR PLAY?! I WAS NOT READY.
HOW'S JOAN DOING?
NEVER BETTER, WALLY.
NEVER BETTER.
COOKIE?

CENTRAL CITY.

FZZZSHHHH!

MR. VICTOR STONE. YOU HOME?

14

VIC!

HEY, SPORT.

WHAT ARE YOU UP TO? YOU DIDN'T RETURN MY CALL.

SORRY. JUST NEEDED SOME TIME ALONE, I GUESS.

GONNA HAVE TO GET A DAY JOB SOON. KEEPING THIS MACHINE WELL-OILED IS EXPENSIVE.

JUST CAME BY TO SAY THANKS FOR ALL YOUR HELP. INVITE YOU TO DINNER.

BROUGHT A SNACK, TOO. COURTESY OF JOAN GARRICK.

GARRICK

-- CAN YOU GET SQUARE CRUST, HOT SHOT?

I KNOW THAT SMILE. SOMEONE'S IN LOVE.

SQUARE CRUST? NO PROBLEM, BABY. BE HOME SOON.

HEY, SPEEDY. HOW ARE YOU?

AFTER EVERYTHING YOU WENT THROUGH. WITH PLUNDER AND ALL. THE REAL QUESTION, DETECTIVE MORILLO, IS... HOW ARE YOU?

WELL. MY WIFE IS OKAY. SO I'M OKAY.

I'M STILL A LITTLE UNCLEAR ON EXACTLY HOW YOU SURVIVED PLUNDER'S ATTACK.

YOU WENT MISSING FOR DAYS. AND CHYRE'S NOT TELLING.

RIGHT...

IT'S... COMPLICATED. I...

YOU KNOW I'VE ALWAYS BEEN *LUCKY*, FLASH. SINCE I WAS A *KID*.

HAD GOOD PARENTS, WAS A NATURAL AT BASEBALL... WHICH GOT ME A SCHOLARSHIP INTO A GREAT SCHOOL.

STUDIED UNDER THE BEST *HOMICIDE* DETECTIVES IN THE COUNTRY WHEN I WAS STATIONED IN *L.A.*

AND THEN MEETING MY *WIFE*...

LISTEN. TAKING DOWN PLUNDER...

LET'S JUST SAY I WAS *LUCKY* THEN, TOO.

NO PARKING

RIGHT.

ALREADY GOT DINNER PLANS, I SEE. GOING OUT FOR *PIZZA*?

YEAH. WANT TO SPEND A NICE, QUIET NIGHT WITH THE WIFE.

STRAIGHT FROM *CAL'S PIZZA* IN DETROIT, MICHIGAN.

BEST *SQUARE PIZZA* IN AMERICA.

ENJOY IT.

FIZZZMTH!

AND *THANKS.*

ALL RIGHT.

DOUBLE CHEESE.

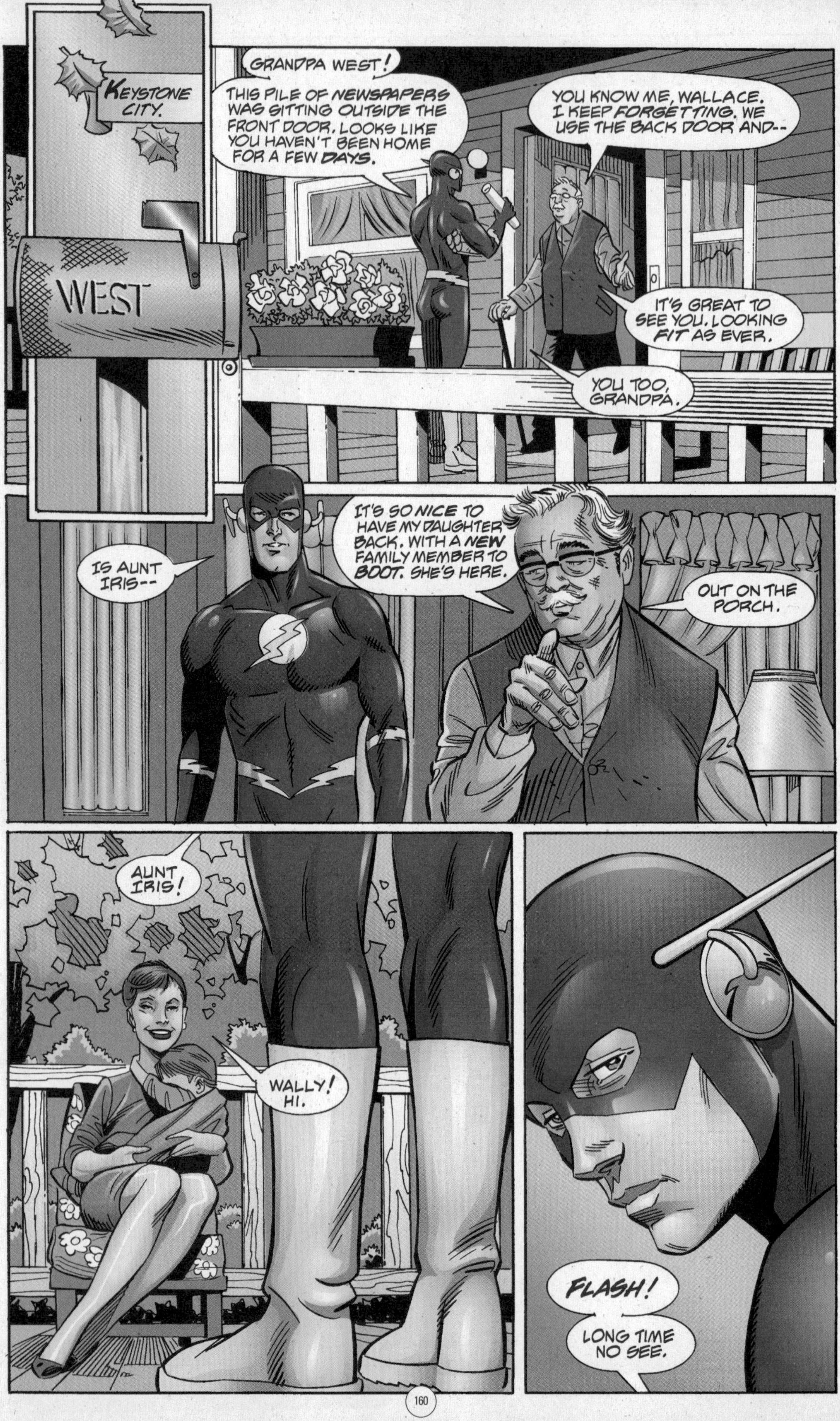
KEYSTONE CITY.
WEST
GRANDPA WEST!
THIS PILE OF NEWSPAPERS WAS SITTING OUTSIDE THE FRONT DOOR. LOOKS LIKE YOU HAVEN'T BEEN HOME FOR A FEW DAYS.
YOU KNOW ME, WALLACE. I KEEP FORGETTING. WE USE THE BACK DOOR AND--
IT'S GREAT TO SEE YOU. LOOKING FIT AS EVER.
YOU TOO, GRANDPA.
IS AUNT IRIS--
IT'S SO NICE TO HAVE MY DAUGHTER BACK. WITH A NEW FAMILY MEMBER TO BOOT. SHE'S HERE.
OUT ON THE PORCH.
AUNT IRIS!
WALLY! HI.
FLASH!
LONG TIME NO SEE.

IRON HEIGHTS PENITENTIARY.

YEAH...

BLACKSMITH AND THE ROGUES SET THEIR PLAN INTO MOTION MONTHS AGO.

THEY SENT PIPER A *BOGUS* E-MAIL FROM HIS FATHER, LURING HIM INTO THEIR GRASP.

MIRROR MASTER POSED AS PIPER, KILLED HIS PARENTS--

--KNOWING THE SECURITY CAMERAS WOULD TAPE IT ALL.

THEY REALLY DID A *NUMBER* ON HIM, FLASH.

THEN HE STRAPPED DOWN PIPER, HYPNOTIZED HIM INTO *BELIEVING* HE COMMITTED THE ACT HIMSELF.

PIPER'S MIND IS FIGHTING THE *PROGRAMMING*. PROBABLY WHY HIS MEMORY'S SO *FUZZY*.

HE'S *NOT GUILTY*, FLASH. EVEN IF HE DOESN'T KNOW THAT HIMSELF.

I HAVE A *PSYCHOLOGIST* LINED UP THAT HE SHOULD SEE. MIGHT BE ABLE TO SORT HIM OUT.

I APPRECIATE YOUR EXPEDIENCE ON THIS, HUNTER. I...

...SORRY. DIDN'T MEAN TO GET AHEAD OF--

IT'S OKAY.

DAMN KNEE.

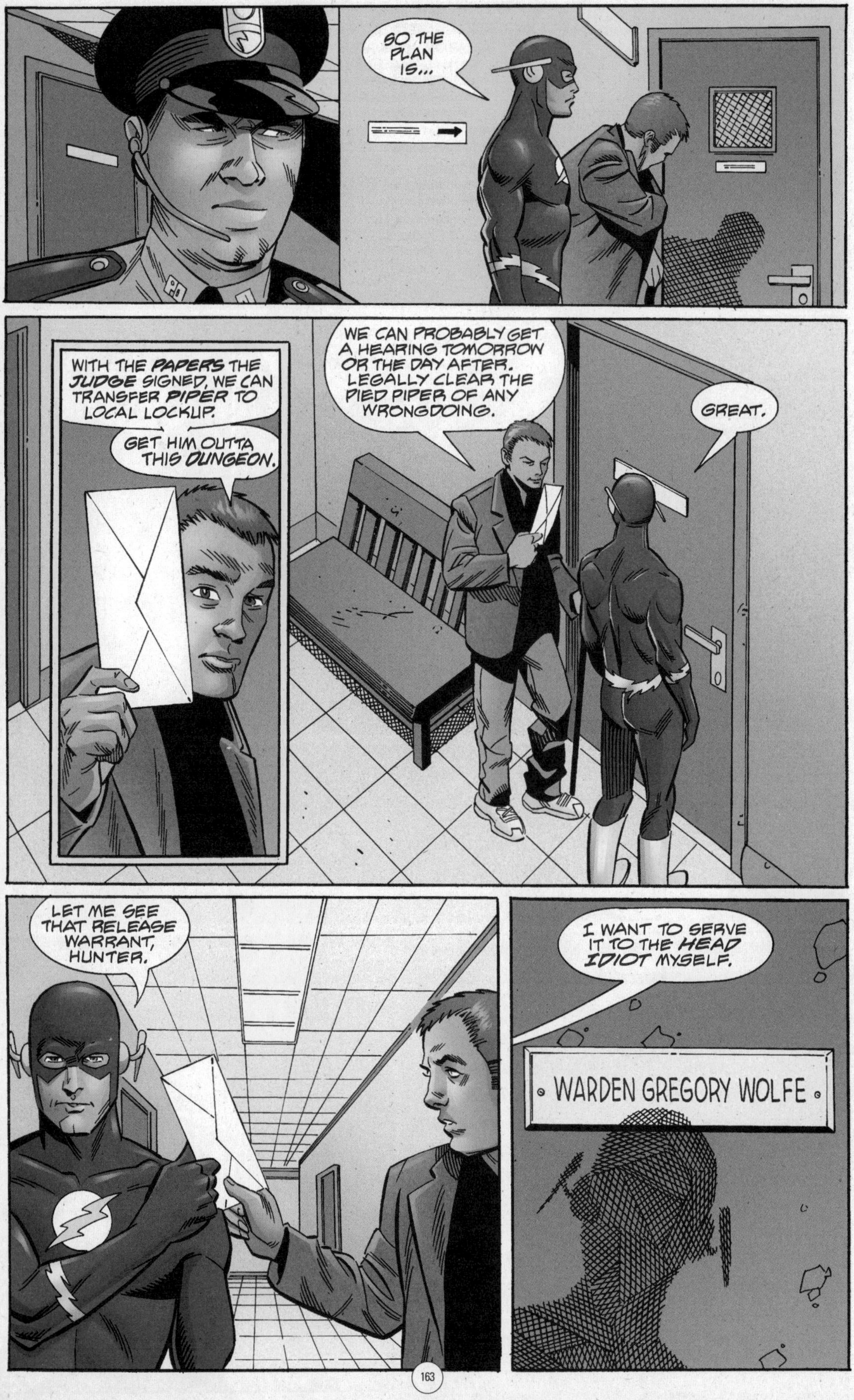
SO THE PLAN IS...
WITH THE *PAPERS* THE *JUDGE* SIGNED, WE CAN TRANSFER *PIPER* TO LOCAL LOCKUP.
GET HIM OUTTA THIS *DUNGEON*.
WE CAN PROBABLY GET A HEARING TOMORROW OR THE DAY AFTER. LEGALLY CLEAR THE PIED PIPER OF ANY WRONGDOING.
GREAT.
LET ME SEE THAT RELEASE WARRANT, HUNTER.
I WANT TO SERVE IT TO THE *HEAD IDIOT* MYSELF.
WARDEN GREGORY WOLFE

I'M SORRY, GOVERNOR.

I'M GOING TO HAVE TO CALL YOU BACK.

THANKS FOR KNOCKING, FLASH.

AND AGENT HUNTER ZOLOMON.

OR IS IT FORMER AGENT? WHAT DO THEY CALL YOU WHEN YOU'RE DISCHARGED FROM THE F.B.I.?

HUNTER IS FINE, WARDEN.

LET ME RUIN YOUR DAY, WOLFE.

SPECIAL DELIVERY.

FWAP!

HNN.

LET'S GO DOWNSTAIRS.

CHNNG

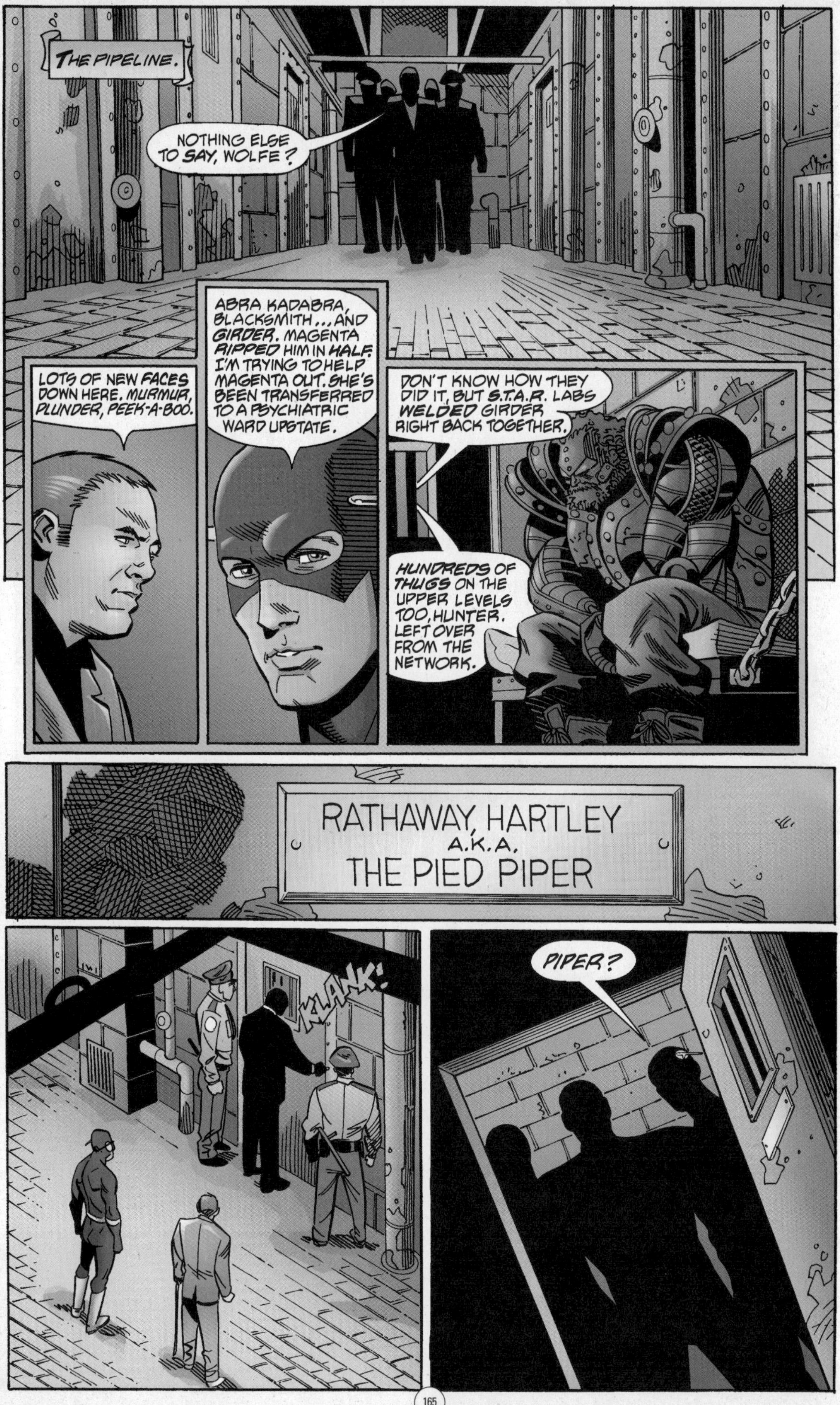
THE PIPELINE.
NOTHING ELSE TO SAY, WOLFE?
LOTS OF NEW FACES DOWN HERE. MURMUR, PLUNDER, PEEK-A-BOO.
ABRA KADABRA, BLACKSMITH... AND GIRDER. MAGENTA RIPPED HIM IN HALF. I'M TRYING TO HELP MAGENTA OUT. SHE'S BEEN TRANSFERRED TO A PSYCHIATRIC WARD UPSTATE.
DON'T KNOW HOW THEY DID IT, BUT S.T.A.R. LABS WELDED GIRDER RIGHT BACK TOGETHER.
HUNDREDS OF THUGS ON THE UPPER LEVELS TOO, HUNTER. LEFT OVER FROM THE NETWORK.
RATHAWAY, HARTLEY
A.K.A.
THE PIED PIPER
KLANK!
PIPER?

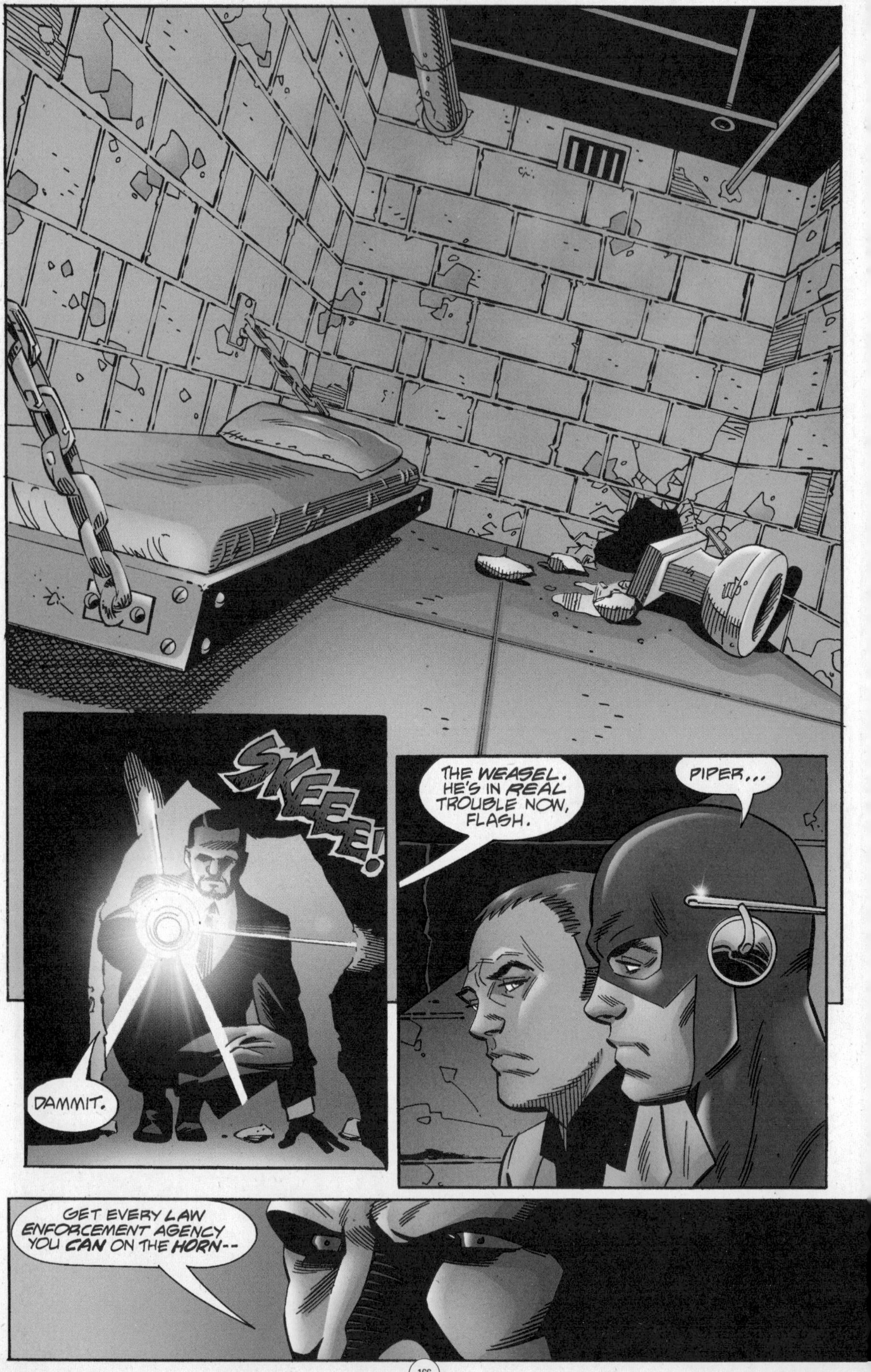
SKEEEE!
DAMMIT.
THE WEASEL. HE'S IN REAL TROUBLE NOW, FLASH.
PIPER...
GET EVERY LAW ENFORCEMENT AGENCY YOU CAN ON THE HORN--

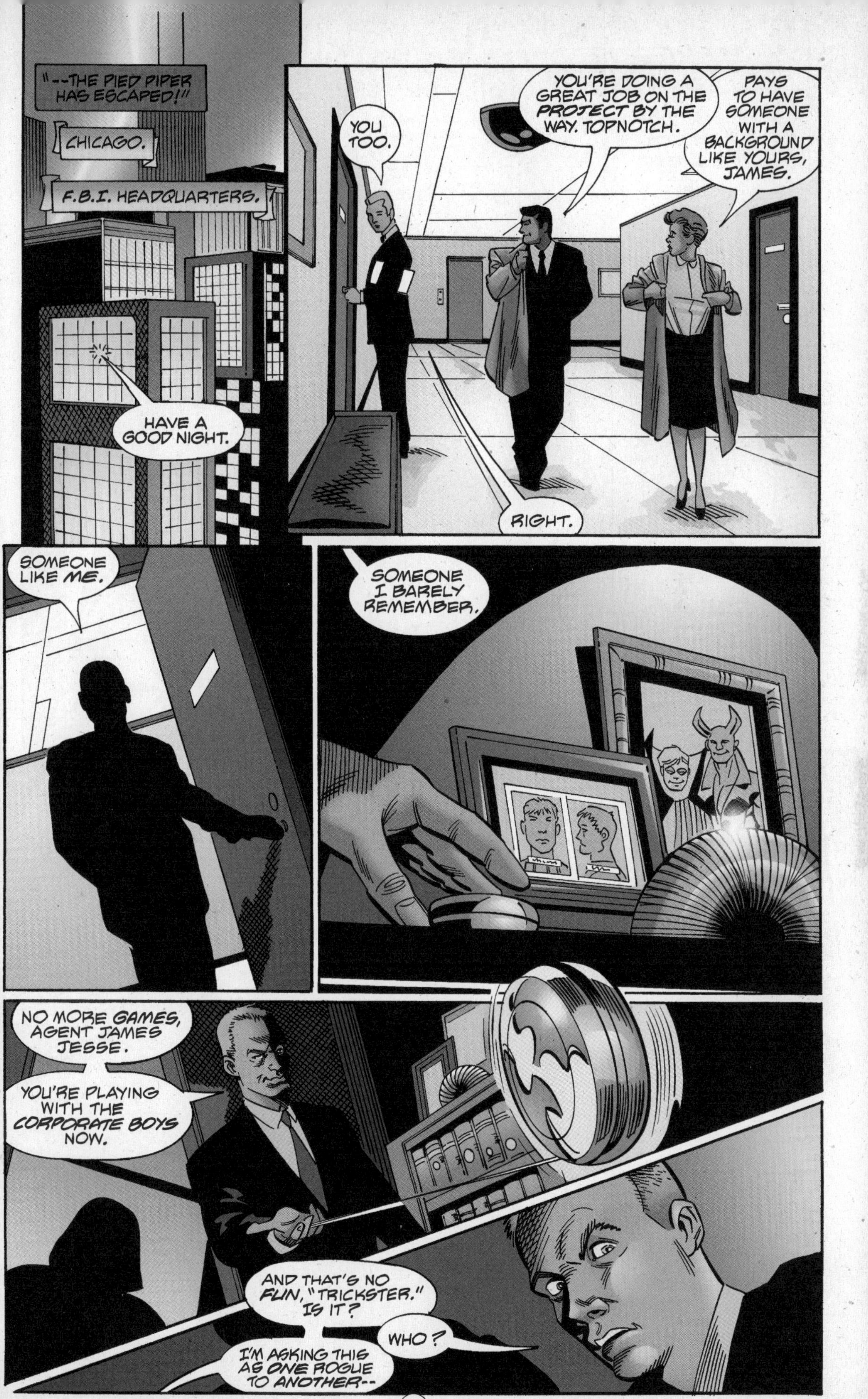
"--THE PIED PIPER HAS ESCAPED!"
CHICAGO.
F.B.I. HEADQUARTERS.
HAVE A GOOD NIGHT.
YOU TOO.
YOU'RE DOING A GREAT JOB ON THE PROJECT BY THE WAY. TOPNOTCH.
PAYS TO HAVE SOMEONE WITH A BACKGROUND LIKE YOURS, JAMES.
RIGHT.
SOMEONE LIKE ME.
SOMEONE I BARELY REMEMBER.
NO MORE GAMES, AGENT JAMES JESSE.
YOU'RE PLAYING WITH THE CORPORATE BOYS NOW.
AND THAT'S NO FUN, "TRICKSTER." IS IT?
WHO?
I'M ASKING THIS AS ONE ROGUE TO ANOTHER--

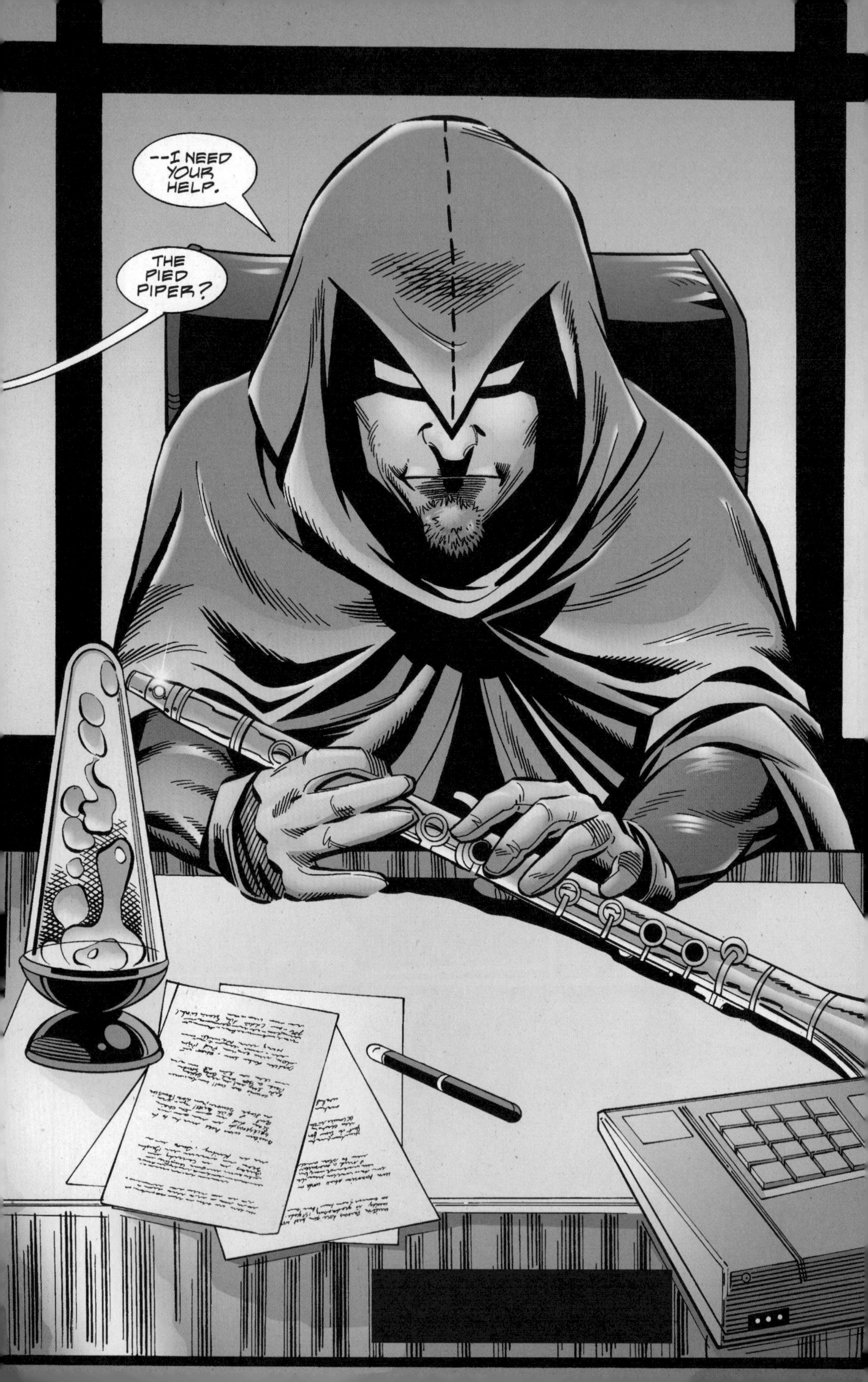
--I NEED YOUR HELP.
THE PIED PIPER?

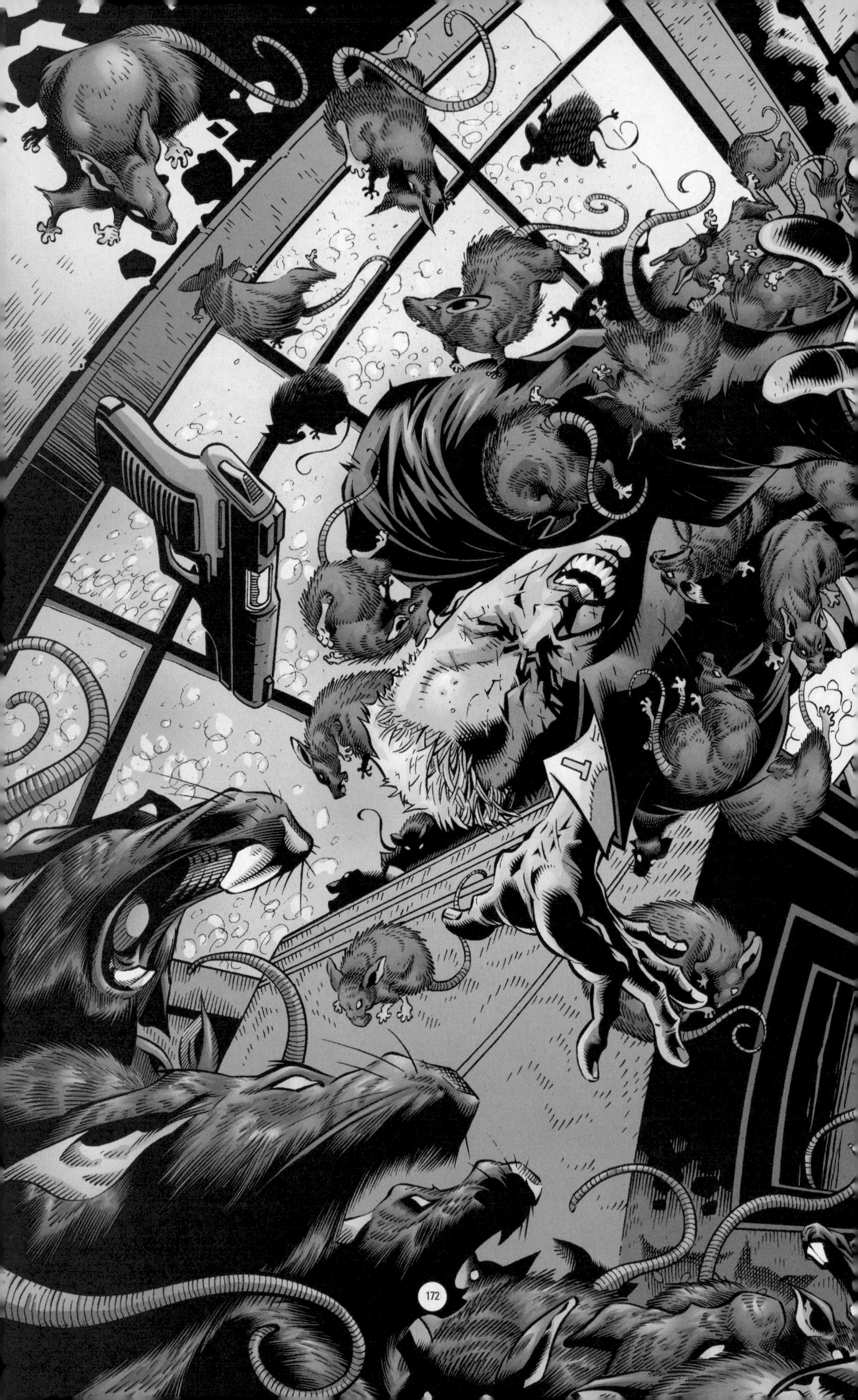

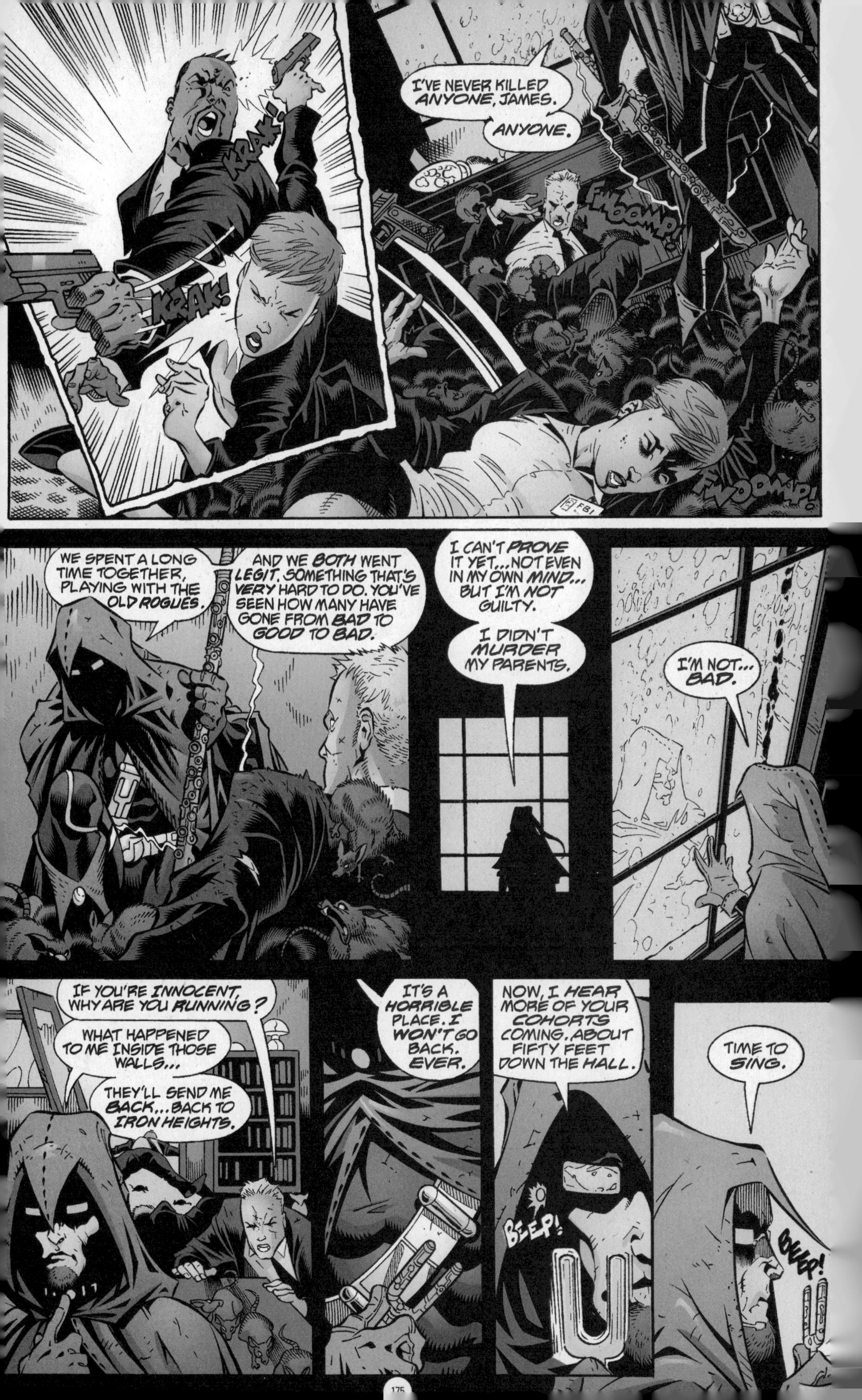

KRAK!
KRAK!
I'VE NEVER KILLED ANYONE, JAMES.
ANYONE.
FWOOMP!
FBI
FWOOMP!
WE SPENT A LONG TIME TOGETHER, PLAYING WITH THE OLD ROGUES.
AND WE BOTH WENT LEGIT. SOMETHING THAT'S VERY HARD TO DO. YOU'VE SEEN HOW MANY HAVE GONE FROM BAD TO GOOD TO BAD.
I CAN'T PROVE IT YET... NOT EVEN IN MY OWN MIND... BUT I'M NOT GUILTY.
I DIDN'T MURDER MY PARENTS.
I'M NOT... BAD.
IF YOU'RE INNOCENT, WHY ARE YOU RUNNING?
WHAT HAPPENED TO ME INSIDE THOSE WALLS...
THEY'LL SEND ME BACK... BACK TO IRON HEIGHTS.
IT'S A HORRIBLE PLACE. I WON'T GO BACK. EVER.
NOW, I HEAR MORE OF YOUR COHORTS COMING. ABOUT FIFTY FEET DOWN THE HALL.
BEEP!
TIME TO SING.
BEEP!

A FEW MONTHS AGO MY PARENTS WERE *MURDERED.* A SECURITY CAMERA CAPTURED *ME* DOING IT... AND I HAVE MEMORIES...

BUT THERE'RE *HOLES* EVERYWHERE. IT FEELS MORE LIKE A *DREAM* THAN *REALITY.*

AND IN MY *HEART,* I *KNOW...* EVEN THOUGH WE DIDN'T GET ALONG *THAT WELL...* I WOULD NEVER *HURT* THEM.

EVERYONE TRIES TO *BLAME* WHAT'S WRONG WITH THEIR *LIVES* ON THEIR *PARENTS.*

MINE WERE *STUCK-UP SNOBS.* STERILE. BUT THEY WEREN'T... *MONSTERS.*

SOMETIMES I THINK BEING *BAD* IS IN YOUR *GENETIC STRUCTURE.*

DESPITE IT ALL, I *LOVED* THEM.

MAYBE I WAS *CURSED* AT BIRTH. AND I'M *FIGHTING* AN *UPHILL* BATTLE.

I NEED TO TALK TO *SOMEONE.* NEED TO BE *HEARD...* BUT I'VE BEEN *IGNORED* SINCE DAY ONE.

I WAS BORN *HARTLEY ROBERT RATHAWAY.* IN CENTRAL CITY. THIRTY *PLUS* YEARS AGO. HAD TWO SILVER SPOONS IN MY *MOUTH.*

I DON'T MEAN TA PRY, MR. RATHAWAY, SIR. BUT YOUNG HARTLEY HAS BEEN HOME FOR A *MONTH* NOW, AND YOU AND THE *MRS.* HAVE GONE OUT *EVERY NIGHT.*

MICK RORY 911 ROCK ISLAND DRIVE— QUAD CITIES ILLINOIS

OH, FOR *HEAVEN'S SAKE.* HE'LL BE THERE WHEN WE GET *HOME.*

DON'T WAIT UP.

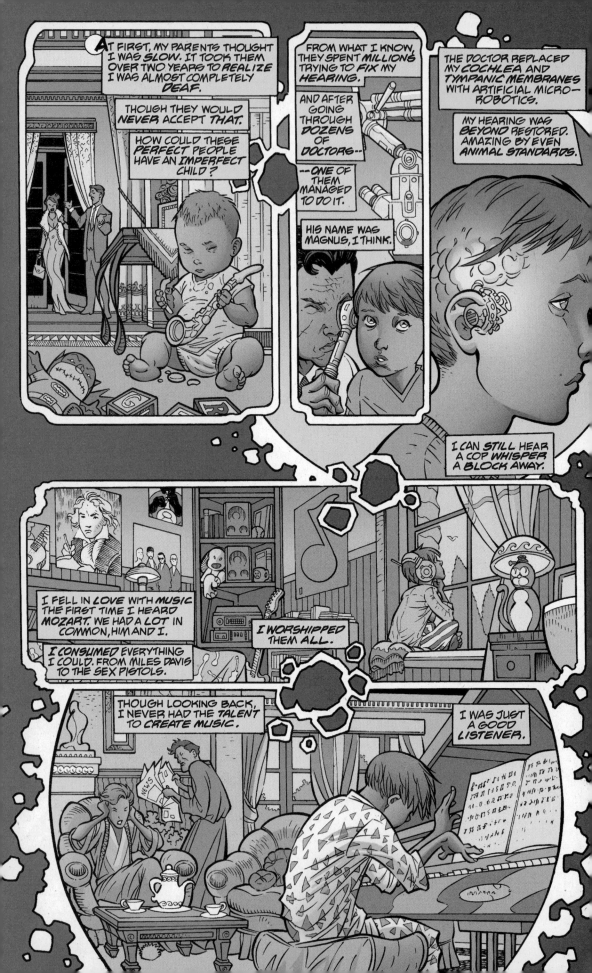

AT FIRST, MY PARENTS THOUGHT I WAS *SLOW*. IT TOOK THEM OVER TWO YEARS TO *REALIZE* I WAS ALMOST COMPLETELY *DEAF*.

THOUGH THEY WOULD *NEVER ACCEPT THAT*.

HOW COULD THESE *PERFECT* PEOPLE HAVE AN *IMPERFECT* CHILD?

FROM WHAT I KNOW, THEY SPENT *MILLIONS* TRYING TO *FIX* MY HEARING.

AND AFTER GOING THROUGH *DOZENS* OF DOCTORS--

--*ONE* OF THEM MANAGED TO *DO* IT.

HIS NAME WAS MAGNUS, I THINK.

THE DOCTOR REPLACED MY *COCHLEA* AND *TYMPANIC MEMBRANES* WITH ARTIFICIAL *MICRO-ROBOTICS*.

MY HEARING WAS *BEYOND* RESTORED. AMAZING BY EVEN *ANIMAL* STANDARDS.

I CAN STILL HEAR A COP *WHISPER* A *BLOCK* AWAY.

I FELL IN *LOVE* WITH *MUSIC* THE FIRST TIME I *HEARD MOZART*. WE HAD A *LOT* IN COMMON, HIM AND I.

I *CONSUMED* EVERYTHING I COULD. FROM *MILES DAVIS* TO THE *SEX PISTOLS*.

I *WORSHIPPED* THEM ALL.

THOUGH LOOKING BACK, I NEVER HAD THE *TALENT* TO CREATE MUSIC.

I WAS JUST A *GOOD LISTENER*.

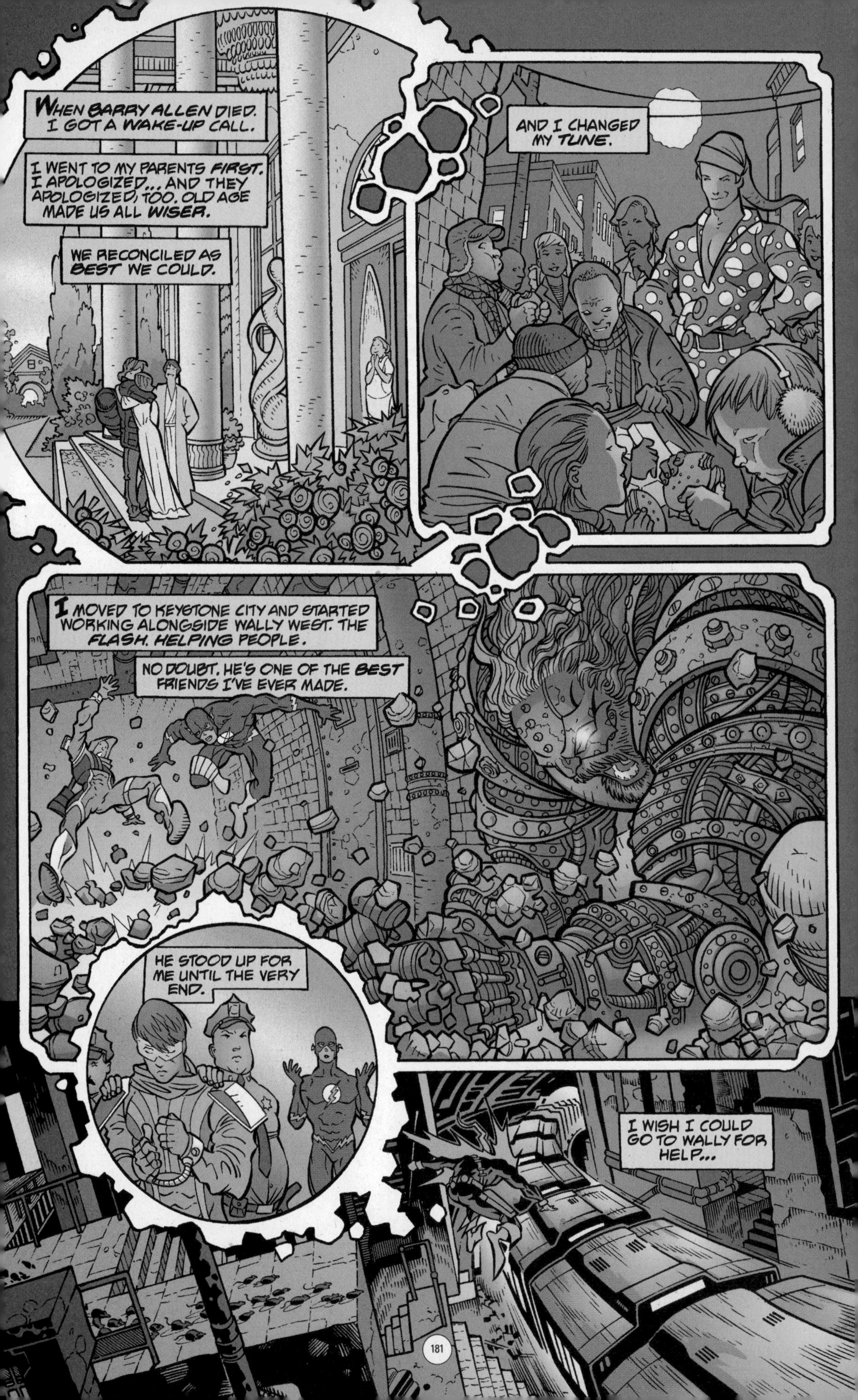
WHEN BARRY ALLEN DIED. I GOT A WAKE-UP CALL.
I WENT TO MY PARENTS FIRST. I APOLOGIZED... AND THEY APOLOGIZED, TOO. OLD AGE MADE US ALL WISER.
WE RECONCILED AS BEST WE COULD.
AND I CHANGED MY TUNE.
I MOVED TO KEYSTONE CITY AND STARTED WORKING ALONGSIDE WALLY WEST. THE FLASH. HELPING PEOPLE.
NO DOUBT, HE'S ONE OF THE BEST FRIENDS I'VE EVER MADE.
HE STOOD UP FOR ME UNTIL THE VERY END.
I WISH I COULD GO TO WALLY FOR HELP...

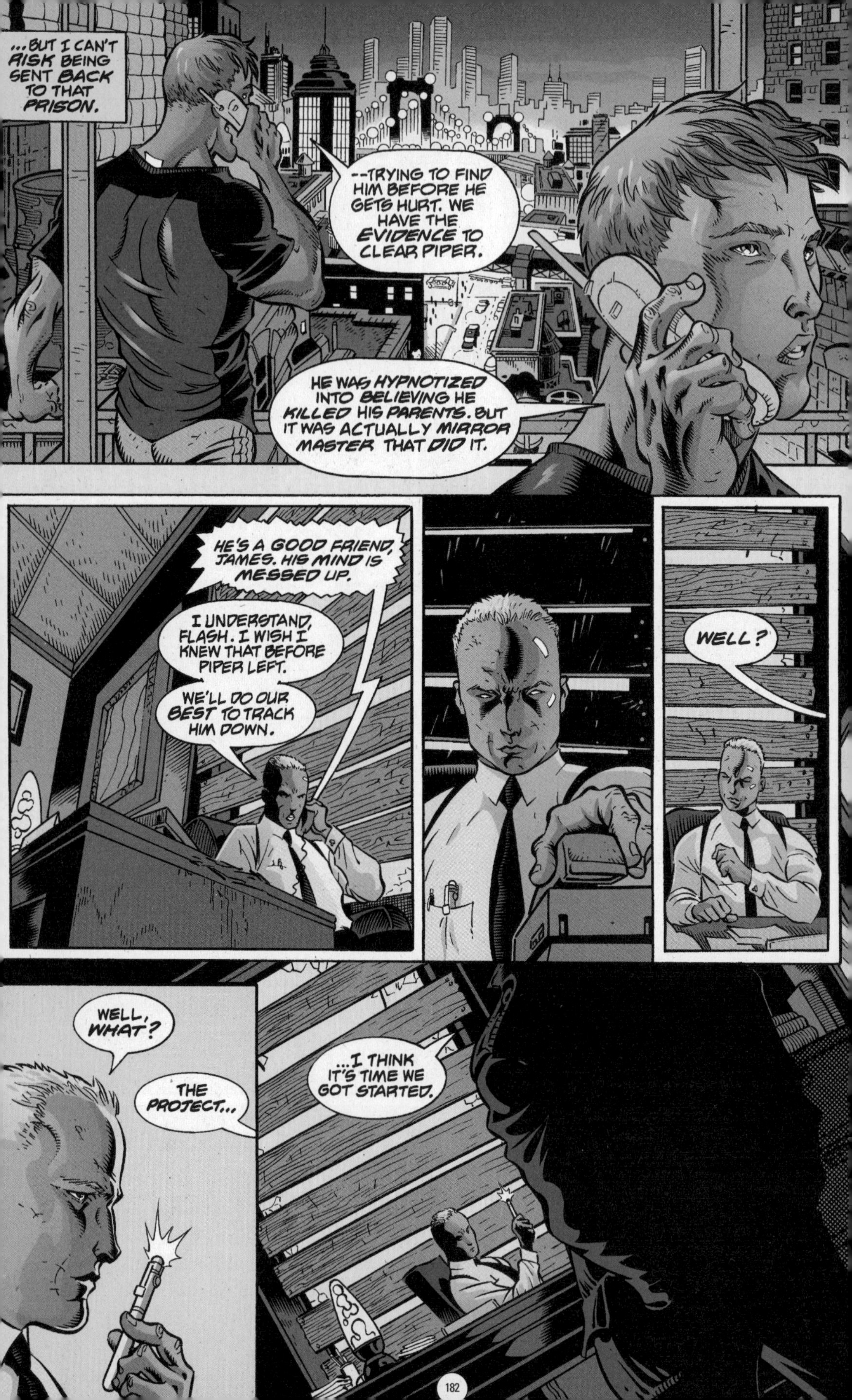
...BUT I CAN'T RISK BEING SENT BACK TO THAT PRISON.
--TRYING TO FIND HIM BEFORE HE GETS HURT. WE HAVE THE EVIDENCE TO CLEAR PIPER.
HE WAS HYPNOTIZED INTO BELIEVING HE KILLED HIS PARENTS. BUT IT WAS ACTUALLY MIRROR MASTER THAT DID IT.
HE'S A GOOD FRIEND, JAMES. HIS MIND IS MESSED UP.
I UNDERSTAND, FLASH. I WISH I KNEW THAT BEFORE PIPER LEFT.
WE'LL DO OUR BEST TO TRACK HIM DOWN.
WELL?
WELL, WHAT?
THE PROJECT...
...I THINK IT'S TIME WE GOT STARTED.

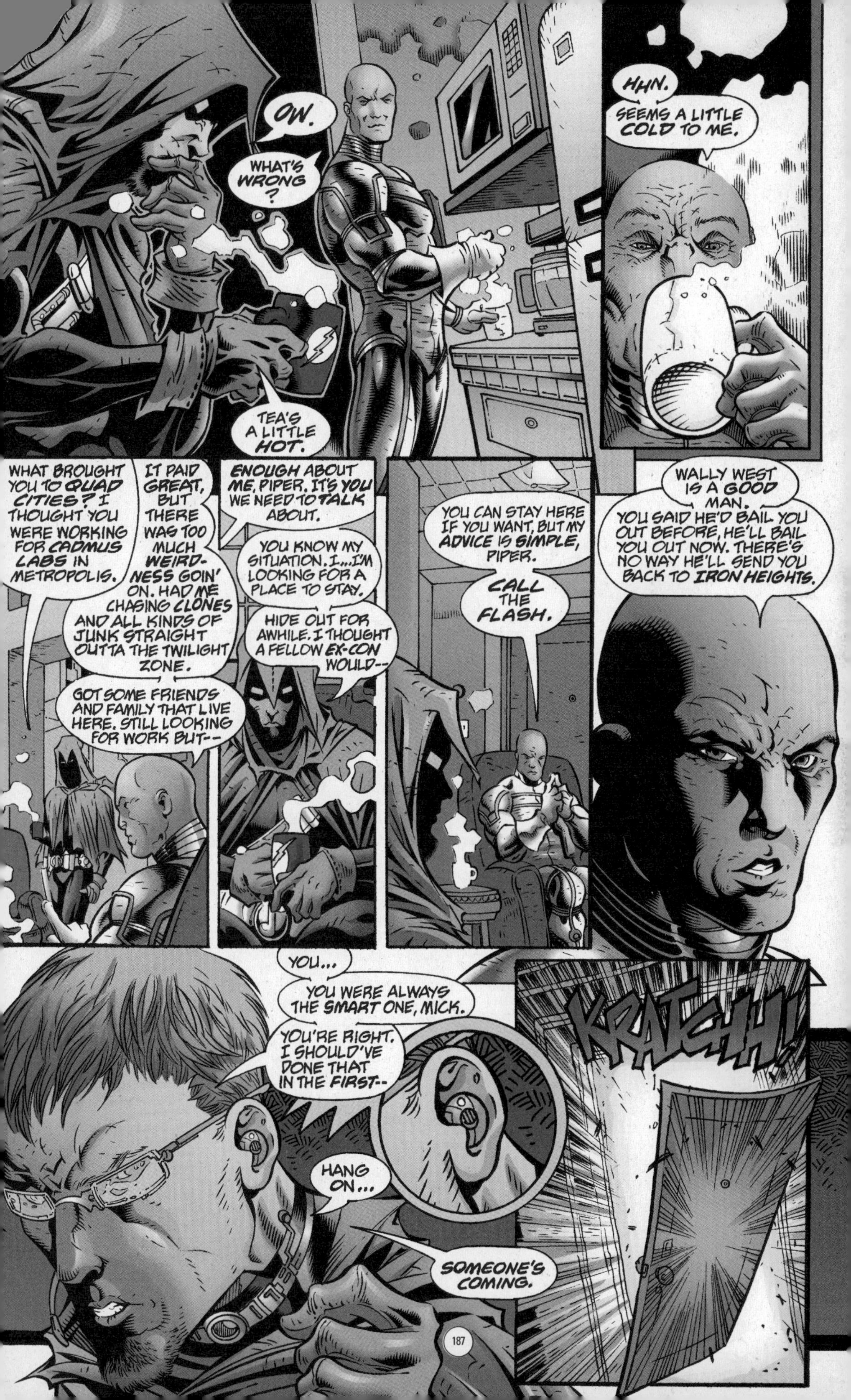
OW.
WHAT'S WRONG?
TEA'S A LITTLE HOT.
HHN.
SEEMS A LITTLE COLD TO ME.
WHAT BROUGHT YOU TO QUAD CITIES? I THOUGHT YOU WERE WORKING FOR CADMUS LABS IN METROPOLIS.
IT PAID GREAT, BUT THERE WAS TOO MUCH WEIRD-NESS GOIN' ON. HAD ME CHASING CLONES AND ALL KINDS OF JUNK STRAIGHT OUTTA THE TWILIGHT ZONE.
GOT SOME FRIENDS AND FAMILY THAT LIVE HERE. STILL LOOKING FOR WORK BUT--
ENOUGH ABOUT ME, PIPER. IT'S YOU WE NEED TO TALK ABOUT.
YOU KNOW MY SITUATION. I...I'M LOOKING FOR A PLACE TO STAY.
HIDE OUT FOR AWHILE. I THOUGHT A FELLOW EX-CON WOULD--
YOU CAN STAY HERE IF YOU WANT, BUT MY ADVICE IS SIMPLE, PIPER.
CALL THE FLASH.
WALLY WEST IS A GOOD MAN.
YOU SAID HE'D BAIL YOU OUT BEFORE, HE'LL BAIL YOU OUT NOW. THERE'S NO WAY HE'LL SEND YOU BACK TO IRON HEIGHTS.
YOU...
YOU WERE ALWAYS THE SMART ONE, MICK.
YOU'RE RIGHT. I SHOULD'VE DONE THAT IN THE FIRST--
HANG ON...
SOMEONE'S COMING.
KRATCHH!

CHAK CHAK! CHAK! CHAK!

JAMES JESSE.

HOW DID YOU--

PUT A *TRACER* ON YOUR *BOOT*, MUSIC MAN.

I STILL HAVE A FEW TRICKS UP MY SLEEVE.

GONNA *ARREST* US THEN, "*TRICKSTER*"?

ACTUALLY, HOT SHOT... I HAVE A *PROPOSITION* FOR THE *BOTH* OF YOU.

KEYSTONE CITY.

POLICE PRECINCT 242.

I APPRECIATE YOU GETTING BACK TO US SO QUICKLY.

WE APPRECIATE ALL YOU'VE DONE, AGENT JESSE.

AND THANKS AGAIN FOR THE INFO ON THE NEW KID THAT'S USING MY SCHTICK. SO WE GOT A DEAL...YOU HEAR ANYTHING MORE ABOUT THIS TRICKSTER-BOY YOU LET US KNOW.

AND I'LL LET YOU KNOW ABOUT THE PIED PIPER.

AFTER YOU CALLED AND TOLD ME THE SITUATION, FLASH--

--WE TRIED OUR BEST TO LOCATE HIM.

BUT SO FAR, THE BUREAU HAS COME UP DRY.

JAMES IS FINE.

ONE

WALKER, AKA

TRICKSTE

GOTTA RUN.

KLIK!

WHAT DO YOU THINK?

YOU'RE THE PSYCHOLOGIST, HUNTER, YOU TELL ME.

JAMES JESSE MAY BE WITH THE F.B.I. NOW--

--BUT THAT DOESN'T MEAN HE'S GONE HONEST. I THINK HE'S LYING ABOUT SOMETHING.

YEAH. HE WAS USING HIS "HAPPY" VOICE.

I STILL HAVE SOME FRIENDS THERE, BACK WHEN I WAS IN THE BUREAU. I'LL MAKE SOME CALLS AND SEE IF I CAN DIG ANYTHING ELSE--

RATHAWAY, HA

PIED PIPE

RRMMMB-KATHOOOM!

WHA--

WHAT THE HELL WAS THAT? EARTHQUAKE?

NO. NOT AN EARTHQUAKE--

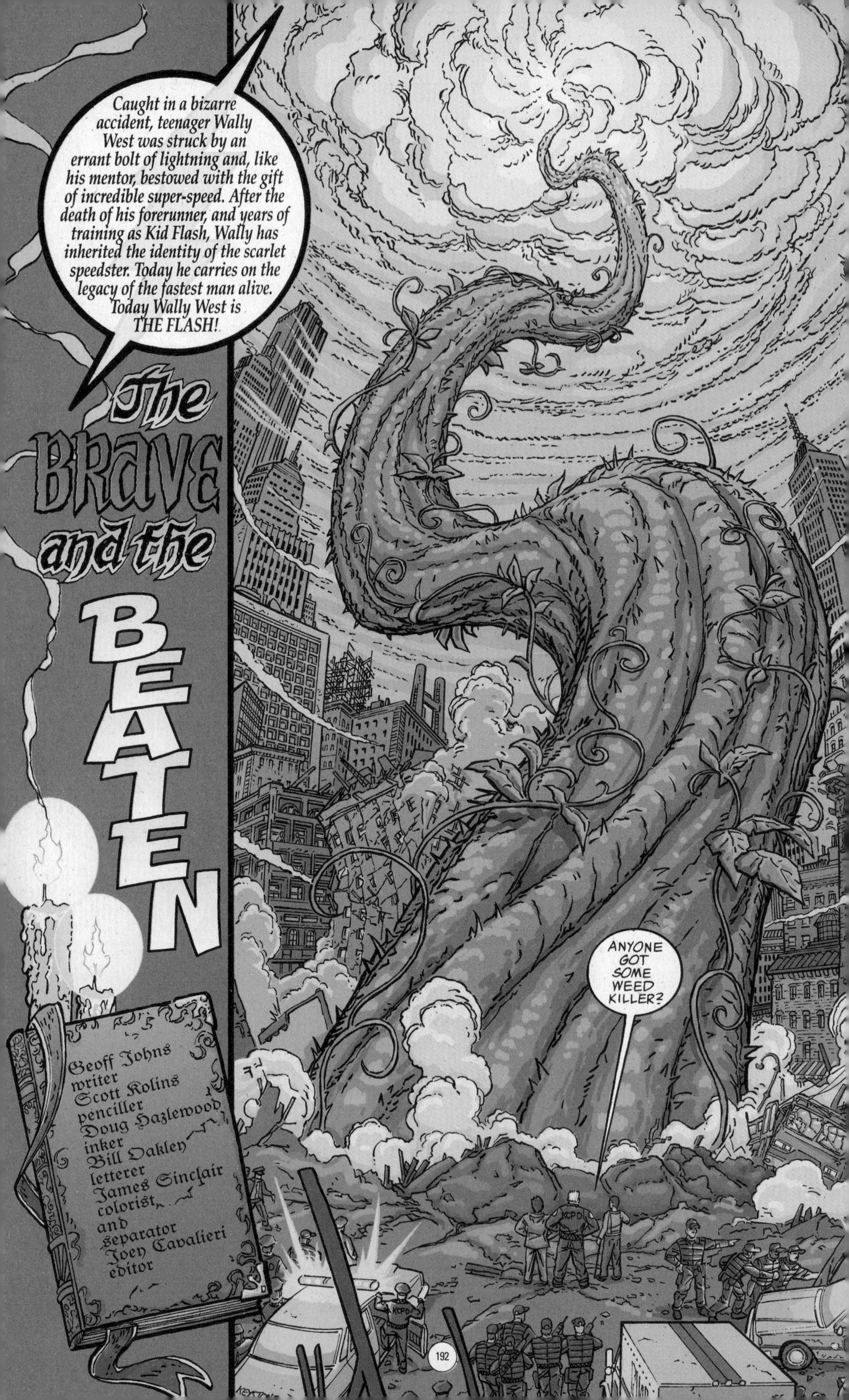
Caught in a bizarre accident, teenager Wally West was struck by an errant bolt of lightning and, like his mentor, bestowed with the gift of incredible super-speed. After the death of his forerunner, and years of training as Kid Flash, Wally has inherited the identity of the scarlet speedster. Today he carries on the legacy of the fastest man alive. Today Wally West is THE FLASH!
The BRAVE and the BEATEN
Geoff Johns writer
Scott Kolins penciller
Doug Hazlewood inker
Bill Oakley letterer
James Sinclair colorist, and separator
Joey Cavalieri editor
ANYONE GOT SOME WEED KILLER?
KCPD

HUNTER? YOU GOT IDEAS?

TRIED SAWING INTO IT, ALREADY TORE UP OVER A *DOZEN* CHAINSAWS. COULDN'T MAKE A *DENT.* WHATEVER THIS IS--

--IT'S JUST A *PIECE* OF THE *PUZZLE* HERE. THOSE... *GREEN* CLOUDS ARE TOO *THICK* TO SEE THROUGH. PLUS THESE *WINDS*--

SO WHAT IS IT?

IT'S A *GIANT BEANSTALK,* CHYRE.

I CAN *SEE* THAT, MORILLO. BUT HOW IN THE HELL DID IT *SPROUT* IN THE CENTER O' DOWNTOWN KEYSTONE?

"--THESE WINDS HAVE SHUT THE AIRPORT *DOWN.*

"WE'VE BEEN *FORCED* TO DECLARE THE ENTIRE CITY A *NO FLY ZONE.*"

FZZZSHHH

FLYING RESTRICTED UNTIL FURTHER NOTICE -K.C.P.D.-

FZZSHH

MY WIFE WAS SUPPOSED TO FLY OUT TO SEE HER *MOTHER* THIS MORNING. THERE GOES *HER GOOD MOOD.*

SO *WHO* PLANTED THE *MAGIC BEANS?* THE *JOLLY GREEN GIANT?*

YOU'RE NOT *THAT* FAR OFF, CHYRE.

BROTHER
...GRIMM?
NO ONE I'VE
PROFILED
BE--

BARBARIAN *KIDNAPPED*
KEYSTONE A WHILE BACK.
TOOK THE WHOLE DAMN
CITY TO SOME KINDA
WONDERLAND.

PLAYED
PUPPETEER
WITH ALL OF
US.

I'VE
SEEN THIS
BEANSTALK
BEFORE.

THE *TROLL*
RESPONSIBLE
IS NAMED
*BROTHER
GRIMM.*

FZZASHH!

GRIMM'S THE *PRINCE*
OF A *REALM* CALLED
EASTWIND. A WORLD
WHERE *FAIRY TALES*
COME TRUE.

HE KILLED HIS BROTHER,
NEARLY DESTROYED EASTWIND
...AND BLAMES *ME* FOR INSPIR-
ING HIM TO DO IT. NOW HE'S
OBSESSED WITH
RULING "MY"
KINGDOM.

BROTHER
GRIMM WANTS TO
BE THE *KING* OF
KEYSTONE CITY.

WHAT'D
YOU DO?

RRRRR

VBMMNBV

IT STARTED...
SHAKING WHEN
I TOUCHED IT. I--

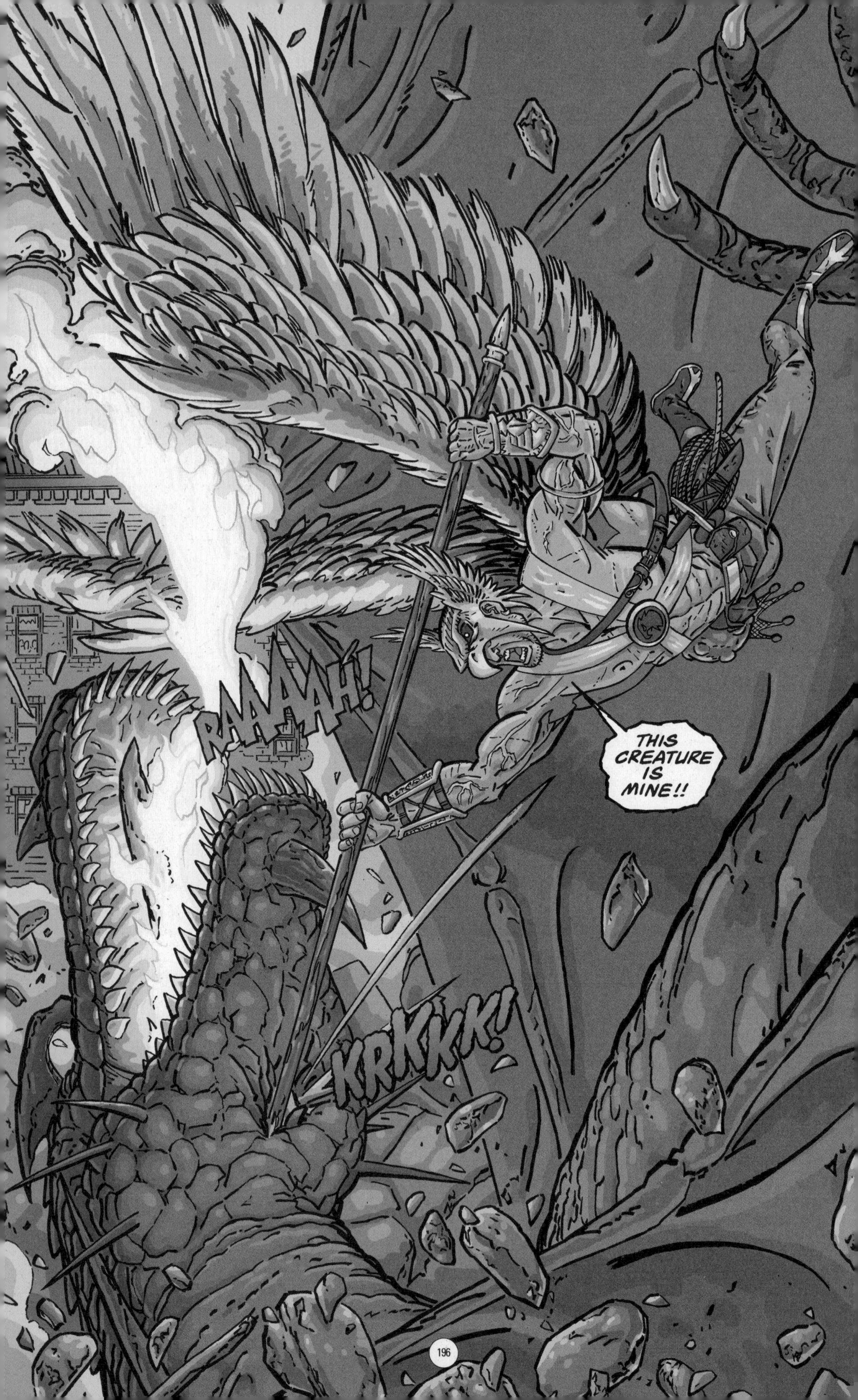
RAAAAH!
THIS CREATURE IS MINE!!
KRKKK!

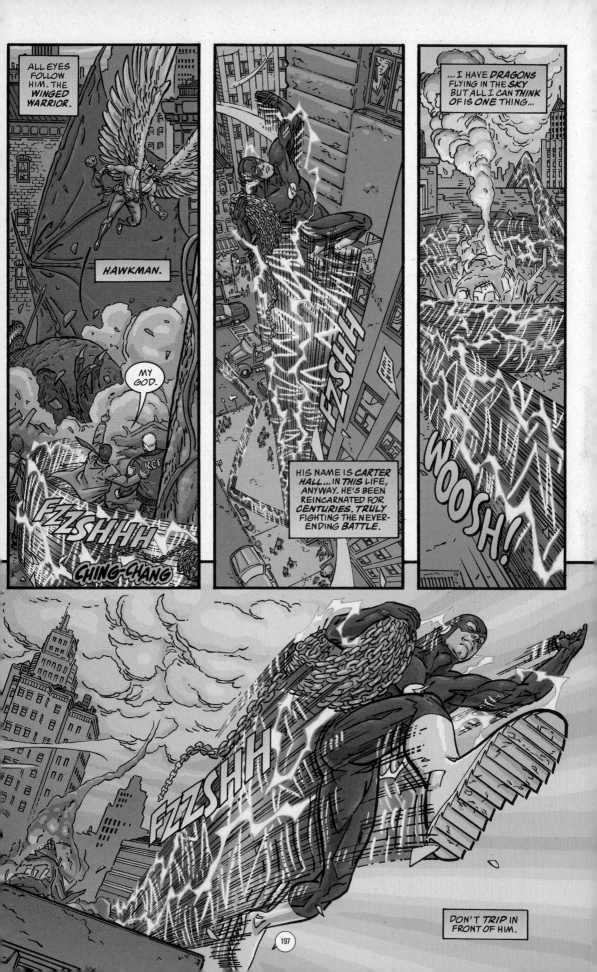

ALL EYES FOLLOW HIM. THE WINGED WARRIOR.

HAWKMAN.

MY GOD.

FZZSHHH

CHING-CHANG

FZSHH

HIS NAME IS CARTER HALL...IN THIS LIFE, ANYWAY. HE'S BEEN REINCARNATED FOR CENTURIES. TRULY FIGHTING THE NEVER-ENDING BATTLE.

...I HAVE DRAGONS FLYING IN THE SKY BUT ALL I CAN THINK OF IS ONE THING...

WOOSH!

FZZSHH

DON'T TRIP IN FRONT OF HIM.

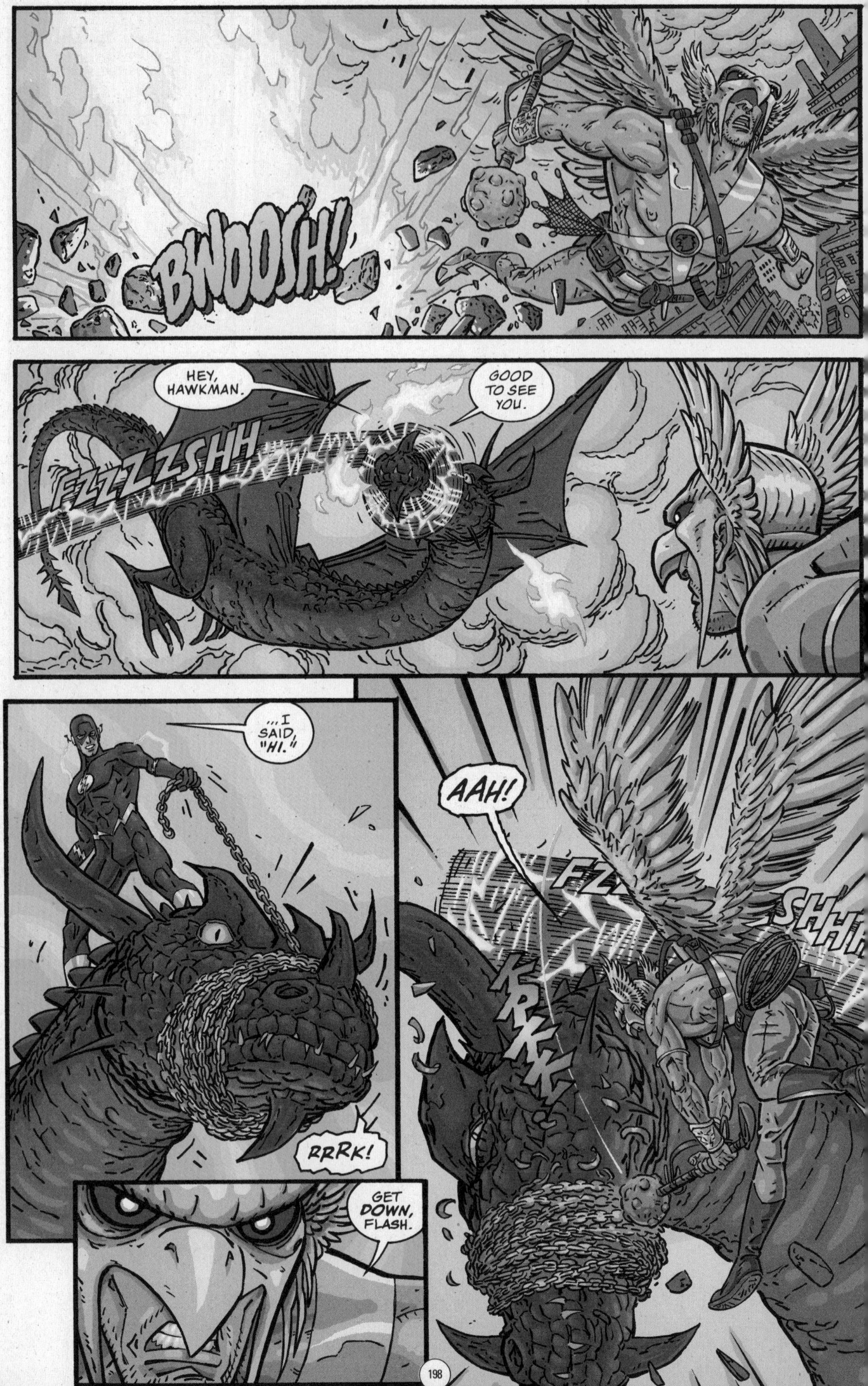
BWOOSH!
HEY, HAWKMAN.
GOOD TO SEE YOU.
FZZZZZSHH
...I SAID, "HI."
AAH!
FZZ
SHH
KRKK
RRRK!
GET DOWN, FLASH.

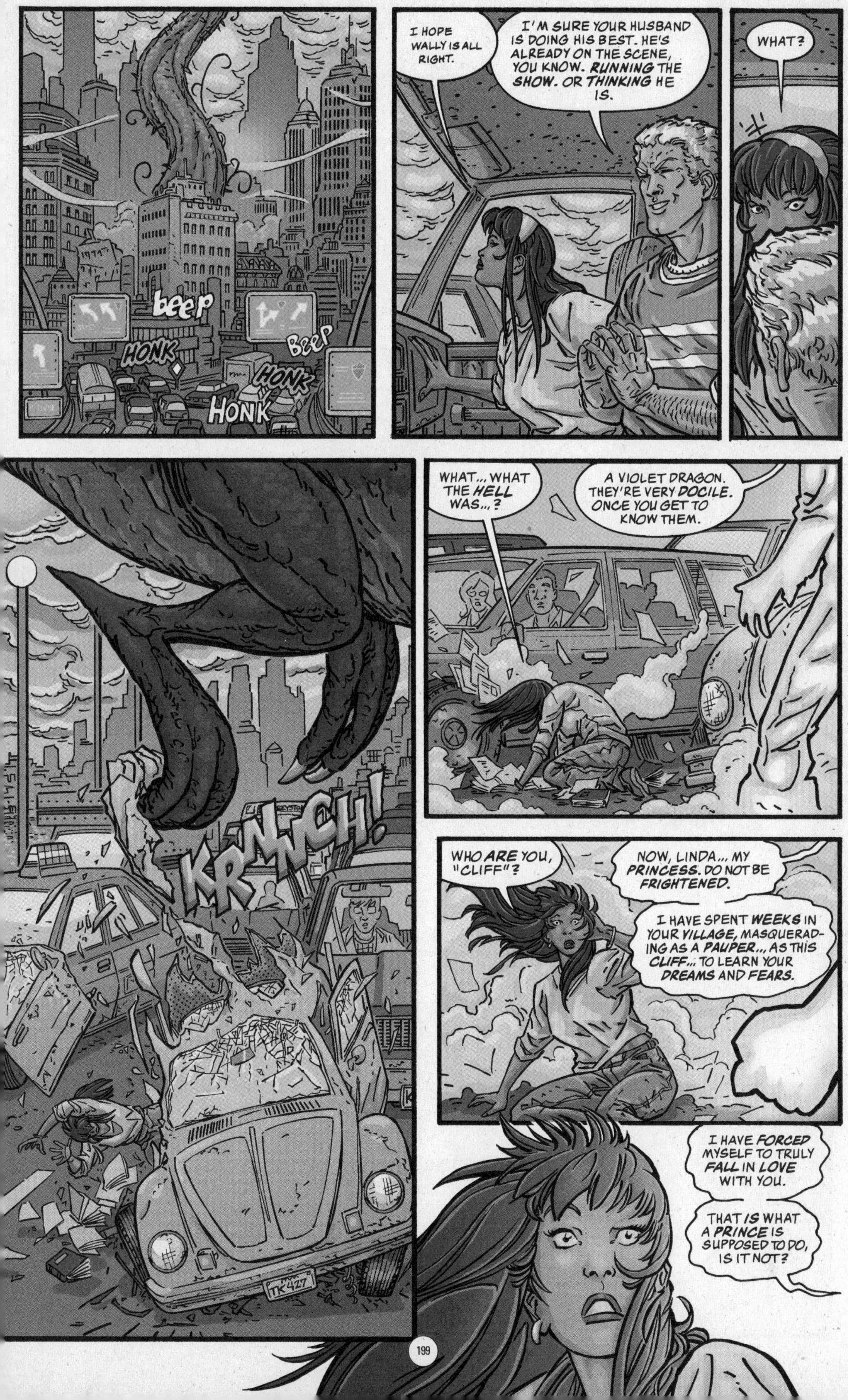

beep
HONK
Beep
HONK
HONK
I HOPE WALLY IS ALL RIGHT.
I'M SURE YOUR HUSBAND IS DOING HIS BEST. HE'S ALREADY ON THE SCENE, YOU KNOW. *RUNNING* THE *SHOW*. OR *THINKING* HE IS.
WHAT?
KRNNCH!
WHAT... WHAT THE *HELL* WAS...?
A VIOLET DRAGON. THEY'RE VERY *DOCILE*. ONCE YOU GET TO KNOW THEM.
WHO *ARE* YOU, "CLIFF"?
NOW, LINDA... MY *PRINCESS*. DO NOT BE *FRIGHTENED*.
I HAVE SPENT *WEEKS* IN YOUR *VILLAGE*, MASQUERADING AS A *PAUPER*... AS THIS *CLIFF*... TO LEARN YOUR *DREAMS* AND *FEARS*.
I HAVE *FORCED* MYSELF TO TRULY *FALL* IN *LOVE* WITH YOU.
THAT *IS* WHAT A *PRINCE* IS SUPPOSED TO DO, IS IT NOT?

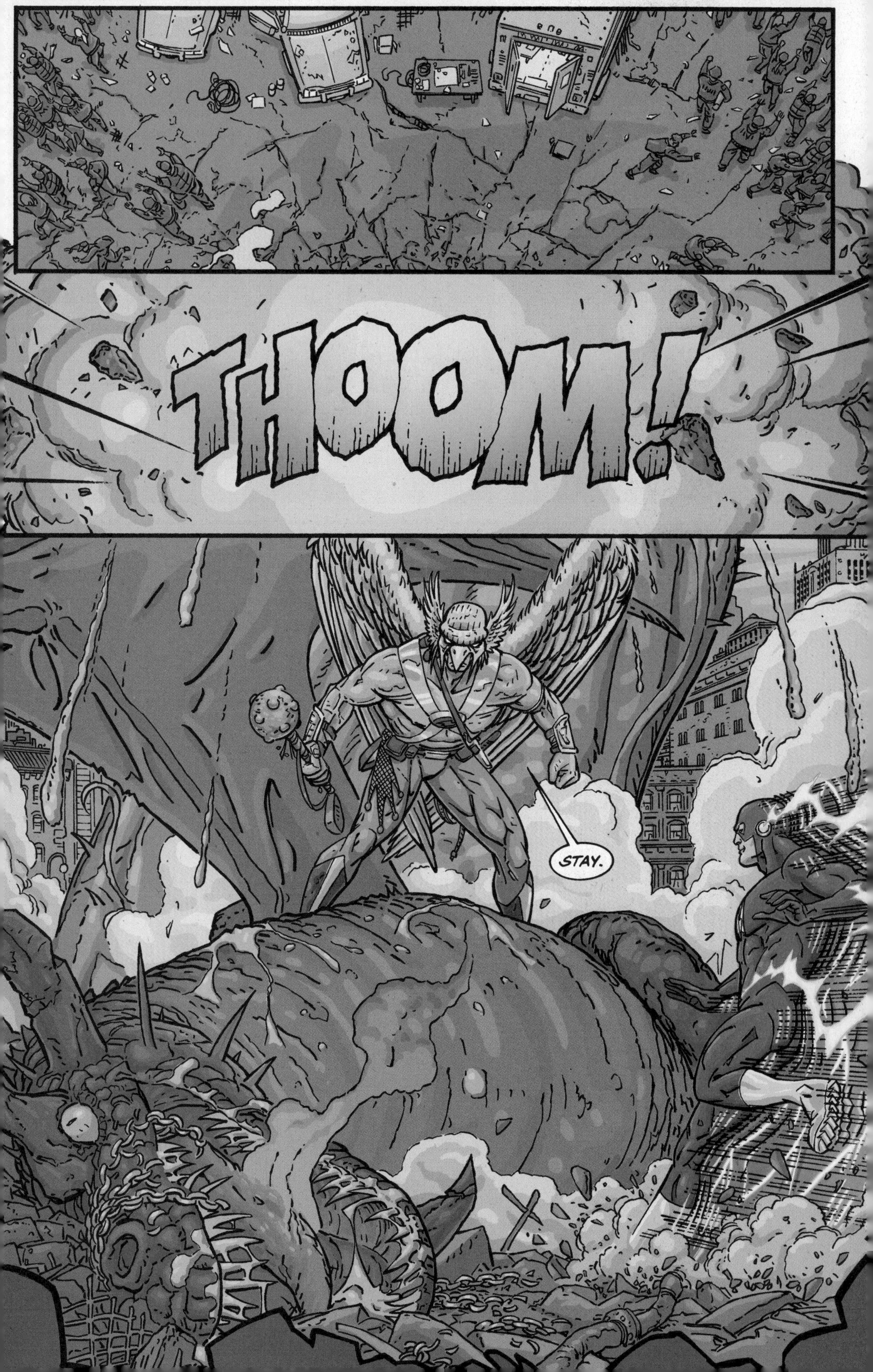
THOOM!
STAY.

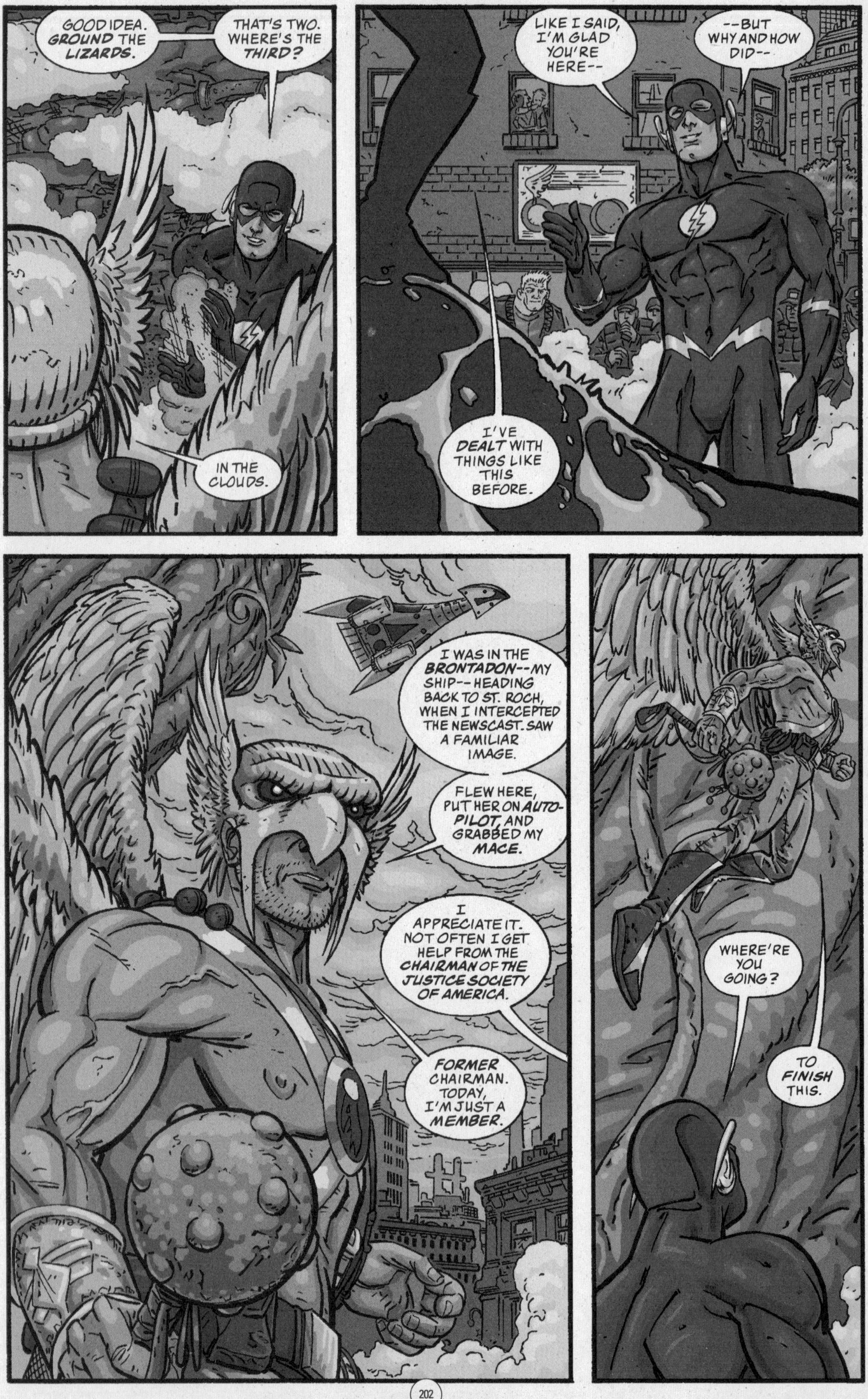
GOOD IDEA. GROUND THE LIZARDS.
THAT'S TWO. WHERE'S THE THIRD?
IN THE CLOUDS.
LIKE I SAID, I'M GLAD YOU'RE HERE--
--BUT WHY AND HOW DID--
I'VE DEALT WITH THINGS LIKE THIS BEFORE.
I WAS IN THE BRONTADON--MY SHIP--HEADING BACK TO ST. ROCH, WHEN I INTERCEPTED THE NEWSCAST. SAW A FAMILIAR IMAGE.
FLEW HERE, PUT HER ON AUTO-PILOT, AND GRABBED MY MACE.
I APPRECIATE IT. NOT OFTEN I GET HELP FROM THE CHAIRMAN OF THE JUSTICE SOCIETY OF AMERICA.
FORMER CHAIRMAN. TODAY, I'M JUST A MEMBER.
WHERE'RE YOU GOING?
TO FINISH THIS.

DON'T YOU WANT SOME HELP?

OF COURSE. I ASSUMED YOU'D *RACE* UP THAT OVERGROWN VINE.

NO. I MEAN, I CAN'T. BUCKS LIKE A *BRONCO* WHEN I GET ANYWHERE NEAR IT. I NEED... A *LIFT.*

THERE'S *TREPIDATION* IN YOUR *VOICE.*

IT'S... I'VE WORKED WITH A LOT OF HEROES. FROM THE ATOM TO ZATANNA.

YOU KNOW, EVERY TIME SOMEONE HAS A "TEAM-UP," *RUMORS* HIT THE SPANDEX GRAPEVINE. WE *ALL* TALK.

THE *RAY* IS A MOOCH, *HALO* WILL TALK YOUR *EAR* OFF, AND *ANIMAL MAN* AND HIS FAMILY ACTUALLY SEND *FRUIT BASKETS.*

SOME SAY YOU'RE *MOODY.* GROWLING LIKE A *SAVAGE* ONE MINUTE, TALKING ABOUT *SHAKESPEARE* AND *OPERA SERIA* THE NEXT.

OTHERS SAY YOU'RE AS *PROFESSIONAL* AS THEY COME. TREATING THEM WITH *NOTHING BUT RESPECT.*

I THINK YOU CAN COME TO YOUR *OWN* CONCLUSION.

DO YOU *KNOW* WHAT *THEY* SAY ABOUT *YOU?*

THEY SAY YOU'D MAKE YOUR UNCLE *VERY* PROUD.

WHAT DO *THEY* SAY?

THE MASTER RETURNS!

WE WELCOME YOU AND YOUR NEW BRIDE. A FEAST IS BEING PREPARED IN THE GREAT HALL.

THANK YOU, MY BEASTS.

THIS IS YOUR NEW HOME, PRINCESS. *OUR* NEW HOME.

I WILL *OVERSEE* KEYSTONE CITY FAIRLY AND JUSTLY, AS I DO EASTWIND.

I WILL *SHOW* THE PEOPLE I AM A *BETTER* RULER THAN THE FLASH.

--LET ME *GO*!

YOU'RE SO *CLUELESS.* NOW I SAID--

A VALIANT BLOW, BUT--

YOU.

YOU ARE *WITH* CHILD.

THE *FLASH'S* CHILD.

I WILL *REMEDY* THAT.

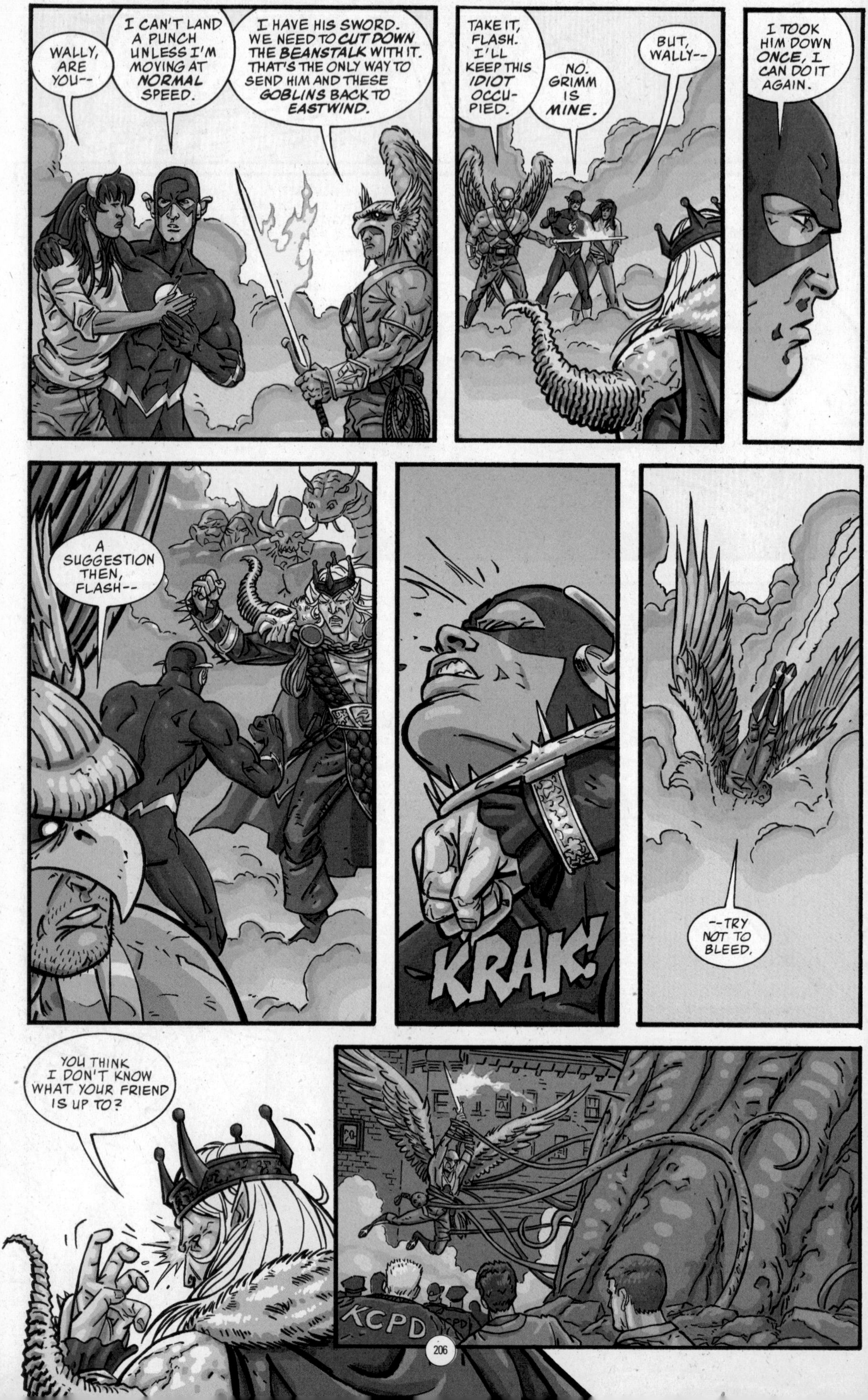
WALLY, ARE YOU--
I CAN'T LAND A PUNCH UNLESS I'M MOVING AT NORMAL SPEED.
I HAVE HIS SWORD. WE NEED TO CUT DOWN THE BEANSTALK WITH IT. THAT'S THE ONLY WAY TO SEND HIM AND THESE GOBLINS BACK TO EASTWIND.
TAKE IT, FLASH. I'LL KEEP THIS IDIOT OCCUPIED.
NO. GRIMM IS MINE.
BUT, WALLY--
I TOOK HIM DOWN ONCE, I CAN DO IT AGAIN.
A SUGGESTION THEN, FLASH--
KRAK!
--TRY NOT TO BLEED.
YOU THINK I DON'T KNOW WHAT YOUR FRIEND IS UP TO?
KCPD

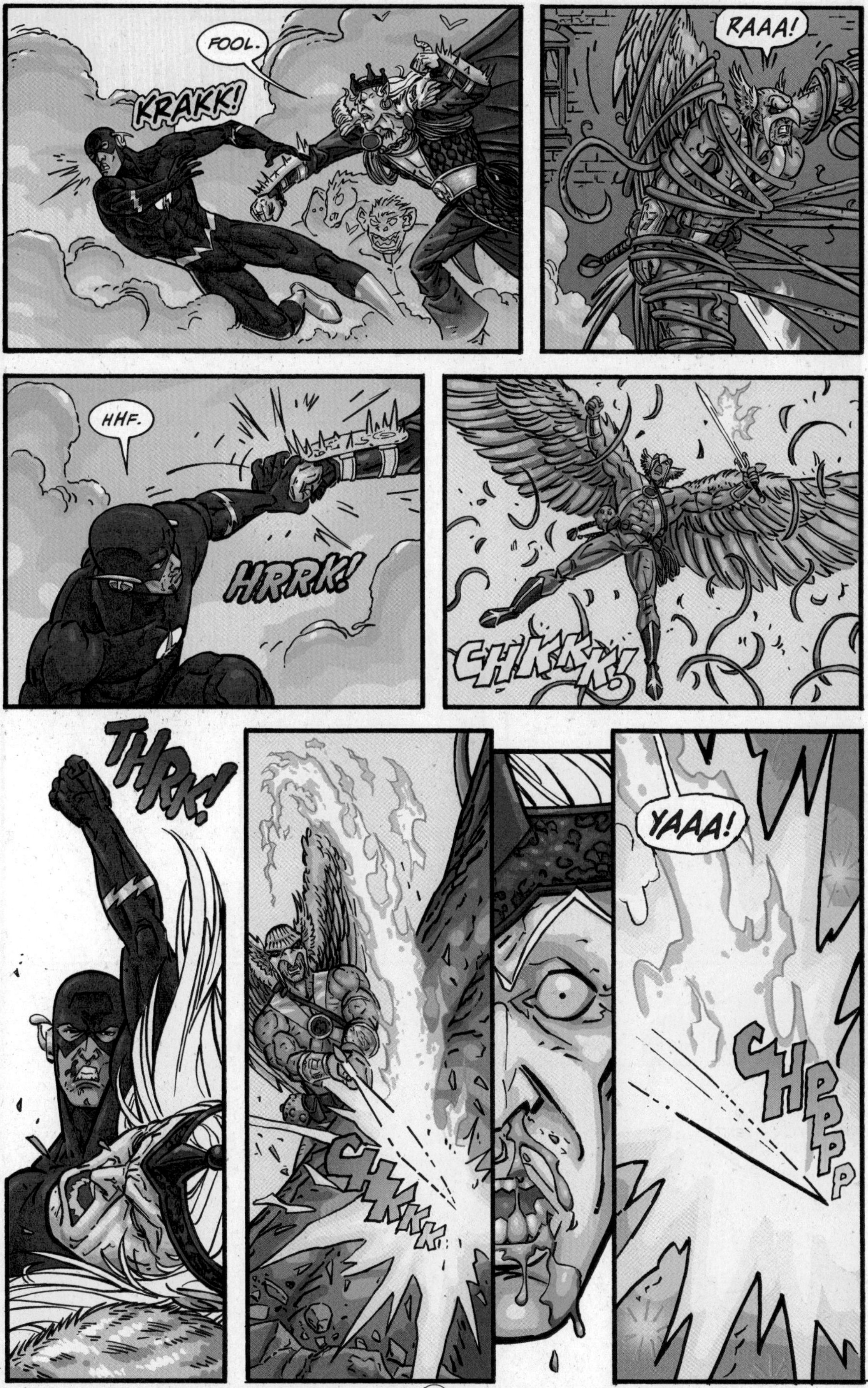
FOOL.
KRAKK!
RAAA!
HHF.
HRRK!
CHKKKK!
THRK!
CHKKKK
YAAA!
CHPPPP

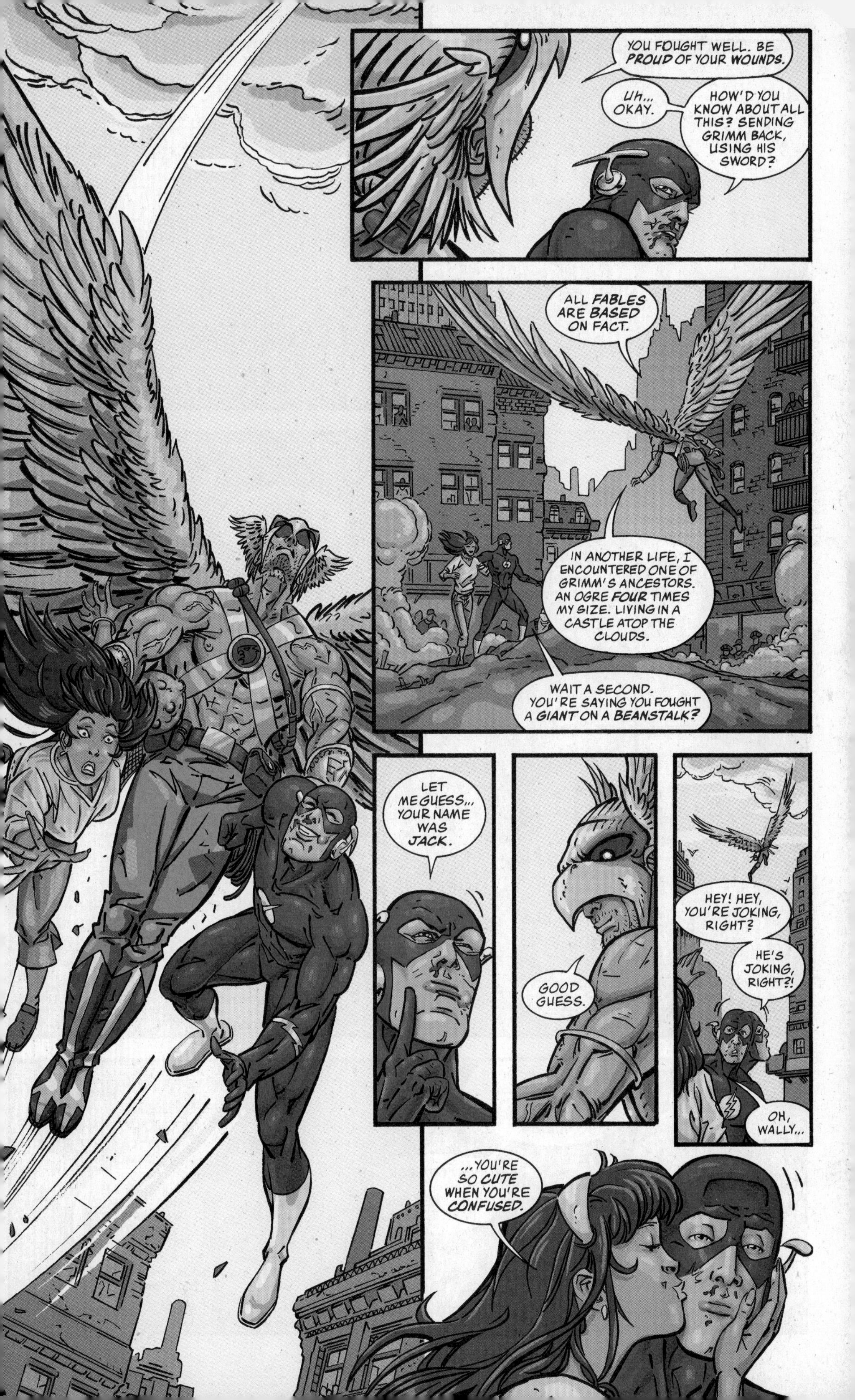
YOU FOUGHT WELL. BE PROUD OF YOUR WOUNDS.
UH... OKAY.
HOW'D YOU KNOW ABOUT ALL THIS? SENDING GRIMM BACK, USING HIS SWORD?
ALL FABLES ARE BASED ON FACT.
IN ANOTHER LIFE, I ENCOUNTERED ONE OF GRIMM'S ANCESTORS. AN OGRE FOUR TIMES MY SIZE. LIVING IN A CASTLE ATOP THE CLOUDS.
WAIT A SECOND. YOU'RE SAYING YOU FOUGHT A GIANT ON A BEANSTALK?
LET ME GUESS... YOUR NAME WAS JACK.
GOOD GUESS.
HEY! HEY, YOU'RE JOKING, RIGHT?
HE'S JOKING, RIGHT?!
OH, WALLY...
...YOU'RE SO CUTE WHEN YOU'RE CONFUSED.

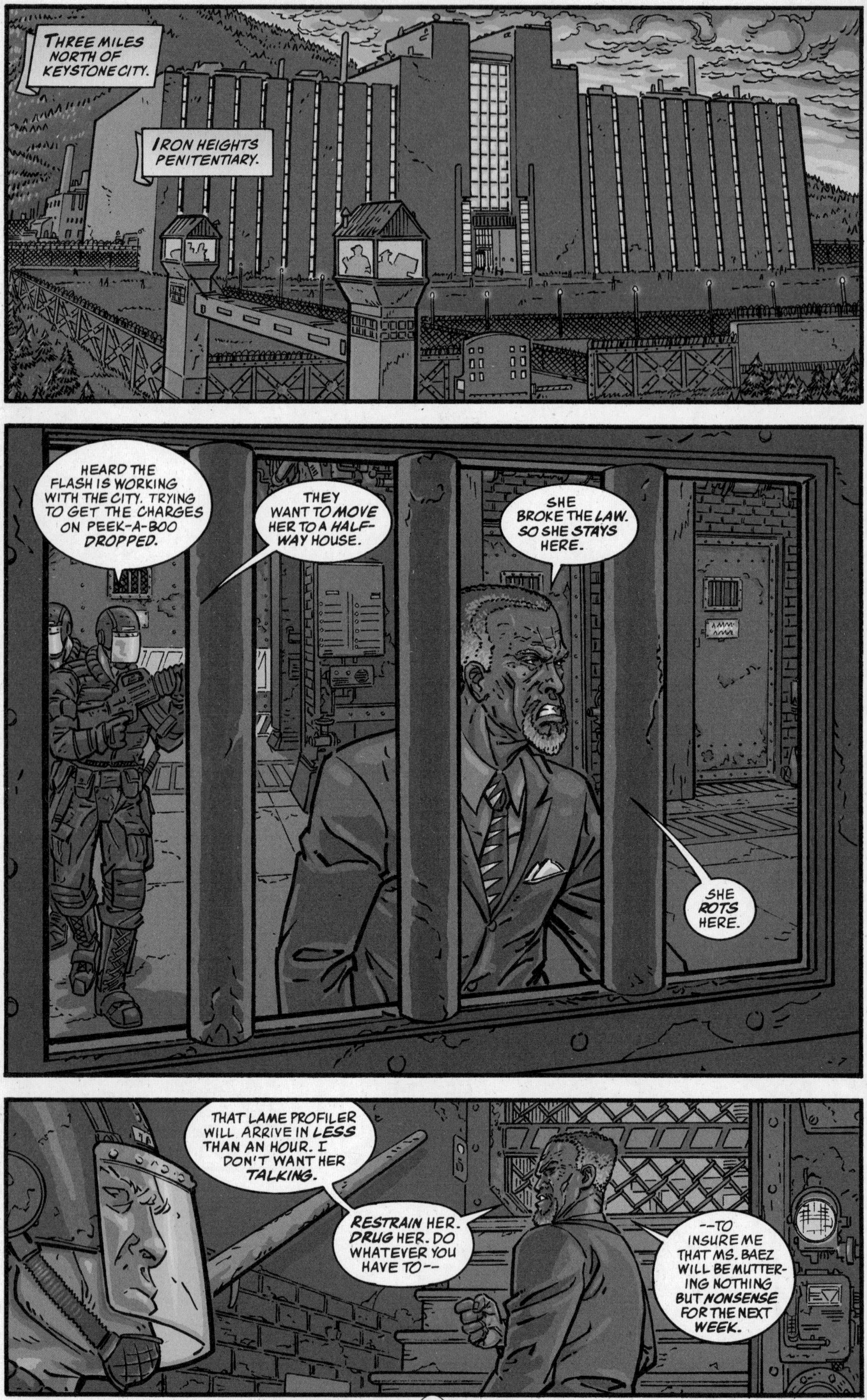

THREE MILES NORTH OF KEYSTONE CITY.
IRON HEIGHTS PENITENTIARY.
HEARD THE FLASH IS WORKING WITH THE CITY. TRYING TO GET THE CHARGES ON PEEK-A-BOO DROPPED.
THEY WANT TO MOVE HER TO A HALF-WAY HOUSE.
SHE BROKE THE LAW. SO SHE STAYS HERE.
SHE ROTS HERE.
THAT LAME PROFILER WILL ARRIVE IN LESS THAN AN HOUR. I DON'T WANT HER TALKING.
RESTRAIN HER. DRUG HER. DO WHATEVER YOU HAVE TO--
--TO INSURE ME THAT MS. BAEZ WILL BE MUTTERING NOTHING BUT NONSENSE FOR THE NEXT WEEK.

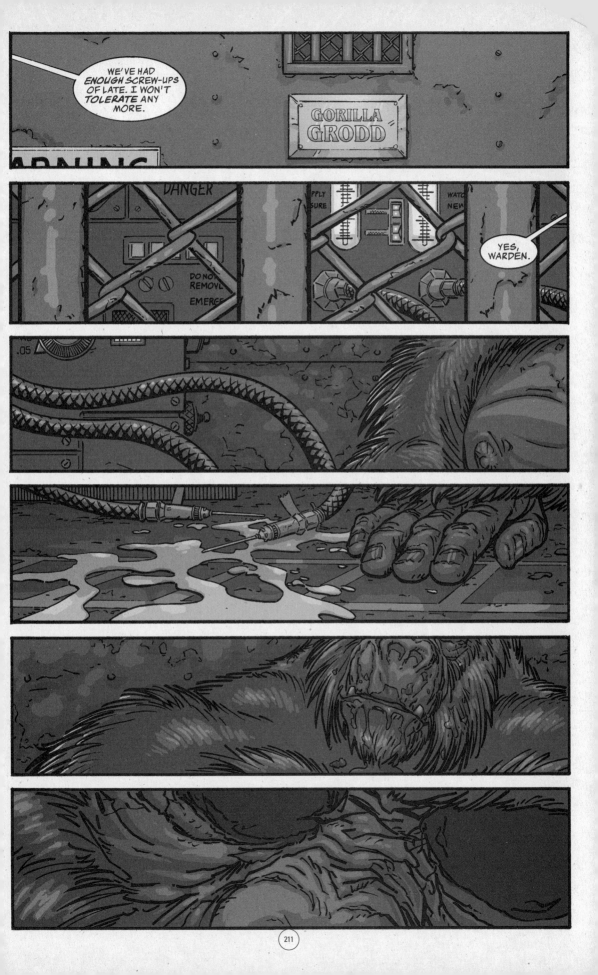

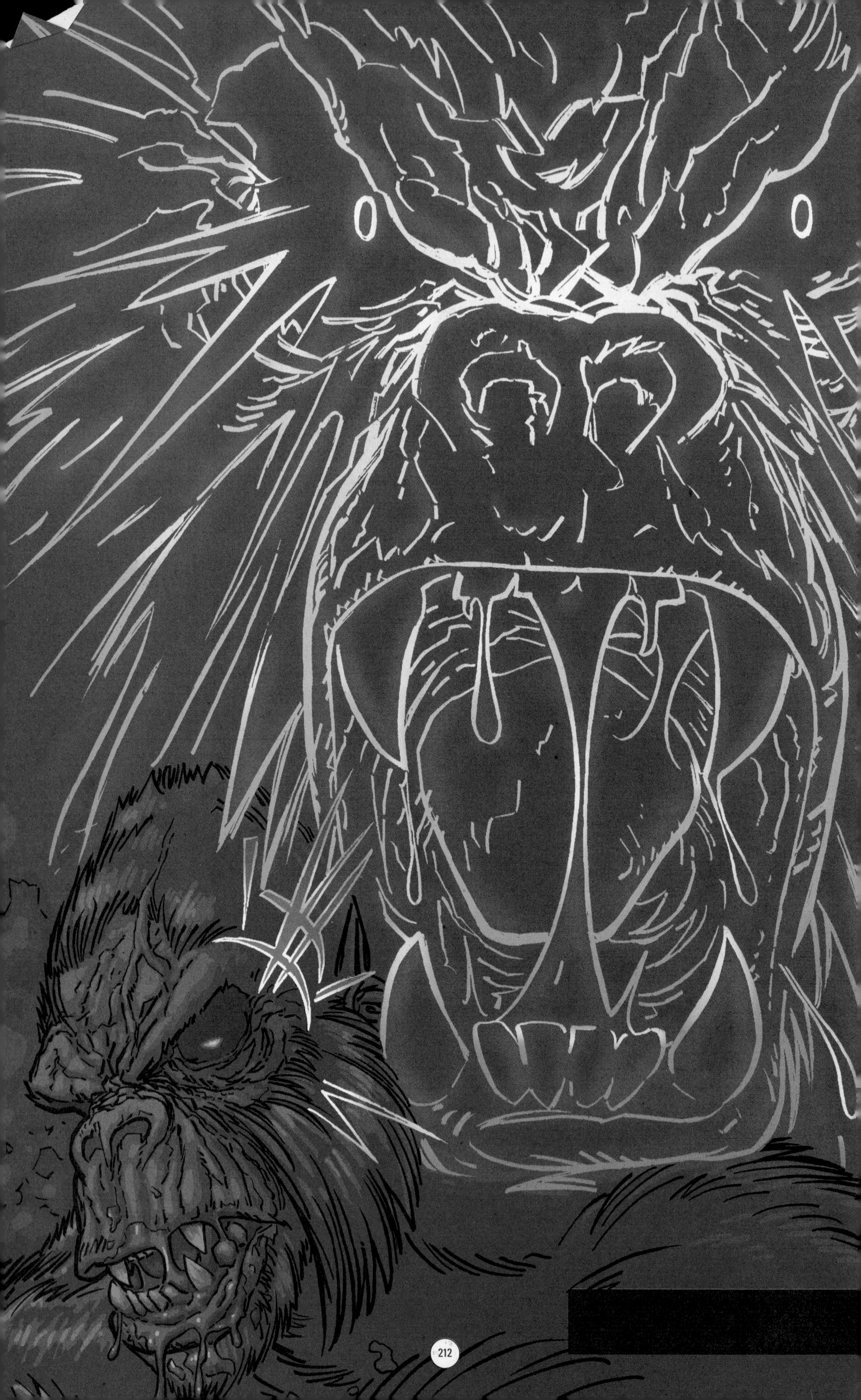

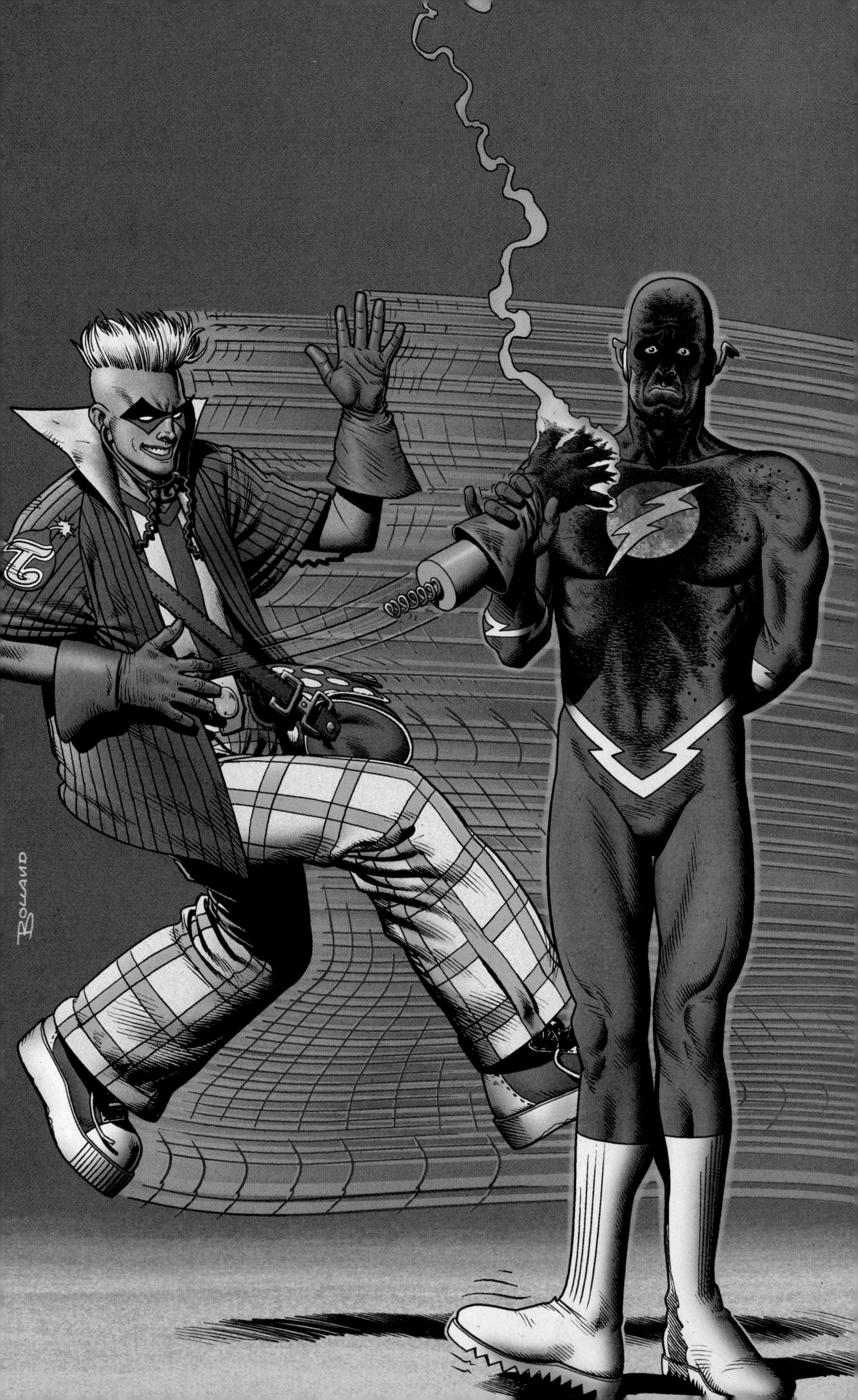
BOLLAND

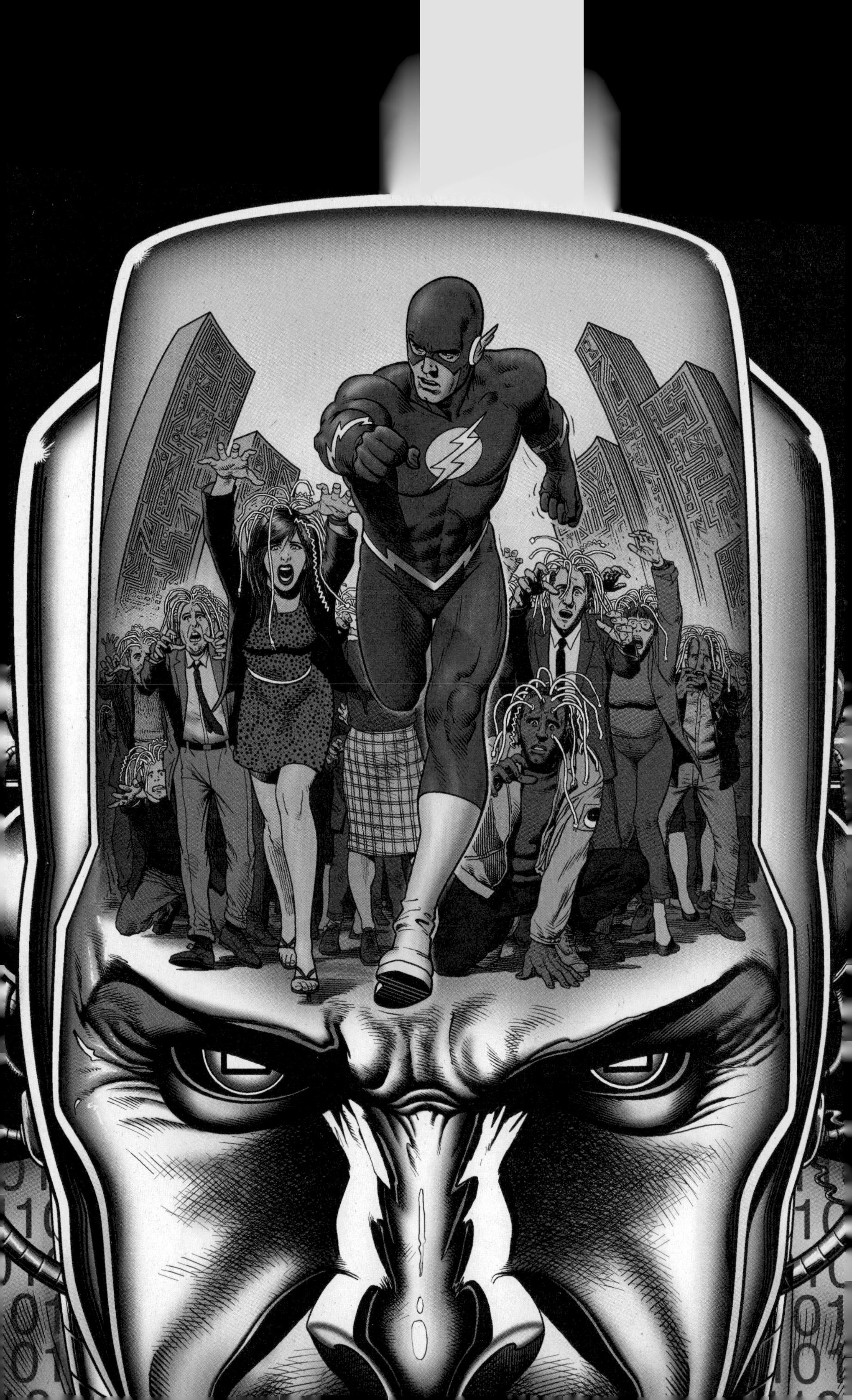

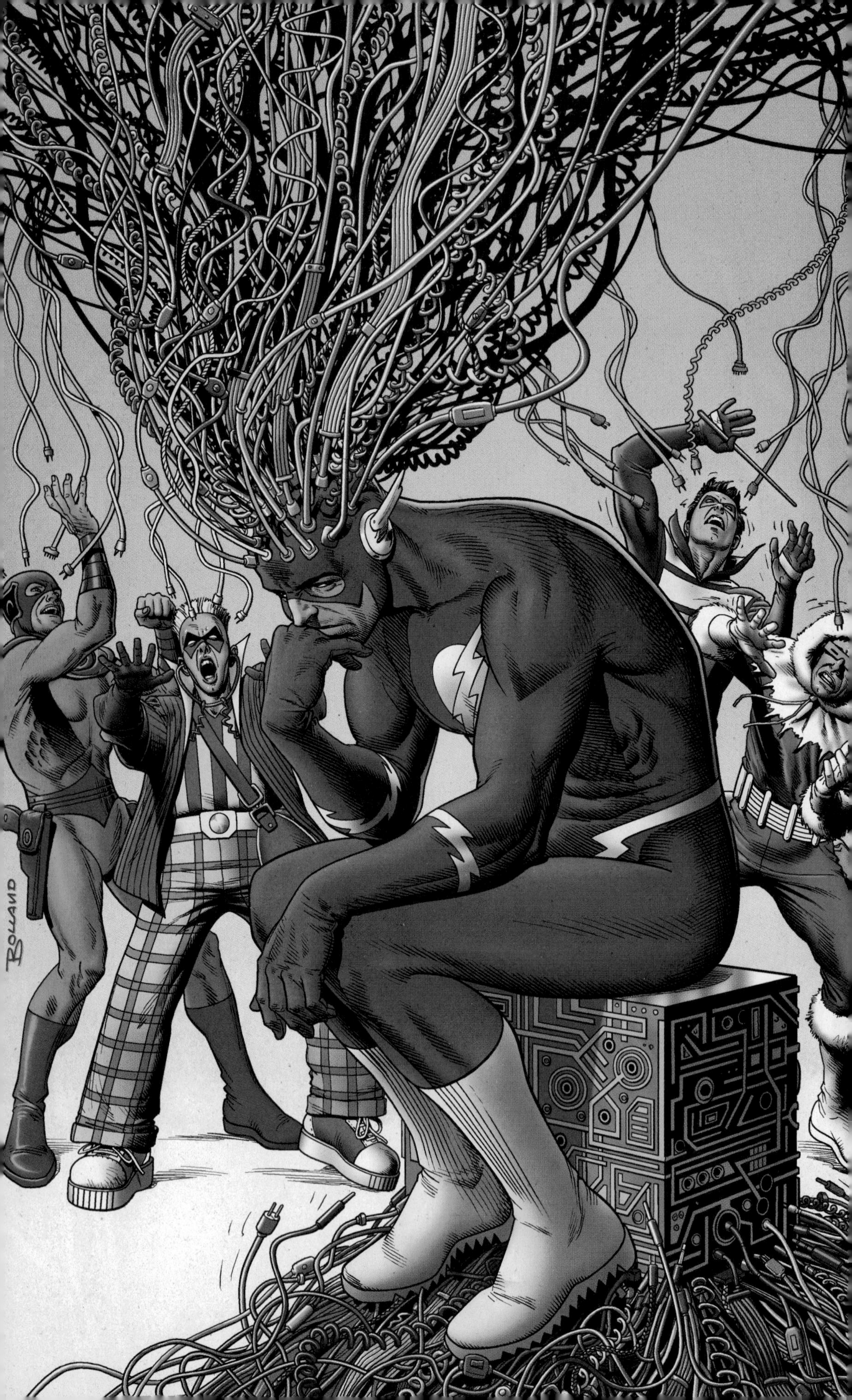
BOLLAND

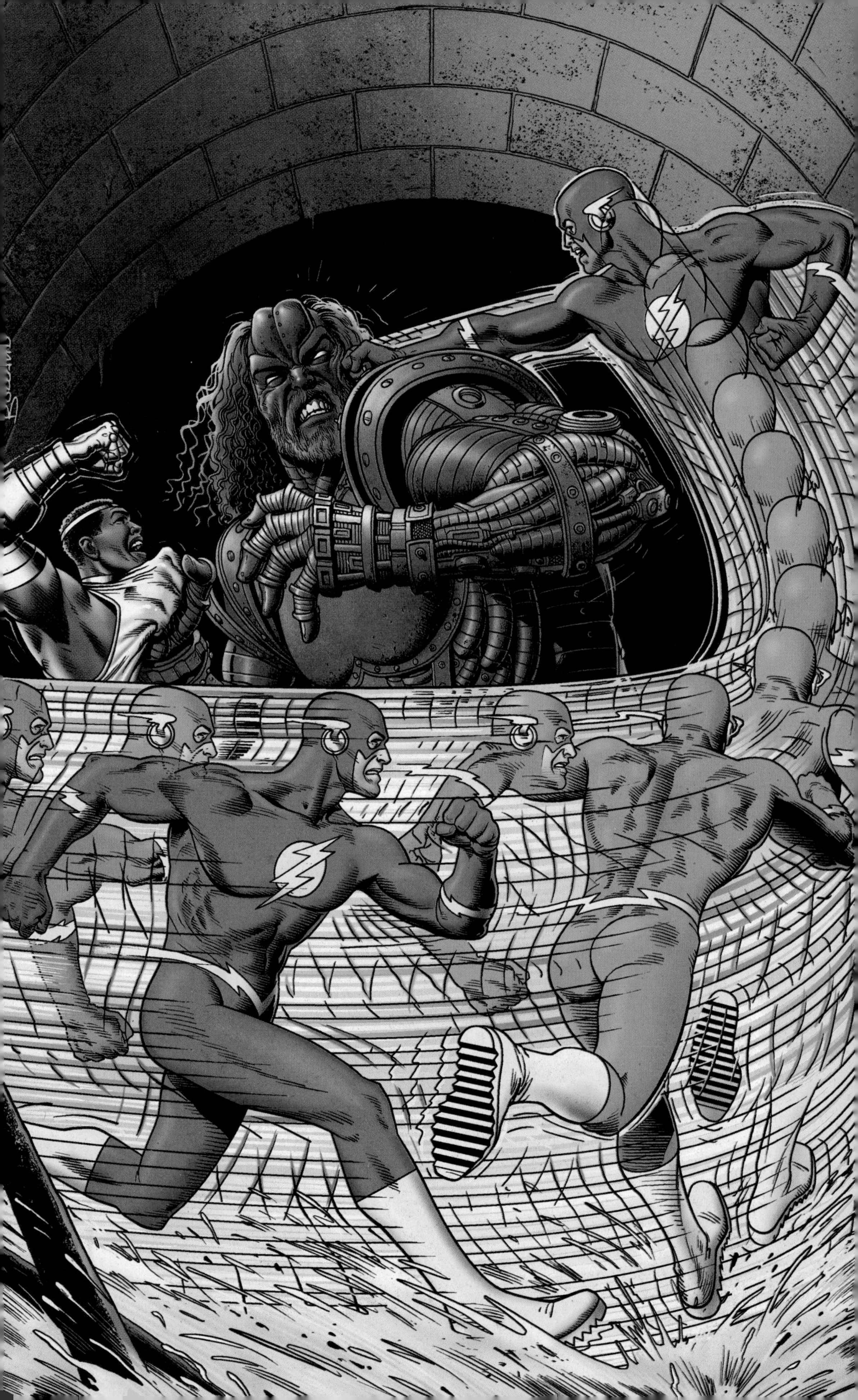

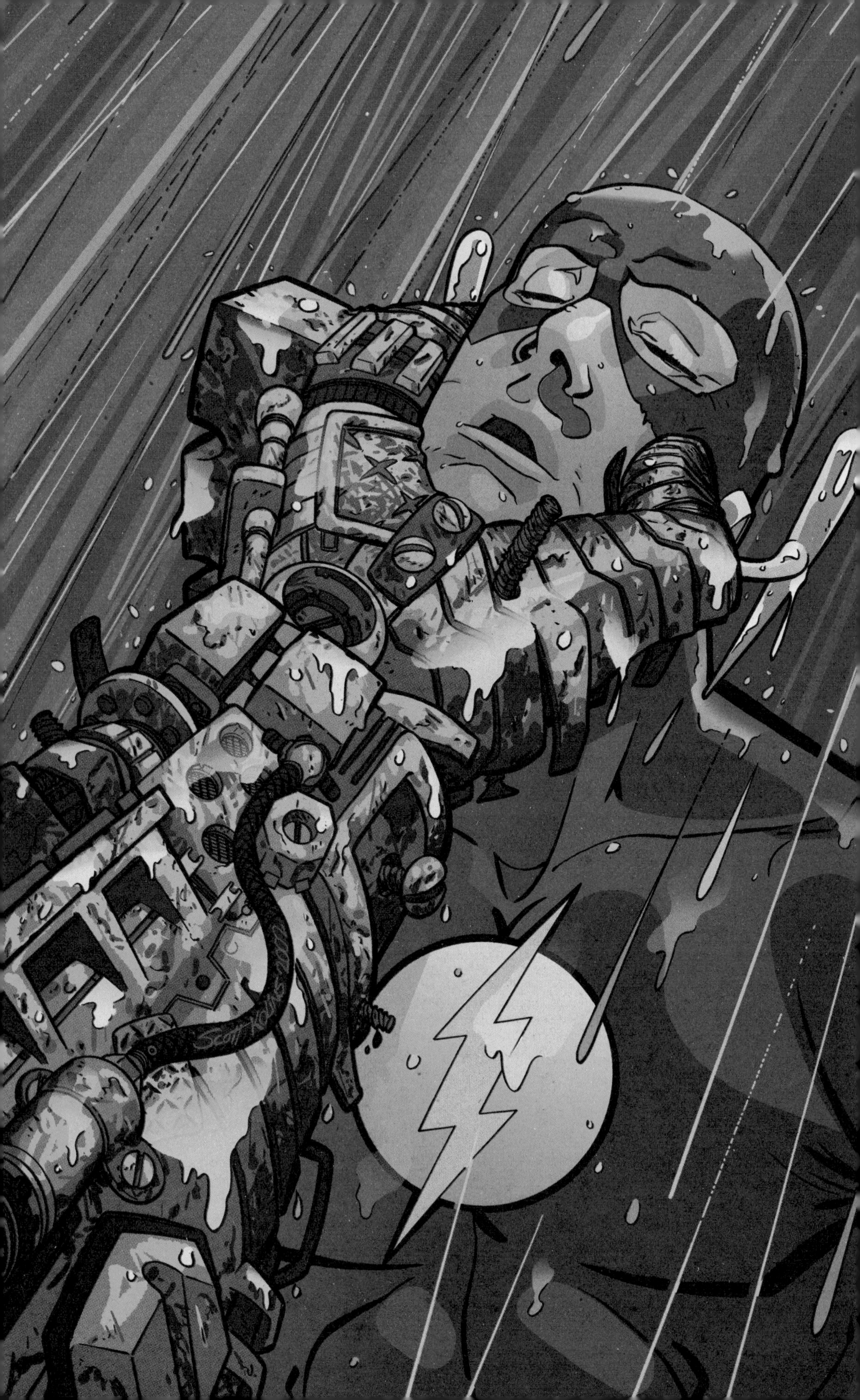

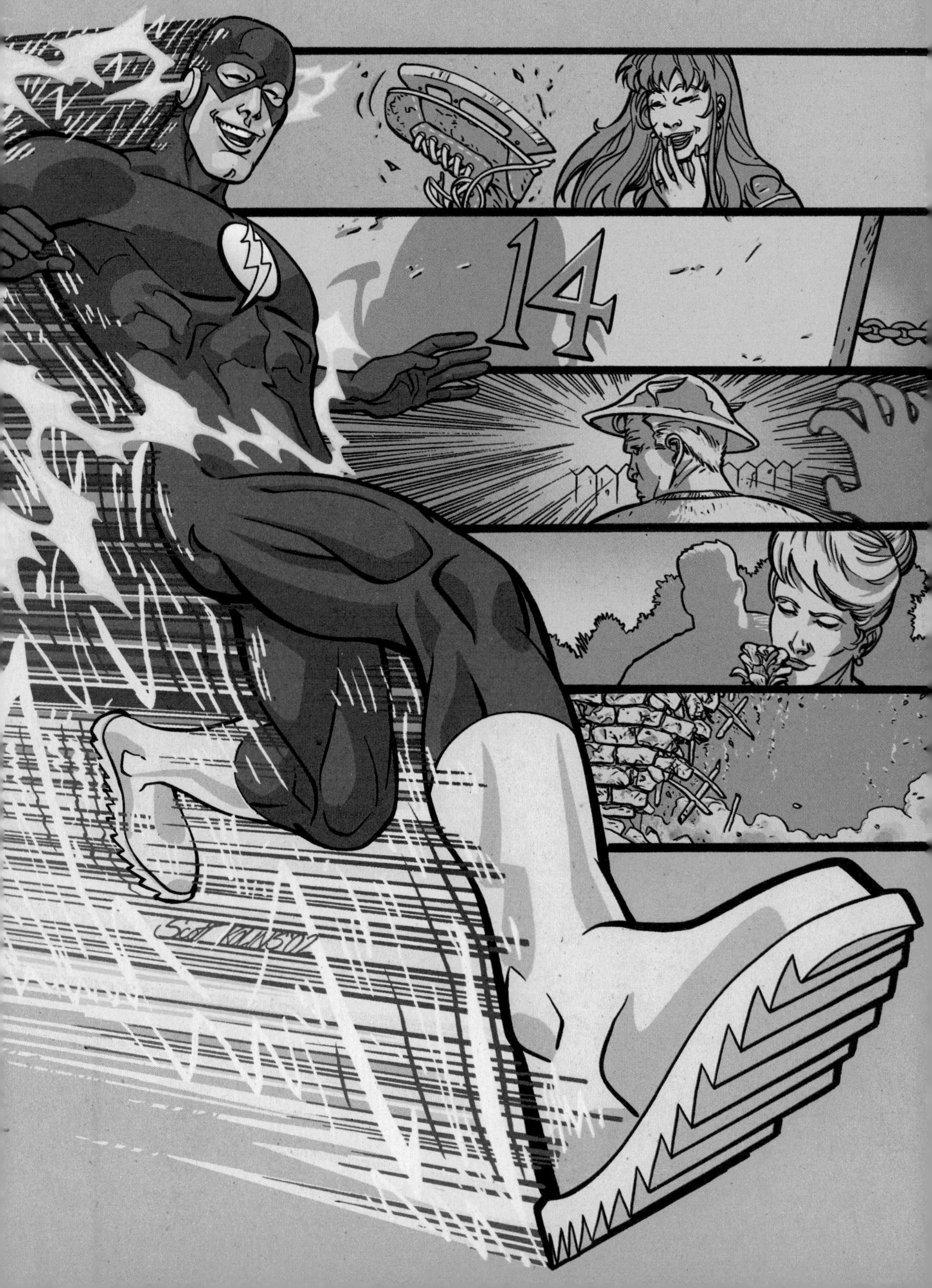
14

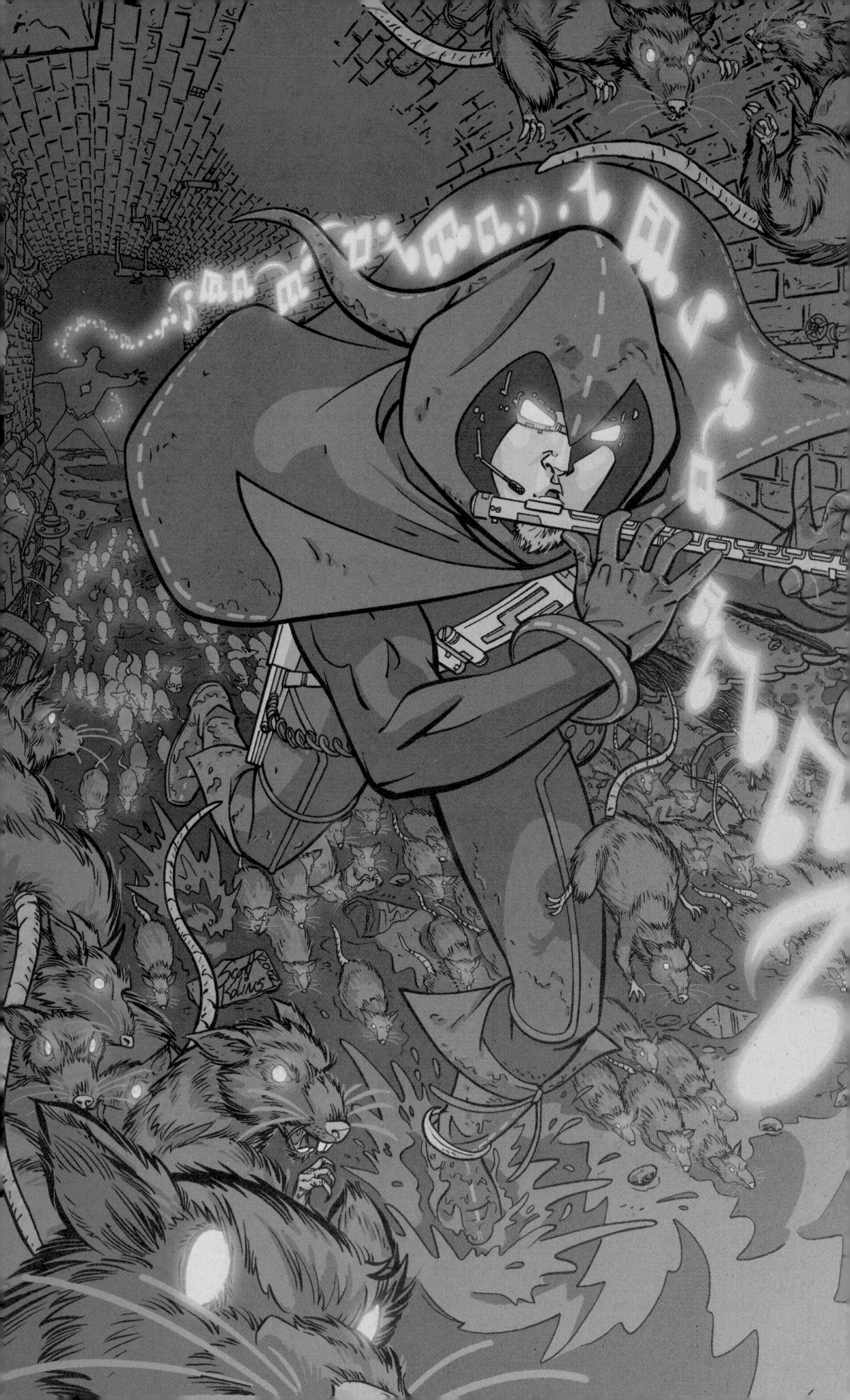
Scott Kolins 2002

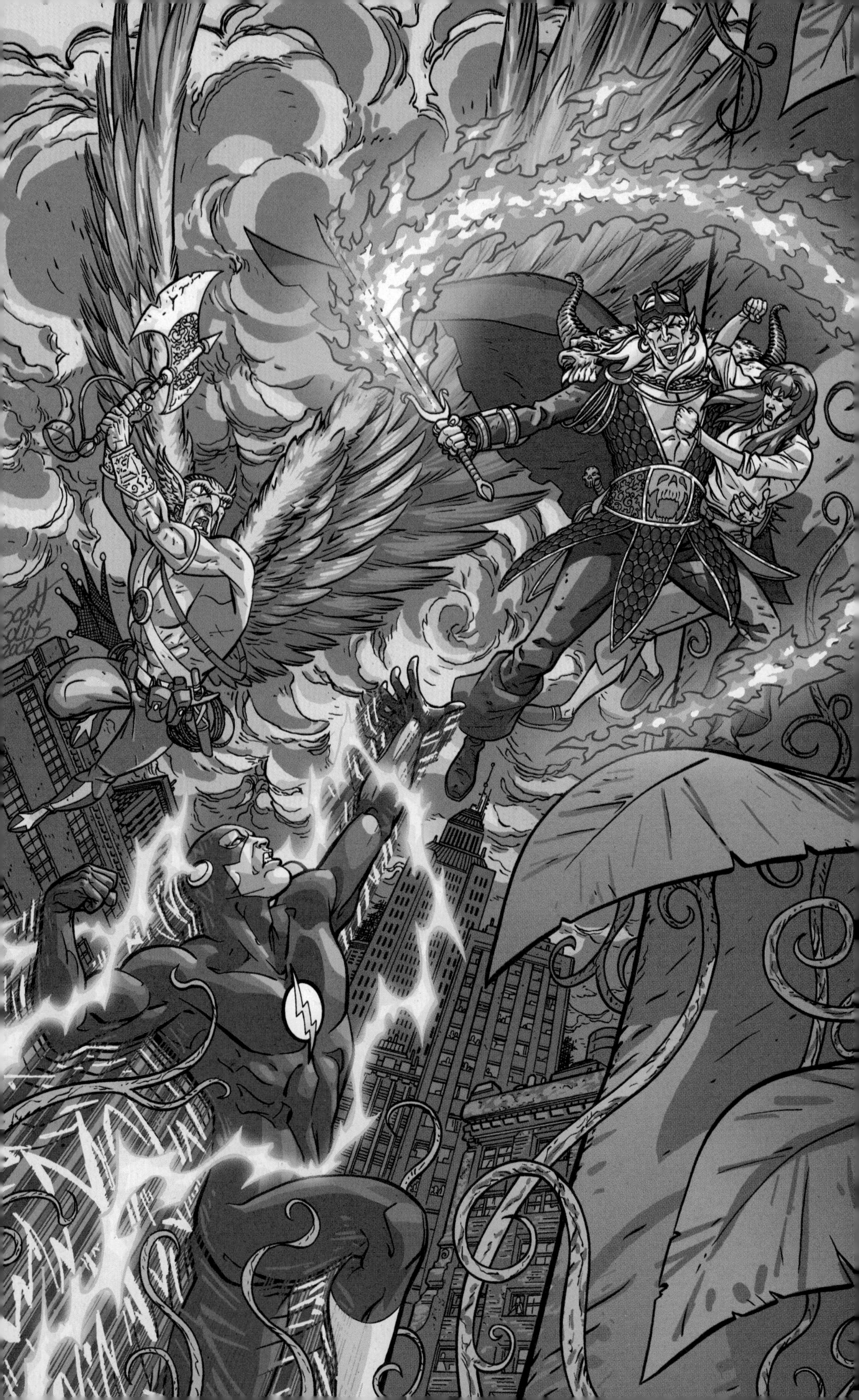
Scott Kolins 2002

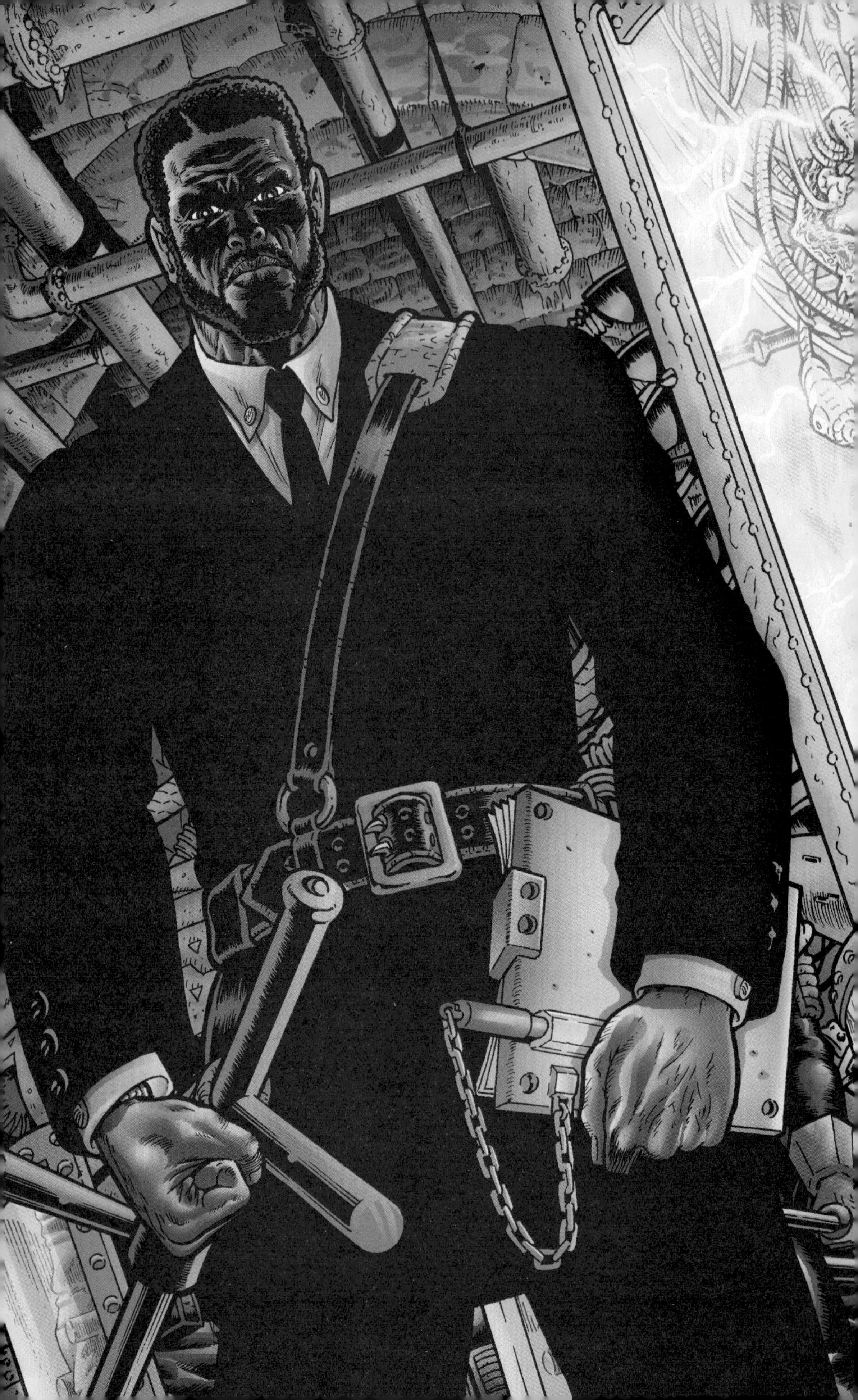

IRON HEIGHTS PENITENTIARY

First Appearance:
THE FLASH: IRON HEIGHTS (October, 2001)

"The only way out of Iron Heights is in a body bag." Up until the recent breakout, this was the motto among Iron Heights' prisoners…and its staff.

Keystone City Penitentiary was a fairly standard institution until Gregory Wolfe took over as warden. Spending a budget of nearly forty million dollars, Wolfe entirely reinvented the prison, transforming it into Iron Heights.

The main structure of the prison houses the worst criminals the surrounding states have to offer, as well as the infirmary – and the Warden's office. Riots are increasingly infrequent, and no guards had ever lost their lives until the recent breakout.

Over forty feet underground, the lower level of Iron Heights is called the Pipeline. Originally just a utility basement, it has since been converted to house metahuman and costumed inmates. The prisoners in the Pipeline are rarely let out of their cells.

Next to the Pipeline is the Power Room. Once, large generators powered the prison. Now, at Warden Wolfe's request, a radioactive rogue named Fallout serves as the power source. The prison saves hundreds of thousands of dollars thanks to his energies.

Currently over one thousand men and women are held within the walls of Iron Heights.

GREGORY WOLFE

Occupation: Warden
Marital Status: Married
Ht: 6' 2"   Wt: 195 lbs.
Eyes: Brown
Hair: Black
First Appearance: THE FLASH: IRON HEIGHTS (October, 2001)

Prior to his role as warden, Wolfe was an infamous prosecutor for the city of St. Louis. He earned a reputation for being hard on criminals and seeking somewhat shady help in accumulating evidence. His methods were controversial, but Wolfe almost never lost a case. The only man Wolfe failed to convict was murdered two days after the trial, a case as yet unsolved.

Because of his friendship with the Governor, Wolfe was offered the job of Warden of Keystone City Prison after the previous warden suffered a heart attack and was forced to retire. Looking for a challenge, Wolfe accepted the position.

Wolfe was instrumental in updating and remodeling the institution, renaming it Iron Heights. His frustration with the "revolving door" nature of many prisons with large metahuman populations has driven Wolfe to ensure his building has been outfitted with the latest in containment technology.

Wolfe takes great care in initiating costumed "super-villains" into the prison. He forces them to wear their costumes, so they'll be easily spotted when mingling with the general population.

Although Wolfe held the Flash in high regard, his first encounter with him left him cold. The Flash accused the Warden of excessive cruelty towards prisoners, outraging Wolfe. Unbeknownst to the Flash – as well as to his superiors – Gregory Wolfe has the metahuman ability to control muscular impulses in living beings and, at a thought, can trigger painful spasms within any part of the human body.

**WRITTEN BY GEOFF JOHNS. ART BY BRYAN TALBOT.
COLOR BY TOM MCCRAW.**